Human Rights in Graphic Life Narrative

New Directions in Life Narrative

New Directions in Life Narrative explores the concept of life narrative across the mediums of written work, oral narratives, photography, documentary film, visual art, performance and social media. The series nurtures theoretical, methodological and interpretive innovation in life writing research, supporting projects that apply new combinations of philosophy, critical theory and methodology to the study of life narrative, providing new ways of reading diverse and always evolving forms. It advances interdisciplinary approaches to life narrative, combining the insights of life writing scholarship with those of cognate fields such as art history, history, anthropology, comparative literary studies, law, sociolinguistics, media studies, medicine, philosophy, psychology and sociology. The series strives towards an international scope that mirrors its community, offering a forum for the study of works in translations not previously studied as well as publishing studies of non-Anglophone works.

Series Editors
Kate Douglas, Flinders University, Australia
Anna Poletti, Utrecht University, Netherlands
John Zuern, University of Hawaii, USA

Editorial Advisory Board
Dr Ebony Coletu (Penn State University, USA); Dr Ana Belén Martínez García (University of Navarra, Spain); Associate Professor Claire Lynch (Brunel University, UK); Professor Pramod K. Nayar (The University of Hyderabad, India); Dr Nick Tembo (The University of Malawi); Professor Jianling Liu (Shanghai Jiao Tong University, China); Professor Gerardo Necoechea (Instituto Nacional de Antropología e Historia, Mexico); Dr Laurie McNeill (University of British Columbia, Canada)

Forthcoming Titles
The Death Memoir in Contemporary Culture, Claire Nally
Refugee Lives in the Archives: A Pacific Imaginary, Gillian Whitlock
Reading Mediated Life Narratives: Auto/Biographical Agency in the Book, Museum, Social Media, and Archives, Amy Carlson
Contemporary Life Writing and the End of Empire, Emma Parker
Life Writing and the Southern Hemisphere: Texts, Spaces, Resonances, edited by Elleke Boehmer and Katherine Collins
Ecological Life Writings from India: Marginalisation, Environmental Justice and Told-to Autobiography, Shalini M. and Moncy Mathew

Human Rights in Graphic Life Narrative

Reading and Witnessing Violations of the 'Other' in Anglophone Works

Olga Michael

BLOOMSBURY ACADEMIC

LONDON · NEW YORK · OXFORD · NEW DELHI · SYDNEY

BLOOMSBURY ACADEMIC
Bloomsbury Publishing Plc
50 Bedford Square, London, WC1B 3DP, UK
1385 Broadway, New York, NY 10018, USA
29 Earlsfort Terrace, Dublin 2, Ireland

BLOOMSBURY, BLOOMSBURY ACADEMIC and the Diana logo are trademarks of
Bloomsbury Publishing Plc

First published in Great Britain 2023
Paperback edition published in 2025

For legal purposes the Acknowledgements on p. viii constitute an extension of this
copyright page.

Series design by Rebecca Heselton
Cover image: Evangelos Konstantelos

A catalogue record for this book is available from the British Library.

A catalog record for this book is available from the Library of Congress.

ISBN: HB: 978-1-3503-2975-1
        PB: 978-1-3503-2979-9
        ePDF: 978-1-3503-2976-8
        eBook: 978-1-3503-2977-5

Series: New Directions in Life Narrative

Typeset by RefineCatch Limited, Bungay, Suffolk

To find out more about our authors and books visit www.bloomsbury.com
and sign up for our newsletters.

Contents

Figures

Acknowledgements

This book has been completed during my two-year post-doctoral fellowship at the Department of English, University of Cyprus, under the supervision of Dr Antonis Balasopoulos, to whom I am grateful for his support. The project has been funded through the ONISILOS post-doctoral grant scheme.

I am also grateful to Lucy Brown and Aanchal Vij from Bloomsbury Academic for their belief in this project and their continuous support. Alongside them, I would like to thank Kate Douglas, John David Zuern and Anna Poletti, the series editors of 'New Directions in Life Narrative' for the opportunity to publish this book under this exciting series.

This book would not have been made possible if I had not found a home and a research direction through IABA, the International Auto/Biography Association. Since my first conference attendance at IABA World in Cyprus in 2016, I have met brilliant people who have introduced me to the value and importance of life narrative. I am deeply grateful for the support, mentorship and opportunities I have received through this association, as well as for the friendships I have made, and I consider myself very lucky for being part of it.

I would also like to thank my family and friends for their continuous support, and my PhD supervisor, Dr Monica Pearl, for teaching me how to write.

And, lastly, as always, I am grateful to the late Dr Nephie Christodulides, for having believed in me when I did not, and for showing me the way.

Introduction

In this book, I propose an interdisciplinary, intersectional methodology for the analysis of online and print graphic life narratives that remediate fictionalized testimonies of othered people's suffering in different geo- necro- and bio-political contexts.[1] I examine graphic accounts of human rights violations through a focus on gendered precarities, death, space and embodied border-crossing experiences, and I argue for the role graphic life narrative can play in social justice, in decolonial, postcolonial and intersectional-feminist literary studies, and in critical race, refugee and migration studies.

In the following chapters, I examine the aesthetics of the visualization of suffering, and how artistic choices complicate the testimonies remediated in print and online texts.[2] Specifically, I investigate the extent to which such choices challenge or reproduce mainstream neo-colonial depictions of othered people that also often justify Western States' 'neo-imperial practices' within their borders and beyond (Slaughter 2007: 37).[3] If vision is affected by 'social energy' and the way we see other people is determined by images reaching us via mainstream

---

[1] These contexts concern the industrialized city of Juarez at the US/Mexico border, and that of Mae Sot at the Burma (Myanmar)/Thailand border, the Sri Lankan and the Israeli/Palestinian conflict, the Vietnam war, as well as undocumented migration and asylum detention in Europe and Australia.

[2] On the potentialities and political implications of fictionalized testimony in life narrative in general and women's graphic memoir in particular, see Jolly 2014; Jensen 2014; Michael 2018, 2023; Jones 2019.

[3] In this monograph, I approach the terms 'other', 'othered' and 'otherness' from a critical standpoint which conceptualizes them as produced through colonial histories and the injurious implications of modernity/coloniality, which I explicate below. The other is not understood as existing in hierarchical relations to the Universal, Western, and Eurocentric Self. Rather, they form the essential part of society-building, or 'sociogenesis' in Walter Mignolo's terms (Mignolo and Gaztambide-Fernández 2014: 201), and of inter-subjective knowledge production that is not Western, Eurocentric, stemming from only rationality and perceived as universal (Grosfoguel 2011). The analysis that follows points to a postcolonial 'possibility of *a politics of fellowship* [whose] precondition [...] is [the] recognition of the Other in his or her difference' (Mbembe 2021: 73, emphasis in the original). For this reason, the act of bearing witness to the other and their testimony moves beyond recognition, which implies hierarchical relations (Oliver 2001). Rather, it is based on 'address-ability and response-ability [...,] the roots of subjectivity, which are damaged by the objectifying operations of oppression and subordination' and, as such, it reinstates the othered person's subjectivity in the witnessing process (Oliver 2001: 7).

media (Oliver 2001: 14), I argue that graphic life narratives accounting for other people's pain and intersectional, decolonized, postcolonial approaches to them, enable a different kind of seeing that can also critically engage with stereotypical injurious images of gendered, racially othered people, which often introduce them as sensationalized spectacles of victimhood or threat. As I do so, I also assess the extent to which graphic life narrative can function as an 'alternative jurisdiction' (Gilmore 2001a: 134) by voicing human rights violations that remain predominantly silenced.

Life narrative, testimony and witness

Issues surrounding social justice, human rights and testimony are core to life narrative, a broad generic category that refers to 'acts of self-representation of all kinds and in diverse media', including comics life storytelling (Smith and Watson 2010: 3; Schaffer and Smith 2004). G. Thomas Couser highlights the presence of others in relation to the authorial and narrating I in such auto/biographical acts, and notes that life narrative is '*built into* [. . .] the formation of individual identity and human relationships' (2012: 23, emphasis in the original). Narrating the self inevitably entails narrating others, and *vice versa*; narrating the lives of others also implies their relational bonds with the authorial and the narrating I.[4] Acts of witness are central in this genre that emerged due to the limitations of canonical autobiography, and offered space for the narration of previously silenced life stories – those of women, (post-)colonized subjects, queer people and sexual abuse survivors among others (Smith and Watson 2010; Whitlock 2015a). Gillian Whitlock, for instance, shows how testimonial transactions contribute to 'the making of the human' in postcolonial life narrative, an auto/biographical category that is core 'for de/colonizing the subject' (2015a: 1, 3).[5] Leigh Gilmore has also extensively written on women's life narrative as an alternative jurisdiction, on the tainting of coloured women's and girls' testimonies, and on the adequate witnessing that can be enabled through one's engagement with difficult literary testimonial trauma narratives (Gilmore 2001b, 2017, 2019; Gilmore and Marshal 2019).

---

[4] Sidonie Smith and Julia Watson explain that 'the self-inquiry and self-knowing of many autobiographical acts is relational [that is, it becomes] routed through others' (2010: 64).
[5] Whitlock defines 'literary testimonies [as] performative, rhetorical acts that "summon and beseech us" as readers', further noting that 'shifting jurisdictions and global transits of testimonial narrative record changing, historical thresholds of subaltern agency and dispossession' (2015a: 8).

For Kate Douglas, literary testimony can 'resist enforced silences and [...] assert previously marginalized narratives' at the same time as inviting 'informed debate upon itself' (2010: 144). This kind of informed debate can stem from acts of reading testimonial life narrative as 'second person' witness (Douglas 2010: 152; Whitlock 2001).[6] Writing from the standpoint of cultural and political memory studies, Sara Jones notes that testimony can often 'be triply mediated, through the secondary witness, through [an] artistic form and [the] figurative language of the medium [via which it is told, as well as] through the location of the medium in a particular culture' (2019: 274).[7] She further points out that such testimonial accounts operate 'as a form of communication between witness and audience that can – perhaps exactly because of that mediation – work to promote an "other-oriented" empathy with the victims and survivors of atrocity that does not risk "over-arousal"' (Jones 2019: 274). It is precisely in the interpretation of the multiple perspectives, gazes, aesthetic choices and the attributes of comics that intervene in, and produce, remediated testimonies that there lies the potential for an informed debate and a critical other-oriented empathy in graphic life narratives accounting for othered people's distant suffering.

In structuring narrated subjects that are other than the author/artist, the graphic life narratives I examine in this book constitute a segment of contemporary 'heterobiography' (Couser 2004: x).[8] The people whose stories they share become implicitly or explicitly linked to the author/cartoonist and the implied reader in relational, hierarchical structures, and the otherness that has been cast upon them often renders them extremely vulnerable.[9] These testimonial texts are written in English and have been published either through traditional publishing outlets or online within the Global North. They target an Anglophone readership, and they aim to raise awareness about invisible distant suffering. The

---

[6] Jones describes the secondary witness as a person who may '"witness" the mediation of [an] event and consider themselves to have knowledge of the event through that mediation' (2019: 269–70). This person may also 'bear witness in the active sense by recounting/presenting this knowledge to an audience' (Jones 2019: 270).

[7] Comics have been marginalized within academic literary research for most of the twentieth century and gained legitimacy in the 1980s with the publication of Art Spiegelman's *Maus* (1986), which narrates the relational life of Vladek, the cartoonist's father and Holocaust survivor. This graphic memoir won the Pulitzer Prize in 1992 (Gardner 2006; Chute 2010, 2011).

[8] In Ancient Greek the word 'ἕτερος' refers literally to the 'other' (Montanari 2016: 833).

[9] Couser unpacks the factors that render specific subjects of life writing vulnerable, which range between 'age-related (extreme youth or age) and [...] physiological (illnesses and impairments, physical or mental) [ones] to membership in socially or culturally disadvantaged minorities' in his analysis of the ethics surrounding the representation of another vulnerable person's life (2004: xii).

vulnerability of their narrated subjects is caused by different reasons: citizenship status, race, socioeconomic background, age, gender, trauma, linguistic competence in English (or lack thereof), and precarious existence within the bio- geo- and necro-political contexts of Juarez, Burma, Vietnam, Palestine, Sri Lanka and the borderzones of Australia and Europe.

The testimonies these texts relate were delivered to English-speaking practitioners, who then remediated them through their creative work. Alternatively, they may be based on events directly witnessed by the agent behind the drawing and/or the writing of the fictionalized testimony. The following chapters introduce my own further removed, theoretically informed, critical acts of reading as secondary witnessing. According to Douglas, 'witnessing [as] as a mode of intelligent, informed, and necessarily empathic reading [has] political power: [it] can raise awareness, challenge historical knowledge, shift power relationships, and redress inequalities' (2010: 152). The purpose of my reading as secondary witnessing is to show how decolonized, postcolonial approaches to print and online graphic life narrative can point not only to its affordances but also to its limitations when it comes to decolonizing the figure of the (post-) colonized other and their testimonies.

Looking elsewhere: graphic testimony and visual witness

In their hybridity, comics display a multiplicity of parameters that determine testimonial remediation both visually and verbally either reproducing or critically unsettling human hierarchies and inequalities, and they can trigger acts of witness that are affectively charged. Rebecca Scherr, for instance, writes that when we experience 'other people's pain [...] that is directly attributable to human rights violations, we are framed as a kind of emotionally invested witness' while engaging with auto/biographical comics (2013: 25). Empathy, grief and compassion are core in testimonial and witnessing transactions, as well as in activist movements and artworks attempting to speak on behalf of othered, marginalized, precarious populations (Whitlock 2011; Polak 2017; Rifkind 2020). However, such affective responses to distant suffering have also been approached from more skeptical standpoints.

Sukhmani Khorana writes that 'the evocation of empathy in refugee narratives is often accompanied by a depoliticisation of systemic issues [, which is reflected in the shift of] responsibility onto the feelings of the ethical citizen rather than the imperative of international obligations and/or the power imbalance in regional relationships' (2015: np; Phelps 2017; Yalouri 2019). Ida Danewid (2017: 1674) also explains that the prevailing affectively-charged focus on bodies in pain in the context of Europe's so-called refugee crisis 'contributes to an ideological formation [...] that turns questions of responsibility, guilt, restitution, repentance, and structural reform into matters of empathy, generosity, and hospitality'.[10] The outcome of this approach, she continues, 'is a veil of ignorance which [...] allows the European subject to re-constitute itself as "ethical" and "good," innocent of its imperialist histories and present complicities' (2017: 1674). While the risk of depoliticization and dehistoricization is indeed present in artistic and activist attempts to raise awareness about other people's distant suffering, as also demonstrated in the following chapters, to ignore the contributions of emotions and affect to knowledge production is to limit the political potential of remediated testimony in graphic life narrative.[11]

The hybridity of comics and the synaesthesia they trigger are core for enriching and complicating acts of witness to the injustices suffered by other people (Scherr 2013). W. J. Thomas Mitchell also argues that because social relations are mirrored in the field of visual and verbal communication, the otherness with which visual images have been invested contrary to verbal text in Western academia, reflects distinctions 'between the freedom to speak and see and the injunction to remain silent and available for observation [thus becoming] transferable from children to women to colonized subjects' (1994: 162). The (post-)colonized otherness of the muted visual spectacle, that is also affectively charged, has significant rhetorical impact in graphic life narratives that account for injustices suffered by othered people.

To foreground this potential, I pursue a methodological approach that consists of close reading in the form of visual, narratological and rhetorical analysis, which is influenced by the principles of decolonial, postcolonial and feminist theories, as well as those of cultural analysis that foregrounds the mediality and performativity of artworks and the socio-political and cultural

---

[10] The term 'crisis' has been criticized for its dehistoricization and depoliticization of the causes of contemporary forced migration (Danewid 2017). I therefore use the term while bearing in mind the (neo-)colonial histories which have been causing this type of migration in Europe, Australia and America (Mbembe 2019a).

[11] The visual/verbal hybridity of comics is productive in triggering affectively-charged responses to issues around justice and human rights. Legal scholar Thomas Giddens, for instance, argues that comics allow inclusive ways of understanding law and justice because they combine aesthetic and rational approaches, which can deconstruct 'hegemonic ways of knowing' triggered by legal texts (2012: 95; 2015b). A significant body of work on comics, social justice and human rights concerns graphic life narrative (Romero and Dahlman 2012; Crawley and van Rijswijk 2012; Donovan and Ustundag 2017; Michael 2019).

situatedness of the critic/reader.[12] The readings I present in the following
chapters, the selections included therein as well as the inevitable omissions,
constitute one possibility among others, which is necessarily limited, and they
are very much influenced by my own geo- and bio-political locus of enunciation.[13]
These readings underscore the usefulness of working in-between testimonial life
writing, comics studies and social justice and they show how graphic life
narrative can popularize but also complicate the negotiation of distant suffering
by triggering both critical thinking about and affective engagement with other
people's remediated testimonies.

A significant body of comics scholarship on graphic life narrative of witness
concerns Joe Sacco's works of graphic journalism, which I also discuss in four of
the five subsequent chapters.[14] In *Disaster Drawn: Visual Witness, Comics, and
Documentary Form*, Hillary Chute notes that Sacco's comics 'acknowledge the
particularity of the witness' since he gives other people's testimony shape through
drawing as opposed to merely quoting it, thus highlighting the appropriateness
of the form for representing other people's oral testimonies (2016: 205; Musleh-
Motut 2019; Mickwitz 2022).[15] Sacco's narratives travel where photography cannot,
and, for this to happen, his imagination must be put in use (Chute 2016). His line,
Chute writes, aspires to be both a record-keeper charged with a 'photographic
function', and to sustain 'the art of the imaginary, the nonobserved' that is connected
to painting (2016: 210).[16] Pramod Nayar also explains that Sacco's work activates a
kind of witnessing that he describes as 'amanuensistic [, which rather than seeking]
indexical referentiality, ensures that we readers see the drawings as mediated
versions of what the artist-storyteller perceived in the faces, events and accounts
[they] encountered' (2021: 130).[17] He thus highlights the mediatory role of the
cartoonist in a body of work that functions as counter-discourse to the silencing

[12] For a detailed description of this model of cultural analysis see Bal 1999.
[13] In decolonial theory, the 'locus of enunciation' refers to 'the geo-political and body-political location of the subject that speaks' that has been erased in Western sciences and philosophy, which have privileged 'the myth of a non-situated "Ego"' (Grosfoguel 2011: np). Establishing and centralizing the 'ethnic/racial/gender/sexual epistemic location [of] the subject that speaks' are essential in decolonizing the Western, Eurocentric production of knowledge (Grosfoguel 2011: np).
[14] I discuss Sacco's *Palestine* (2001) and *Footnotes in Gaza* (2009).
[15] Chute makes the same argument in *Graphic Women: Life Narrative and Contemporary Comics* where she discusses contemporary women's self-referential graphic life narrative, noting that the 'innovative textual practice offered by the rich visual-verbal form of comics' makes it suitable for productive and ethical representations of trauma and testimony (2010: 3).
[16] Chute draws from Charles Baudelaire's (1980) discussion in 'The Modern Public and Photography'.
[17] Nayar draws from Charles Hatfield's (2005: 125) notion of 'ironic authentication' in autobiographical comics whereby the cartoonist 'makes a show of honesty by denying the very possibility of being honest' that is reflected through the plasticity of the cartoon self and concerns the mediation of emotional rather than literal truths.

of distant suffering and human rights violations in the Western media (Kozol 2011). As I hope to also show in the subsequent chapters, Sacco's work foregrounds the potentialities of comics for densely packed remediations of othered people's testimonies, and for performing the turn of the Western gaze, both that of the reader and the artist, elsewhere in a deeply political manner.[18]

In *Distant Wars Visible: The Ambivalence of Witnessing*, Wendy Kozol writes of 'the call to "look elsewhere" [, which] is designed to [...] expose the human costs of military conflict, [and constitutes] a temporal and spatial turn toward outside/elsewhere/not here/not now' (2014: 6).[19] In this monograph, I examine how the selected graphic life narratives display their creators' gazes elsewhere, at the suffering of othered people in the military conflicts of Palestine/Israel, Sri Lanka, Burma and Vietnam, and within European and Australian borderzones. In addition, I investigate their depictions of Western gazes at the human cost of industrialization and globalized neoliberal economy in two cities of the Global South – Juarez and Mae Sot. In so doing, I respond to Kozol's question regarding 'what happens to visual knowledge [...] when we move from here to there' (2014: 6), and I highlight the value of graphic life narrative in illustrating the (neo-)colonial interconnections between the West (Europe, North America and Australia) and the distant suffering of its others.

According to Scherr, the 'haptic visuality' of comics enables nuanced representations of suffering and pain, which can 'reformulate standard forms of looking at "the other"' (2013: 19). In her discussion of Sacco's work, she notes that the frame, a core attribute of the form, which can have both an inclusive and an exclusive function, becomes utilized to foreground the artist's 'highly ambivalent attitude towards the human rights field that he both participates in and critiques' (Scherr 2015: 111).[20] The ambivalence that Scherr identifies in Sacco's graphic journalism and his framings of other people's testimonies is a core attribute of 'looking elsewhere', an act of visual witness that is nevertheless also charged with the possibility of rupturing 'the authoritative power of Western visuality' (Kozol 2014: 17).[21]

Looking elsewhere, Kozol writes, 'makes evident that contemporary artists, filmmakers, and other cultural producers often remain deeply imbricated in the

---

[18] Kozol notes that the Western 'witnessing gaze [...] is implicated in histories of imperialism, militarization, and the inequalities of citizenships' (2008: 70; Mohanty 2003).
[19] Kozol writes from the US context and its military interventions elsewhere.
[20] Scherr's discussion draws from Judith Butler's work in *Frames of War* where she deconstructively approaches the objectivity of photography, noting that 'the frame implicitly guides the interpretation [and it can enable] a false accusation' (2009: 8).
[21] According to Kozol, 'ambivalence provides an analytic framework through which [one can] explore the radical possibilities and limitations of' bearing witness to distant suffering (2014: 7).

dominant visual regimes of imperialism and orientalism that they critique'
(2014: 10). In its ambivalence, this form of witness demonstrates that 'visual
politics [are not] necessarily progressive, antiracist, antisexist, or anti-imperialist,
but [instead they] function as contested sites that as readily destabilize as
secure hegemonic ways of seeing and knowing' (Kozol 2014: 12). My purpose
in this book is to illustrate how my primary corpus displays such destabilizations
and affirmations of hegemonic ways of seeing and knowing, and how decolonized,
postcolonial reading acts can unsettle them. In exposing the wounding
implications of Western ways of seeing and knowing, the selected texts, and
critical approaches to them, can open up spaces towards healing. At the
same time as doing so, they also demonstrate how the popular culture of visual
witness is currently evolving, and what the contribution of graphic life narrative
therein is.

Further to describing the potentialities of comics alongside Sacco's ethical
positioning, Chute (2016) also embeds his work in the tradition of Naji al-Ali's
political cartoons. A Palestinian refugee who settled as a boy at a refugee camp
in Lebanon, al-Ali published cartoons for three decades prior to being
assassinated in London (Chute 2016). The iconic figure drawn by al-Ali that
embodies Palestinian struggle and resistance is a boy named Handala – a silent
child witness to the atrocities inflicted against Palestinian people. The boy, who
is barefoot, with spiked hair, and in ragged clothes, has been deprived of the right
to a safe home and family life and is always drawn with his back turned at readers
as he bears witness to Palestinian suffering (Sacco 2009a). His creator made the
promise 'that once the Palestinian people were free and allowed to return home,
Handala would grow up and the world would see his face' (Abdelrazaq 2015: 11).
With al-Ali having been assassinated for his political views, and with the
Palestinian people still being deprived of the Right to Return, in addition to
further human rights violations suffered by those living in the Occupied
Territories (Human Rights Watch 2021), Handala is yet to grow up and to face
the reader.[22]

Al-Ali's cartoons and Sacco's graphic journalism belong in the same global
'popular tradition [. . .] of drawing as a sophisticated yet accessible circulating

---

[22] In her analysis of Sacco's work, Scherr discusses the exceptional status of Palestinians who, despite
being uprooted from their land, do not fall under the category of the refugee in International Human
Rights and Refugee Laws. Palestinians, she writes, 'are in fact refugees while being denied the official
status of refugees as a result of international political intervention; they are, in short, caught in a
deadly legal loophole in which their very "humanness" is put under question' (2015: 115; Albanese
and Takkenberg 2020).

form that brings attention to the witness' (Chute 2016: 212). It is alongside this tradition, which has also moved to online digital spaces, that I situate the graphic life narratives examined in this monograph. In being positioned alongside al-Ali's political cartoons, this work becomes charged with the responsibility to bear witness to other people's suffering in the industrialized border cities of Juarez and Mae Sot, in the Sri Lankan and the Israeli/Palestinian conflicts, in the Vietnam war, in asylum detention in Australia and in asylum-seeking journeys from Africa and the Middle East into Europe. As such, it demonstrates the global reach, the political impact and the transformations of contemporary (graphic) life narrative.

Sidonie Smith and Julia Watson write that 'as the global reach of graphic memoirs expands as a popular form of witnessing to histories of trauma and marking the need to remember, new issues for scholars of life narratives arise' (2010: 173). These issues include, among others, the ways in which 'autographics call us to know and see otherwise; how they produce us as different kinds of readers; how they witness and with what effects' (Smith and Watson 2010: 173).[23] In her explication of 'autographics', Whitlock explains that the intertext of 'autobiographics', a term coined by Gilmore in her investigation of women's life narrative, allows one to think about the aforementioned genre as connected to 'the shifting jurisdictions and limits of autobiography that is a consistent feature of [her] attention to the production and consumption of life story' (Whitlock 2008: 967; Gilmore 1994). As such, Whitlock shows how intersectional feminist life narrative scholarship contributes to the conceptualization of the political potentialities of graphic life storytelling, testimony and witness.

While autographics primarily encompass self-referential graphic life narrative, 'biographics', a term introduced by Eva C. Karpinski, presents 'a shift of focus onto biography's "principal character," who occupies a distinct ontological plane from the narrator/author' (2016: 237; Rifkind and Warley 2016). Karpinski notes that 'in studying the rules of engagement with other people's lives and the choices of visual and textual strategies of representation, we can appreciate how comics provide opportunities for the creative reinvention of their biographical subjects' (2016: 237). Simultaneously, the genre's 'double legacy of biography and comics [...] calls for an inquiry into issues related to the ethics

---

[23] Whitlock and Anna Poletti introduce 'autographics [as] life narrative fabricated in and through drawing and design using various technologies, modes, and materials [and as a] practice of reading the signs, symbols and techniques of visual arts in life narrative' (2008: v).

and politics of biographic(al) telling, hearing, seeing, and representing, and their compatibility with the goals of historical commemoration and commercialization, pedagogy, and entertainment' (Karpinski 2016: 238). It is precisely these aspects of graphic life narrative that the following chapters examine through their focus on its distinct sub-genres, which range between print and online graphic journalism and reportage, graphic memoir, the ethno-graphic novel, children's refugee literature and online cartoons.

Primary texts and graphic life narrative sub-genres

The primary texts I examine in this monograph have been selected because of their contribution toward re-conceptualizing issues around bearing witness to other people's distant suffering, human rights violations and global distributions of injustice, and because they demonstrate the interdisciplinary reach of contemporary graphic life narrative. They come from different artistic traditions, they display different relations between the artists and their biographical subjects, and they zoom in on diverse geo- bio- and necro-political locations across the globe.

Joe Sacco's *Palestine* (2001) and *Footnotes in Gaza* (2009) account for Palestinian suffering at the same time as critiquing its Western framing through conventional journalistic and historical scripts. *I Live Here* is a four-volume project edited by Mia Kirschner, J. B. MacKinnon, Paul Shoebridge and Michael Simons (2008), and it bears witness to suffering and injustices occurring in Ingushetia, Burma, Juarez and Malawi through graphic novellas, journal entries, collage, photography and fabric art.[24] In this monograph, I discuss its second and third volumes, which include, further to Kirschner's journal entries, two graphic novellas by Kamel Khélif and Phoebe Gloeckner entitled 'The Story of Mi-Su' (vol. 2) and 'La Tristeza' (vol. 3), respectively. The two volumes have been selected because they zoom in on similar forms of suffering, namely sex work and gendered violence, in the industrialized border cities of Juarez and Mae Sot.

In addition, I discuss *La Lucha: The Story of Lucha Castro and Human Rights in Mexico* by John Sack (2015), which casts a different perspective on gendered violence, femicide and activism in Juarez, and *Vanni: A Family's Struggle through the Sri Lankan Conflict* by Benjamin Dix and Lindsay Pollock (2019), which

---

[24] Following Whitlock and Poletti, in this monograph, I refer to graphic life narrative as a broad genre that uses visual and verbal means that can be other than the language of comics, which is based on speech and thought bubbles, gutters, panels and narrative captions.

mediates a Tamil man and his family's experiences prior to, during and after the escalation of the Sinhala/Tamil conflict in Sri Lanka in 2009. As I show through the close decolonized postcolonial readings that follow, these texts establish connections, either explicitly or implicitly, between othered people's present suffering and Western States' past and present (neo-)colonial interventions elsewhere. In so doing, they highlight the injurious impact of these connections, and they refrain from decontextualizing and dehistoricizing contemporary distant suffering. I also examine Thi Bui's *The Best We Could Do* (2018), which accounts for her family's suffering prior to, during, and after the Vietnam war, and for their undocumented border crossing into the United States, and Francesca Sanna's *The Journey* (2016), a fictionalized life story of a family's asylum-seeking journey from an unnamed city, possibly located in the Middle East, to Europe. This picture book is based on the testimonies of two girls the author met at a refugee camp in Italy and on others she subsequently collected.

The following analysis starts with an exploration of suffering in Juarez, Burma, Palestine, Sri Lanka and Vietnam, and it moves to graphic accounts of suffering closer to the Global North, but still further removed due to its invisibility. *The Journey*, alongside the online graphic life narratives I examine in the last two chapters of this monograph, is concerned with othered people's suffering in detention and in asylum-seeking journeys through Western borders. These online texts include Safdar Ahmed's 'Villawood: Notes from an Immigration Detention Centre' (2015) and 'Affective States' (2024), as well as three cartoons by the Iranian cartoonist Ali Dorani, who was detained in Manus Island, Australia's offshore detention centre, and is known by the pseudonym Eaten Fish. Moving from Australia to Europe, I discuss a short webcomic by Gabi Froden entitled 'Empty Promise' (2017), which accounts for a Nigerian woman's undocumented border crossing through Libya and the Mediterranean to Italy. At the same time as understanding life narrative as a pluralistic, shifting and porous genre (Couser 2012), in delineating the sub-categories in which the aforementioned texts belong, I mean to underscore the interdisciplinary reach of its potential.

Filial graphic memoir

Bui's *The Best We Could Do* constitutes a daughter's attempt to tell the story of her parents, and to thus understand her own. Her autobiographical avatar is often depicted asking her parents questions and trying to make sense of their ideological stance, emotions and decisions. In being familial, the relational bonds existing between the cartoonist/autobiographical self and her biographical subjects are more intimate than those displayed in other texts, where Anglophone artistic practitioners visit conflict zones to collect testimonies or to directly witness the otherwise distant suffering of other people. *The Best We Can Do* thus stands as a 'filial' graphic memoir and, at the same time as being self-referential, it also constitutes a 'patriography' – a type of life narrative by sons or daughters about their fathers – and a 'matriography', its equivalent about mothers (Couser 2012: 259).

Graphic journalism

Palestine, Footnotes, La Lucha and 'Villawood' constitute samples of graphic journalism.[25] Sacco first introduced this term 'in the mid-1990s [. . .] to describe his nonfiction comics about current events' (el Refaie 2022: 65; Sacco 2012a). Graphic journalism highlights the impossibility of journalistic objectivity by making the political standing of the journalist/autobiographical subject through whom events are filtered clear in the *mise-en-scène* realm.[26] This life narrative sub-genre constitutes 'an increasingly popular way to bear witness to a range of socio-political events and circumstances, with a focus on the experiences of ordinary, subaltern people in crisis situations' (el Refaie 2022: 65). Graphic journalism has been commended for its ability to trigger 'reader engagement and empathy through the use of multiple viewpoints, the mixing of realistic and symbolic elements, and the tensions between distinct semiotic modes' (el Refaie 2022: 66).[27]

In addition to the above, and despite its differences in terms of form, *I Live Here* (Kirschner et al. 2008) can also be embedded in this graphic life narrative sub-genre.[28] This four-volume project has been marketed as a 'paper documentary

---

[25] *La Lucha* was published in the framework of the public outreach efforts of the NGO Front Line Defenders to increase visibility about the precarity of human rights defenders in Mexico. For information about the Front Line Defenders see https://www.frontlinedefenders.org/en/who-we-are.

[26] Elisabeth el Refaie (2022: 66) writes that most practitioners of graphic journalism 'include themselves as a character, thus emphasising the interpretative nature of all journalistic processes and challenging established notions of professional objectivity and authenticity'.

[27] Graphic journalism has emerged from the tradition of new journalism, which acknowledges the existence of fiction in journalistic work and has led to the establishment of relevant literary genres such as journalistic and historical fiction (Keeble and Wheeler 2007).

[28] *I Live Here*, like Sanna's *The Journey*, was endorsed by Amnesty International. Together with Jovana Mastilovic, I have written elsewhere on the injurious ambivalences of the NGO's approaches to representing other people's suffering in the context of Greece's refugee crisis (Michael and Mastilovic 2022).

that raises the specter of cinematic conventions and the ethical struggles around the point of view, objectivity, and selectivity associated with film' (Goldberg and Moore 2011: 235). With *I Live Here*, Kirschner, the main editor of the project, tried to reconfigure the ethics of film-documentary objectivity through a paper documentary that allows for the conventions of the former to be put on paper, for moments to freeze and for subjects to become visually or verbally marked in their aesthetic placement across pages. However, this attempt, as also shown in the following chapters, frequently runs the risk, and at times falls into the trap, of presenting 'formulaic' depictions that contribute 'in perpetuating structural imbalances between gendered citizens of the safe and vulnerable worlds' (Goldberg and Moore 2011: 246). In this sense, *I Live Here*, like the other texts examined in this monograph, reflects 'the imbalance [existing] between those who have the power to represent and those who are represented' (Yalouri 2019: 227). Despite claims to objectivity, authorial stance is also clearly marked, particularly in Kirschner's journal entries as per relevant genre expectations, while figuration and fictionalization have a core rhetorical function in this four-volume graphic life narrative.

The ethno-graphic novel

While peritextually situating *Vanni* in the same tradition as Sacco's graphic journalism, Dix has written it as part of his PhD, 'which examined methods of adapting complex testimony into sequential art' in social anthropology (Dix and Pollock 2019: np). Together with Raminder Kaur, Dix refers to the '"graphic narrative turn" that has emerged in anthropology in recent years' and argues for the usefulness of visual images alongside words in ethnographic research that attempts to represent other people and cultures in ways that can 'create synchronous affective intensities' in broader audiences (2019: 76).[29] Dix and Kaur introduce 'a theory and practice for graphic novel production', which they term '*vérités graphiques* (literally, graphic realities)' (2019: 76). With this term they refer to 'the collaborative and interactive engagement with people's contributions and views, and their distillation and fictionalization through the ethno-graphic form', which can negotiate 'a truth-fiction spectrum that further

---

[29] Dix and Kaur's reference to the graphic narrative turn in ethnographic research constitutes a milestone in a longer trajectory which includes the literary turn in the discipline in the 1980s, which acknowledged the existence of fiction and impossibility of objectivity in ethnographic work (Fagerlid and Tisdel 2020).

challenges the presumed objectivity of what is seen, experienced, co-created, and revealed' (Dix and Kaur 2019: 76). Works that fall under this category, like *Vanni*, highlight the value of comics as a form and the 'ethno-graphic novel' as a genre for providing 'a more subjective, self-reflexive, and interactive method for the anthropological endeavor' (Dix and Kaur 2019: 90).

Documentary webcomics of asylum-seeking journeys and detention

Further to the above, Dix is also the founder of PositiveNegatives, an NGO that addresses Anglophone audiences and uses comics to raise awareness about social issues such as conflict, climate change and undocumented migration, *inter alia*. Further to comics and animation videos, which are created through the approach previously described, the organization's website includes educational resources that can be used in diverse teaching contexts (Wong et al. 2020). Johannes Schmid refers to short online comics, such as those shared through PositiveNegatives, with the term 'documentary webcomics' and notes that they aspire to 'influence public opinion and transform society, thus presenting an effort in media activism' (2019: 73).[30] Like Shannon Sandford, in this monograph, I also show how 'webcomics on human rights [can] reshape what it means to be citizens of the Internet, and simultaneously, citizens of the places we live' (2022: 187), as well as of a globalized, (post-)colonized, hierarchically divided world.

The online existence of such work increases its visibility through its shareability, at the same time as offering readers opportunities to respond by liking the texts they read, or by posting their comments about them. As such, contemporarily, book-long graphic life narratives have transformed into 'predominantly short-form webcomics [offering] a sympathetic fit with practices of online reading, viewing, and browsing that tend to be characterized by shorter bursts of attention' (Mickwitz 2016: 145; Humphrey 2017).[31] In her analysis of online comics about the suffering and trauma caused by Australia's asylum detention system, Golnar Nabizadeh points out that even if they are indeed significantly shorter than print graphic narratives, 'like their paper counterparts, [they] frequently require the reader to lengthen their reading

---

[30] Karin Kukkonen defines webcomics as 'comics (primarily) published on and distributed through the Internet. Some, but by far not all, of these comics make use of the affordances of digitalization' (2014: 521).
[31] For a distinction between digital and webcomics see Kleefeld 2020. In this monograph, I will be using the terms webcomics, online comics and graphic life narrative interchangeably.

time and concentration to comprehend the bi-ocular messages before them'
(2019: 163).[32]

As Nina Mickwitz usefully reminds us, however, particularly when it comes
to 'refugee stories' told via comics, it is important to remain cautious of the risk
entailed in generalizing about the affordances of the form (2020a: 459). Like
print graphic life narratives accounting for human rights violations suffered by
othered people, online ones may fall into the trap of reproducing rather than
undoing the (neo-)colonial wounds, hierarchies and injustices they seek to
counter. Refugee stories, like the ones remediated in Froden's and Ahmed's
webcomics, are the product of humanitarian advocacy, a term that implies
speaking 'on behalf of or in solidarity with someone who is not able
to speak for themselves' (Mickwitz 2020a: 459). Advocacy, Mickwitz goes on to
explain, 'is motivated by an ethical response and is, presumably, intended to
support or effect social change' (2020a: 459). And while 'the formal construction
of comics has been described as acutely congruent with witnessing and trauma,
and has been credited with inviting readerly positions that are "ethically
nuanced"' (Mickwitz 2020a: 459), the risk of generalizing about the affordances
of the form is still present. For this reason, even if online graphic life narratives
share the rhetorical potential of their print counterparts, 'such qualities require
consideration on a case-by-case basis' (Mickwitz 2020a: 459), and it is this
approach that I pursue in the following chapters.

Froden's webcomic 'An Empty Promise', which was published via
PositiveNegatives, and that I examine in Chapters 4 and 5, consists of twenty-five
full-page panels and it evokes the style of children's illustration. In order to move
from one page/panel to the next, the reader must click on it or swipe right if they
are reading on a mobile device. In her analysis of webcomics shared via
Instagram, Sandford refers to the carousel as one among other 'aesthetic strategies
[that can be used to] expand and subvert the [...] conventions of comics, most
notably, to denote new tangible meanings to the notion of sequence' (2022: 14).[33]
Carousels, she further explains, 'manipulate the natural aporias, gutters, and gaps

---

[32] Marianne Hirsch refers to comics' 'visual-verbal biocularity', which enables complex mediations of
'traumatic seeing' in Art Spiegelman's *In the Shadow of No Towers*, a graphic memoir that describes the
cartoonist's witnessing of the fall of the World Trade Center (2004: 2013). She writes that the form blurs
'clear differentiations between word and image. With words always already functioning as images and
images asking to be read as much as seen', she points out, 'comics are biocular texts *par excellence*', and
as such they ask 'us to read back and forth between images and words [revealing] the visuality and thus
the materiality of words and the discursivity and narrativity of images' (Hirsch 2004: 2013).
[33] In her analysis of autobiographical webcomics of illness, loss, trauma and human rights, Sandford
(2022: iii) makes a case for 'the visual-verbal-digital idiom of webcomics as a subversive and
underrepresented site for life narrative'.

of comics, broadening the parameters for reading "sequentially", by presenting a more tangible sense of how comics' transitions unfold scene-to-scene' (Sandford 2022: 114). 'An Empty Promise' is based on the utilization of this strategy, and, thus, crossing the gap between panels and moving between narrative fragments, takes the form of clicking or swiping right while looking at the screen.

Mickwitz writes that, contra to vulnerable victimhood refugee representation tropes found in media and humanitarian campaigns, those encountered in the webcomics of PositiveNegatives 'illustrate clear attempts to address some of the criticisms levelled at not just news media, but also humanitarian aid campaigns' (2020b: 288).[34] These comics, she continues, are characterized by 'deliberate and measured quality, [while] the absence of visual hyperbole pre-empts charges of sensationalism' (Mickwitz 2020b: 288). Their drawing style often evokes that of 'children's illustration' even if the protagonists are adult and often male, and their 'friendly and unthreatening' appearance invites empathy at the same time as presenting an alternative to sensationalistic representations of refugees (Mickwitz 2020b: 289).

While this is true, and without questioning the creative practitioners' intentions, I am skeptical about the turn to this drawing style, which may run the risk of mediating child-like or infantilized depictions of othered people, and I therefore see it as charged with the ambivalence that marks the Western visual witnessing of distant suffering. As Dragoș Manea and Mihaela Precup also write in their analysis of Kate Evans's graphic memoir, *Threads: From the Refugee Crisis*, drawing refugees 'in a manner that likens them to children in terms of their facial features and posture to render [them] less threatening to Western audiences [...] resists a tradition that has framed refugees, and particularly refugee men, as physically and sexually dangerous' (2020: 481–2). At the same time, however, this approach also evokes 'an older Orientalist representational tradition that has wilfully framed such men as childlike in order to bolster Western claims to superiority' (Manea and Precup 2020: 482).[35] It is precisely for this reason that drawing styles evoking children's illustration when addressing an adult readership become vested in ambivalence.

Additionally to Froden's webcomic, I also examine Ahmed's 'Villawood' and 'Affective States', which utilize a different visual approach to the remediation of other people's suffering in Australian asylum detention that is not marked by the

---

[34] For an analysis of problematic media portrayals of refugees see Chouliaraki and Stolic 2017.
[35] This does not apply for children's picture books like *The Journey*, which represent difficult matters for younger audiences.

same ambivalence. 'Villawood' came out of the 'Refugee Art Project [...], a grassroots non-profit organisation that promotes the creativity and freedom of expression of asylum seekers and refugees in the Western Sydney area', by providing 'weekly art workshops inside the Villawood Immigration Detention Centre, with men, women and children from such countries as Afghanistan, Burma, Iran, Iraq and Sri Lanka' (Ahmed 2014: 24).[36] 'Villawood' was first released in *The Shipping News*, and it includes illustrations drawn by some of the detainees alongside Ahmed's comics, centralizing their creative, testimonial contribution in the creation process.[37] As opposed to being based on a conventional comics page set-up, it takes the form of 'a scrolling webcomic' (Sandford 2022: 188). In 'Villawood', Sandford writes, 'the vast territory of the screen is what Ahmed leverages to speak about asylum seeker traumas and intimacies, by inviting readers to interpret the details of a scene without stipulating the edges and seams of that scene' (2022: 188).

A more extended version of this online comic was published in book form in 2021 under the title *Still Alive* (Ahmed 2021). As the title of the book implies, in Ahmed's work, asylum seekers and refugees held in Australia's detention system find ways to resist their dehumanization and to reclaim their dignity and humanity. Ahmed's second online text, 'Affective States', was created as an artistic contribution to the special issue of the academic open-access journal *Image [&] Narrative* entitled 'Border Crossings and Human Rights in Graphic Narratives', and it relates the autobiographical subject's affective bonding through music making with Kazem Kazemi, an Iranian refugee who was held in Manus Island. As such, it oscillates between graphic memoir and journalism, crossing generic borders in its testimonial account. It is based on a more conventional comics page set-up, and the reader can engage with the text through a top-down, left-to-right movement while navigating the space of the page.

The last webcomics artist whose work I explore is Eaten Fish, who was awarded the annual Award for Courage in Editorial Cartooning by the Cartoonist Rights Network International (Humphrey 2020). Upon his award, the executive director of the network, Robert Russell, noted that Eaten Fish's comics 'will some day be recognised as important, world-class chronicles of the worst human behaviour since the World War II concentration camps' (quoted in Perera

---

[36] 'Villawood' received a Walkley award in 2015 in acknowledgement of its original journalistic work (Humphrey 2017).
[37] *The Shipping News* is 'an investigative arm of the online publishing platform *Medium* [working] in collaboration with Australian political activist group GetUp' (Sandford 2022: 179).

and Pugliese 2016: np). From his precarious body-political and geo-political positionality, Eaten Fish exposes the Australian State's (neo-)colonial border violence via his colourful webcomics. This violence is also reflected by how people like him 'are at further risk of violence each time they create, speak, draw or write' (Cartoonists Rights Network International, quoted in Bui 2018: 191).[38]

For this reason, after having secured asylum in Norway, further to his own suffering and that which he witnessed, Eaten Fish also bears witness, through his blog and online comics, to the pain of those whose rights continue being violated in Australia's offshore detention centres.[39] And while comics have been devalued and disregarded both as an artform and as a legitimate source of historical and journalistic information, when it comes to their exposure of border violence, they seem to matter in ways that can be injurious for asylum seekers and refugees, who choose to speak out through this artform. This is why the fictionalization of graphic testimony is crucial in such cases.

Children's refugee literature

Further to graphic life narratives addressing adult readers, I also discuss *The Journey*, which falls into the generic category of 'children's refugee literature' (Sifaki 2019: 1).[40] This genre consists of picture books and literary narratives that 'explicate the reasons why, and the conditions under which, refugees and migrants move and re-settle, aiming to trigger child readers' affective responses in relation to this difficult matter and to educate them about human rights' (Sifaki 2019: 1). Whereas in refugee narratives addressing adult readers 'harsh realistic scenes do not constitute a problem, and educational censorship does not apply', this is not the case for texts addressing child readers (Zervou 2020: 3).[41] How can we then depict this difficult reality for younger readers without falling into the trap of its 'excessive beautification?' (Zervou 2020: 3).

---

[38] A postscript to an article written for *The Conversation* on the work of Eaten Fish explains that after publication 'Mr Fish has told the authors that he has been subjected to further violence' during his detention at Manus Island (Perera and Pugliese 2016: np).

[39] Ruth Page (2014: 42) defines 'blogs [as] web pages in which dated entries appear in reverse chronological order [and as] multimodal genres'. In being freely available, they have enabled the increased public exposure of the cartoons of Eaten Fish. As such, they reflect what Whitlock (2015b: 245) has described as 'the hospitality of the cyberspace [in] mobilizing asylum seeker testimony online'. Whitlock (2015a: 195) also refers to the 'hospitality of fiction' for refugee testimony. In this monograph, I also mean to point to the potentialities lying in the fictionalization of othered people's testimony and its online circulation in graphic life narrative.

[40] My translation from Greek.

[41] My translation from Greek.

Vassiliki Vassiloudi writes that most discussions on children's picture books about refugee journeys present them as 'opportunit[ies] to educate non-refugee children into engaging in acts of humanity, rather than urging them to unearth the roots of the refugee crisis' (2019: 35). Such texts are often characterized by their politically sanitized depictions of the refugee crisis and their 'attempt to fix the reader in the position of the Western benefactor', while at the same time avoiding references to the political causes of this social issue (Vassiloudi 2019: 37). She further urges her readers to ask themselves 'in whose best interest we act when promoting such distorted images of rapturous acceptance and benevolence' in our roles as parents, critics and educators (Vassiloudi 2019: 39). 'Even if non-refugee child readers are our primary focus, how are we benefiting them by giving them half-truths and watered-down stories?', she wonders (Vassiloudi 2019: 39). Evgenia Sifaki (2019) proposes that it is best for children's refugee literature to be read alongside historical and testimonial texts, and in parallel to other activities in the classroom and beyond, which could help fill in knowledge gaps regarding the cultures from which refugees come. Such acts of informed reading can also expose the diachronic (neo-)colonial violence that causes contemporary forced migration and the excessive precarity that comes with it. While silences about Western border violence often characterize graphic life narratives targeting adult readers as well, these can be unsettled through decolonized, postcolonial reading practices, which I explicate below.

Even though picture books and graphic novels have been seen as distinct art and literary forms, I understand *The Journey* as part of the broad spectrum of visual/verbal life narratives that remediate othered people's suffering, and through my analysis I hope to undo stereotypical assumptions about the simplicity of picture books due to their connection to childhood. As such, I pursue an argument similar to Douglas's in her recently published *Children and Biography: Reading and Writing Life Stories*, where she foregrounds the role of children's refugee picture books as a life narrative sub-genre for offering new 'historical, social and cultural knowledge on the experience of child asylum seekers' (2023: 15).

Nathalie op de Beeck writes that picture books are often 'pitched to a preliterate audience [, they become] associated with functional literacy [and their] reputation for cuteness and didacticism can cancel out their rich signifying potential' (2012: 468). For this reason, 'they may seem unworthy of literary or art-historical scrutiny' (Op de Beeck 2012: 468). Graphic novels, in contrast, are often 'understood as instilling critical and political literacy, serving a countercultural function unwelcome in the ostensibly sweet and safe picture book form' (Op de Beeck 2012: 476). As I show, however, approaching *The Journey* from a critical standpoint can foreground the political implications of its visual/verbal mixing, and the ways in which the picture book 'can promote critical in addition to basic literacy' (Op de Beeck 2012: 472).[42] Like Douglas (2023), in analysing this book, I mean to point to the contribution of graphic life narrative in children's education about human rights, social justice and forced migration.

Aspects of injustice and suffering

Further to the generic overview that points to the contribution of graphic life narrative in disciplines such as (children's) literature, journalism, social anthropology, social justice and migration studies, below I unpack the kinds of injustice and suffering I address and the reasons why I do so. As mentioned, I discuss precarious othered femininities and masculinities, as well as depictions of the dead, and their rhetorical implications in relation to the limitations of human rights. In addition, I investigate graphic displays of the (back)ground – of space, place, and the environment – to examine its own narrative potential in relation to exposing global distributions of injustice. Lastly, I look at bodies and objects circulating within the borders of Europe and Australia in contexts of asylum detention and forced migration journeys at sea and on land. By zooming in on these different aspects of othered people's distant suffering, I demonstrate how graphic life narrative brings it closer, while also triggering critical thinking about, and affective responses to it.

Gendered violence

The examination of gendered violence is core to this book since the visuality of comics can facilitate complex testimonies of vulnerable and precarious femininities and masculinities. Initially, women's and girls' 'to-be-looked-at-ness', that is, their status as spectacles under the male gaze, was first introduced by Laura Mulvey, who also delineated the status of Man as 'the bearer of the look' (1989: 19–20;

---

[42] In her analysis of the figure of the child in Canadian graphic life narrative, Cheryl Cowdy writes that 'bringing together the material and the semiotic, the textual and the pictorial, the hybridity of graphic life narratives and the formal strategies associated with it make [...] a regenerative reading practice possible, emphasizing as well the centrality of childhood to both life writing and comics' (2016: 292). Through my analysis of *The Journey*, I also hope to underscore the centrality of childhood in contemporary refugee life narrative.

Berger 1972).[43] Within this gendered dichotomy between the owner of the gaze and the visual spectacle, women and girls are conceptualized as primarily looked at, observed and deciphered while remaining silent. Women and girls of colour, who may also be religiously othered, become further silenced and objectified in this schema. Human rights violations inflicted upon them occur within, and become determined by, complex networks of hegemonic and dominant masculinities at public and private, as well as national and international levels. These violations either remain invisible or become spectacularized through their staging in political and media discourses in ways that justify Western countries' neo-colonial interventions elsewhere. For instance, while Muslim women have been perceived as docile, passive victims in need for a Western male saviour to free them from patriarchal oppression, Muslim men are seen as embodying and enacting this oppression (Mohanty 1988; Spivak 1988; Abu-Lughod 2002).

In her analysis of how women's rights have constituted the excuse for America's post-9/11 neo-colonial intervention in Afghanistan, Miriam Cooke introduces 'the four-staged gendered logic of the empire [whereby] (1) women have inalienable rights within universal civilization, (2) civilized men recognize and respect these rights, (3) uncivilized men systematically abrogate these rights, and (4) such men (the Taliban) thus belong to an alien (Islamic) system' (2002: 485). This neo-colonial outlook, Cooke continues, 'genders and separates subject peoples so that the men are the Other and the women are civilizable' (2002: 485). Further to its gendered divisions, it thus produces two masculinity categories in juxtaposition to each other: that of the ethical white Western saviour, and that of the monstrous male other, who threatens Muslim women and the West, both of whom need to be defended. Such discursive formations of othered femininities and masculinities create 'hierarchies of humanity' whereby those deemed most innocent are the ones most worthy of dignified and respectful treatment and protection, suffering less hostility and suspicion (Fassin 2010: 239).

Another outcome of this logic is linked to how white Western men 'are allowed to ignore their complicity in creating a category of people who need saving, and they need never ask whether these brown women actually want saving, since as innocents they are understood to lack desire [and] agency' (Ticktin 2017: 583).[44]

---

[43] In *Graphic Women*, Chute refers to the connections between femininity and visuality, and introduces the 'risk of representation' autobiographical comics take in graphically accounting for sexual trauma, arguing that the genre 'is invested in the ethics of testimony' (2010: 3).

[44] As Ticktin usefully explains, 'while the Latin etymology of innocence focuses on harm (in- + nocens, "not harmful" [...]), the etymology of in- + noscere, "not to know," is perhaps even more significant' because it configures innocent women and children as pure but also lacking in terms of knowledge, and thus unable to decide and to act for themselves (2017: 578).

Contrarily brown, as well as other non-white men become interpellated as oppressive monstrous extremists and violent misogynists, whose monstrosity is associated with their non-Western origins, their non-Christian (Islamic) religion, and most importantly, with their othered masculinities.[45] As Lilie Chouliaraki and Tijana Stolic note, while representations of women and children cast 'refugees as objects of care, the physical proximity of dark-skinned men turns them into "*les enrages*", intimidating "others" who threaten "our" safety' (2017: 1169; Boltanski 1999; Buchanan et al. 2003). Such injurious discursive formations of othered men ignore and silence their vulnerabilities, traumas and precarities.[46]

These are also often ignored in legal, migration and humanitarian discourses (Ticktin 2017; Griffiths 2015). Lara Stemple, for instance, accounts for the multiple ways in which 'numerous instruments in the human rights canon, including U.N. treaties, resolutions, consensus documents, and general comments address sexual violence while explicitly excluding male victims' (2008: 605–6). Even though the protection of women and girls from violence is essential, it is also crucial for it to include men because failing to do so 'reifies hierarchies that treat some victims as more sympathetic than others, perpetuates norms that essentialize women as victims, and imposes unhealthy expectations about masculinity on men and boys' (Stemple 2008: 606). Such exclusions derive from preconceptions about the threat of aggression as always-already male, which exists in opposition to vulnerability, passivity and innocence that are imagined as linked to femininity and childhood. In this monograph, I look into whether the selected graphic life narratives undo or reproduce such (neo-)colonial takes on othered men, which heavily impact their reception as asylum seekers and refugees in Western host countries (Charsley and Wray 2015).

Indeed, Melanie Griffiths mentions that the deceiving, unworthy asylum seeker is usually imagined as male, and that this results from 'gendered suspicions

[45] In *The Novel of Human Rights*, James Dawes also writes that there is an 'insistent and vivid representation of injured women' and of female bodies in need of salvation (2018: 168). This category of female victims produces the autonomous, invulnerable (presumptively male) subject speaking for the collective human subject as well as this subject's inhuman other, the male perpetrator (Dawes 2018; Wilcox 2015). Such neo-colonial discursive formations of male as well as the female otherness are understood in this monograph as instances of performative speech acts that produce particular subjects at the same time as linguistically wounding them through their 'interpellative force', which stems from human beings' 'linguistic vulnerability' (Butler 1997: 1–9).
[46] In 'Violent Conflict and Gender Inequality', for instance, Mayra Buvinic et al. write of 'the human effects' of conflict and violence, which have gendered implications and of the high mortality rates that typically affect men (2013: 2). Men also constitute 90 percent of the world's missing people, leaving a high percentage of women and children forced into internal displacement (World Bank 2011). They suffer high disability rates due to their increased exposure to mass violence, they undergo particular kinds of torture, and as a result, they suffer psychological injuries and PTSD, which often remain silenced due to gendered shame (Krug et al. 2002).

and expectations regarding agency' (2015: 468). Migration scholarship also tends to either 'sideline men or to present them as oppressors, fanatics, or criminals' and to connect 'black men [. . .] with criminality, violence, and hypersexuality' (Griffiths 2015: 469, 471). Men from Asia and the Middle East are also increasingly becoming linked to 'fundamentalism and security threats' (Griffiths 2015: 471; De Hart 2009; Wray 2009). Such attitudes are representative of broader Western perspectives on racially and religiously othered adult male refugees and asylum seekers.[47]

By looking at the human rights violations suffered by women and girls on the one hand, and men and boys on the other, and while by no means pretending to present an exhaustive discussion of gender and sexuality issues in contexts of war, persecution, incarceration, conflict and forced migration, I hope to highlight the usefulness of graphic life narrative in illustrating why such injustices and corresponding in/visibilities should be taken into consideration. On the one hand, the human rights violations suffered by men and boys in prison, war and asylum detention, as well as their relationalities and vulnerabilities, remain largely invisible in the human rights canon when it comes, for instance, to their protection from sexual torture, as well as in migration and humanitarian discourses. On the other hand, men become visible first and foremost as monstrous perpetrators of violence. For these reasons, I seek to investigate the ways in which their graphic depictions can unsettle this in/visibility.

Death

Further to gendered precarities and their rhetorical potential in relation to the global distribution of injustice, dead bodies in different geo-, bio- and necro-political contexts have significant implications regarding the limitations of human rights discourses and the unequal distribution of violence across the globe. Antoine Pécoud, for instance, discusses the border deaths of the Mediterranean in the context of undocumented migration from Africa and Asia to Europe, and argues that their political significance lies in how they expose 'the deadly consequences of the politics of migration in Europe' and in how they 'embody the diffuse violence that underlies the control of peoples' mobility and the rejection of foreigners outside European borders' (2020: 383). The dead are

[47] Sara Dehm and Jordana Silverstein discuss similar 'gendered archetypes', among which 'the aggressive male, the caring mother, the innocent child' in a TV film commissioned by the Australian government in 2015 in the framework of its deterrence policies which aimed at convincing people to stop entering the country by boat 'without state authorization' (2020: 427).

also charged with political impact in the Israeli/Palestinian, the Tamil/Sinhala and the Burmese/Karen conflicts, as well as in the context of the Juarez femicides, the Vietnam war and asylum detention in Australia. By zooming in on graphic displays of death through a thanatopolitical and necropolitical perspective, I mean to illustrate how and why the dead relationally matter in the remediated testimonies of the living.

Spatial injustice

While we tend to focus on human bodies that suffer, rather than on the spaces where suffering occurs when examining depictions of human rights violations in graphic life narrative, injustice, inequality and the violence that comes along with them 'have a spatial dimension, which [also] requires attention and sensitivity' (Madanipour et al. 2022: 808). Spatial justice concerns 'the interactions between space and society' and the ways in which inequalities become 'geographically distributed' (Rauhut 2018: 109). It encompasses 'territorial justice, environmental justice, the urbanization of injustice, [and] regional inequalities', *inter alia* (Soja 2009: 1). Edward W. Soja writes that 'thinking spatially about justice not only enriches our theoretical understanding, [but] it can [also] uncover significant new insights that extend our practical knowledge into more effective actions to achieve greater justice and democracy' (2009: 1).

For this reason, it is important 'to emphasize explicitly the spatiality of justice and injustice, not just in the city but at all geographical scales, from the local to the global' (Soja 2009: 1). In the last decades, the spatial turn has provided fruitful insights into the workings of space and place in literary studies (Tally 2017). In life narrative research, 'autotopography' refers to diverse forms of writing the self on and through space both literally, via graffiti for instance, and metaphorically, through the arrangement of objects in a given place (González 1995; Bal 2002; Heddon 2002, 2007), while 'topobiography' foregrounds the 'triad [between] place, memory, and time' (Karjalainen 2015: 101).[48] Such generic types have helped unpack the significance of spatial rhetorics in life storytelling.

Attention to space and place is relatively recent in comics scholarship. In *Urban Comics: Infrastructure and the Global City in Contemporary Graphic Narratives*, for instance, Dominic Davies illustrates how 'graphic narrative [can] capture the political forces that solidify into the material infrastructure of

---

[48] Pauli T. Karjalainen (2015: 101) defines biography as 'the description in words or otherwise of one's course of life [and] topobiography [as] the expression of the course of life as it relates to the lived spaces'.

contemporary urban spaces' (2019: 11). Through his analysis, he also demonstrates how 'the visual-narrative vocabulary of comics' allows artists and readers 'to "re-vision" – that is, "to see again, to look at afresh" [...] – the social and spatial injustices that are built into the infrastructural layouts of twenty-first-century cities' (Davies 2019: 3). In my analysis of Miranda Hoplaros and Lara Alphas's work of 'graphic docufiction', *The Sign-Maker*, I have also explored the rhetorical potential of buildings and monuments in terms of narrating the 'national topobiography' of the postcolonial, partitioned island of Cyprus, and I have argued for the suitability of comics for nuanced spatial articulations (Michael 2020a: 405).[49] Scherr, too, explores the workings of the 'ground' in graphic narratives structured around 'tropes of suffering and witnessing' (2020: 475). In this book, I also look into the rhetorical implications of space and place to point to the potential contribution of graphic life narrative in better understanding the workings of spatial injustice.

Border violence

Lastly, I examine border violence and its embodied experiences. According to the *World Migration Report*, at the end of 2020, there were 26.4 million refugees across the globe (IOM 2022a: 45). This unprecedented number only seems bound to increase in the years to come.[50] In addition to those whose asylum claims were successful, close to 4.1 million asylum seekers were awaiting State decisions concerning their refugee status, with the USA being the first recipient country, followed by Germany (IOM 2022a). People crossing liquid and territorial borders without documents to seek asylum in countries across the Global North, away from their homelands in the Global South, are charged with excessive precarity. This happens because, as Özgün E. Topak writes, in the borderzones that divide the East from the West, 'human rights are suspended in favor of sovereign practices' (2014: 816).[51] On the one hand, Western borders have been excessively surveilled and monitored in the context of migration governmentality. On the other, human rights violations inflicted upon undocumented border crossers remain largely veiled under, and justified by,

---

[49] Elsewhere, I have also discussed the role of the family home in Alison Bechdel's *Fun Home: A Family Tragicomic* as Bruce's Wildean autotopography (Michael 2020b).

[50] According to the *Ukraine Internal Displacement Report*, by 17 April 2022, an estimated 7,707,000 people have been displaced internally, while the total number of people on the move, including 'refugees fleeing across borders' has reached 12,641,000 (IOM 2022b: 1).

[51] Topak makes this statement in his analysis of the border of the Evros river between Greece and Turkey.

deterrence and security discourses. As Davies phrases it, this system thus 'prioritizes the rights of a national citizenry over the rights of a universal humanity' (2020: 384). As a result, the refugee, that 'exceptional figure that should have been the most essential recipient of human rights [...] comes instead to embody their failure' (Davies 2020: 384). The violence of Western borders therefore lies in how they deprive refugees, asylum seekers and stateless people of the 'right to have rights' (Arendt 1976: 296; Agamben 2008).

The populations that are deemed undesirable are increasingly becoming deprived of 'a right to mobility' (Pécoud and de Guchteneire 2006: 69).[52] This deprivation charges them with excessive precarity that is caused by the legal production of the 'illegality' of undocumented migration, the only border-crossing option available for them, which in turn recasts them as 'deportable' by creating the ever-present risk of their deportation (De Genova 2002: 419). As a result, the lives of these people are always liminal, in limbo and characterized by uncertainty. If, as Achille Mbembe writes, 'to be alive, or to remain alive, is increasingly tantamount to being able to move' (2019a: 8), those who systematically become deprived of this ability, and consequently, of the right to mobility and asylum, are not quite humanly living (Veit and Strass 2021).[53] While their 'biological life' is injuriously sustained at the border, their 'biographical life [is put] on hold' (Jacobsen and Karlsen 2021: 12). In this monograph, I explore the potential of graphic life narrative for depicting undocumented border-crossers as other than silent victims deprived of agency and biographical life in the face of Western sovereign State violence. As I do so, I show how the notion of the border itself can be reconfigured and reconceptualized through its displays in the selected graphic life narratives.

As Johan Schimanski writes, every time a border is crossed, 'new narrative borders are created and crossed in the crosser's own story, and in the story of the border itself' (2006: 47). Borders are ideological, cultural, political, social, and they can be parts 'of *B/ORDERING* processes of *EXCLUSION* and inclusion'

---

[52] Antoine Pécoud and Paul de Guchteneire introduce the 'right to mobility' as what would potentially 'counterbalance the uneven access to mobility among peoples and nations. Mobility', they explain, 'is a privilege that is unevenly distributed among human beings; citizens from developed countries may travel and settle down almost anywhere in the world, while their fellow human beings from less-developed countries depend upon the uncertain issuance of visas and residence permits to migrate' (2006: 75). In this sense, 'a right to mobility is not about adding one more right to a long list of rights; rather, it is about fostering respect for existing human rights' (Pécoud and de Guchteneire 2006: 74).

[53] Distinguishing between the refugee and the asylum seeker, Nicholas de Genova writes that the latter 'is always already predicated upon a basic suspicion of all people who petition for asylum within a European asylum system that has routinely and systematically disqualified and rejected the great majority of applicants, and thereby ratifies anew the processes by which their mobilities have been illegalized' in the name of state protection (2017: 8).

(Schimanski and Wolfe 2017: 149, emphasis in the original).[54] They are liminal, in-between spaces 'caught between the *LAW* and that which transgresses the law, between fixity and change' (Schimanski and Wolfe 2017: 149, emphasis in the original). Their embodied experiences can reconfigure their meanings, and, at the same time, 'cultural and discursive processes allow them to surface as aesthetic figurations – narratives or tropes – [that] can also interrogate their including/excluding function' (Schimanski and Wolfe 2017: 149). It is precisely for these reasons that there is potential in the examination of their violence in graphic life narratives accounting for human rights violations inflicted against those who become othered at, and in/visibilized by them.[55]

In/visibilities

According to Benno Herzog, there exists in society 'the invisibilization *of* suffering, but also suffering *from* invisibilization' (2020: 72, emphasis in the original). In other words, 'invisibilization can signify social exclusion from the space where conditions of suffering are negotiated and produced', while the inability to express, and thus process and heal from suffering, can cause new kinds of wounding (Herzog 2020: 72–3). In the graphic life narratives examined in this monograph, causal links between invisibilization and suffering emerge through artistic choices made for the staging of other people's testimonies of human rights violations. In some cases, because of these choices, the visual itself may paradoxically cause their invisibilization, thus acquiring injurious, silencing implications. As such, narratives of this kind expand, in the artistic field, the injustices against those on whose behalf they seek to speak.

Chiara Brambilla and Holger Pötzsch also analyse the ways in which 'audio-visuality' and literal as well as metaphorical borders produce 'different forms of in/visibility' (2017: 68). This analysis is useful in identifying the ways in which people who belong in different racial, ethnic and religious groups become othered in the

[54] Didier Fassin distinguishes between borders and boundaries, defining the former as territorial and the latter as 'social constructs establishing symbolic differences (between class, gender, or race) and producing identities (national, ethnic, or cultural communities)', further noting the impact of borders on social relations (2011: 214).
[55] In their introduction to *Transnational Perspectives on Graphic Narratives: Comics at the Crossroads*, Shane Denson et al. note that 'a transnational perspective on graphic narratives must take into account their medially constitutive infractions of […] formal borders – the spatiotemporal hybridities that result from the intersection of visual and verbal forms and that define narration itself as a series of transgressions, moving from one panel to another, violating the borders of individual images, and crossing the expanse of the gutter' (2013: 18). Such a perspective would potentially suggest 'that the internal functioning of the medium is not so different, formally, from its external imbrications in transnational exchanges' (Denson et al. 2013: 18). It is precisely such an approach that I pursue in this monograph as well.

sense of being perceived as mute, but at the same time terrifying and monstrous (if male) or passive (if female) spectacles. For Brambilla and Pötzsch (2017: 68), Western borders can veil 'certain subjectivities and their respective articulations while promoting others'. Visibility, they point out, can be both 'empowering' in offering recognition to someone, and 'disempowering', when enabling one's control (Brambilla and Pötzsch 2017: 71). Refugees, the stateless and the displaced are burdened with the predicament of manifesting the 'simultaneity of two pathologies of political action and citizenship: *public invisibility* and *natural visibility*' (Borren 2008: 214, emphasis in the original; Arendt 1958). In other words, refugees, the stateless and the displaced are excessively visible because their appearance becomes marked in predominantly white Western host societies; at the same time, they are banned from access to political life.[56] The same is true for the othered gendered subjects whose suffering occurs elsewhere but becomes remediated in Anglophone graphic life narratives for readers in the Global North.

Brambilla and Pötzsch (2017: 72) explain that such structures prevent 'the emergence of [...] competing perspectives and points of view in the hegemonic discourse'. As a result, 'the hegemonic audio-visual borderscape of the global war on terror [produces a] pathologic visibility of one particular version of the Other's complex and dynamic subjectivity – the terrorist', denying them 'agency and self-articulation' and reducing them 'to a mere object of communication' (Brambilla and Potzsch 2017: 72, 73). This also applies to the female other, who is frequently reduced to the position of the helpless mute victim in need of a saviour. As a result of these structures of in/visibility, 'a productive and potentially subversive first-to-second person discourse where the response of the Other actually matters' becomes impossible (Brambilla and Pötzsch 2017: 73). Instead, there appears an 'objectifying exchange about the Other, who is bound to remain silent – a form of discourse that narrowly frames the Other' (Brambilla and Pötzsch 2017: 73). The questions I seek to respond to in this monograph are therefore as follows: What is it that graphic life narratives of the human rights violations suffered by othered people can do to challenge their inaudibility and public invisibility? To what extent can a subversive first-to-second person discourse emerge in graphic life narrative where Anglophone artists remediate the testimonies of others and, is there radical potential therein? What would the usefulness of graphic life narrative be in the study of globalization, conflict and migration through the lens of social justice, human rights, life narrative and comics studies? To respond to these questions, I pursue, as explained, a decolonized postcolonial approach.

[56] Marieke Borren describes such cases as illustrative of 'pathologies of in/visibility' (2010: 151).

Decolonial theory, social justice and the decolonization of human rights

While the post- of postcolonialism signals the era after colonization, decolonial theory sees the implications of the latter as morphing into different power structures that still sustain the global, spatial, cultural and human hierarchies established through Western States' past colonial projects (Bhambra 2014).[57] Coloniality, according to Nelson Maldonado-Torres, refers to power dynamics that 'define culture, labor, intersubjective relations, and knowledge production well beyond the strict limits of colonial administrations' (2010: 97), and it constitutes the dark side of modernity within the modernity/coloniality paradigm (Quijano 2007; Mignolo 2011). Whereas Western modernity is celebrated as growth, progress and development, its dark side, coloniality, which encompasses 'poverty, misery, inequities, injustices, corruption, commodification, and dispensability of human life,' remains silenced (Mignolo 2011: xviii). Western imperial countries have instituted the 'colonial matrix of power', determining how power and knowledge are produced and how they geopolitically shape human and national relations (and divisions) across the globe (Mignolo 2011: xviii).[58]

This Eurocentric 'colonial matrix of power' (Mignolo 2011: xviii) has established hierarchies between metropolitan centres and their peripheries, and it has structured knowledge as rationality and as something to be possessed by and from within the European Self, rather than becoming inter-subjectively achieved (Quijano 2007). Knowledge as rationality became configured as a Eurocentric and thus universal product, and thus 'the world became unthinkable beyond European (and, later, North Atlantic) epistemology' (Mignolo 2002: 90).[59] These colonial dynamics 'left profound marks not only in the areas of

---

[57] Coloniality explains how 'historical colonialisms have been a constitutive, although downplayed, dimension' of Western civilization, which emerged with the Renaissance and Humanism (Mignolo 2011: 2).

[58] The coloniality of being, for instance, influences both 'colonial subalterns [...] who are belittled and dehumanised, and [...] those who imagine themselves as superior and as embodying the paradigm of humanity' (Restrepo and Rojas 2010: 158). My translation from Spanish.

[59] Such a consequence of the production of knowledge in the context of Western modernity also concerns trauma theory, which as Stef Craps convincingly argues, 'rather than promoting cross-cultural solidarity, risks assisting in the perpetuation of the very beliefs, practices, and structures that maintain existing injustices and inequalities' (2013: 2). It does so because it tends to 'favour or even prescribe a modernist aesthetic of fragmentation and aporia as uniquely suited to the task of bearing witness to trauma, [while disregarding] the connections between metropolitan and non-Western or minority traumas' (Craps 2013: 2). Contra to this model, Craps proposes a culturally-sensitive and inclusive 'decolonized trauma theory [that would allow] us to recognize and attend to the sufferings of people around the world [and that would] expose situations of injustice and abuse, [opening] up ways to imagine a different global future' (2013: 8). It is precisely this kind of witnessing that I pursue in this monograph.

authority, sexuality, knowledge and the economy, but on the general understanding of being as well' (Maldonado-Torres 2010: 96). María Lugones, for instance, refers to the failures of white Western feminism and the 'the modern/colonial gender system' (2010: 371), which she defines as 'a violent [colonial] introduction consistently and contemporarily used to destroy peoples, cosmologies, and communities as the building ground of the "civilized" West' (Lugones 2007: 186; Schiwy 2010). In the following chapters, I examine the manifestations of modernity/coloniality across different geographical contexts, and I unearth their implications in regard to gendered precarity and violence, as well as spatial injustice and border violence.[60]

As I do so, remain conscious of the fact that human rights discourses have emerged in the context of Western, Eurocentric knowledge that is understood as rationality, and as connected to patriarchal *logos* (Quijano 2007; Mignolo 2013). This discourse remains blind to gendered injustices that have been inflicted by (neo-)imperial European powers upon people beyond the West, and omits Third-World, as well as intersectional feminist perspectives on the history of human rights (Barreto 2012). In addition, it excludes emotions, which are understood as irrational, and as associated with otherness, as well as with femininity and the body that exist in contradistinction with masculinity and the mind.[61] The separation between text and image neatly corresponds to these dichotomies (Kooistra 1995), as human rights discourses still remain predominantly preoccupied with the white, Western (male) self.[62] Martin Woessner proposes that to counter this preoccupation and to thus decolonize human rights, we should look 'at the messier margins of provincial suffering' (2013: 68). But as mentioned, when emerging from the West, this gaze at the margins is charged with ambivalence.

Margaret McLaren explains that human rights perspectives on injustices suffered by women in the Global South are limiting because they do not consider

---

[60] I perceive border violence both as literal – that occurring in asylum detention and difficult sea crossings – and metaphorical – that which is manifested in Western States' exploitation of othered people and distant places in the context of neoliberal economy, and in structural racism and religious discrimination within their borders.

[61] Lynda Hutcheon refers to the 'dualistic organising mechanisms of Western thought [whereby] Self/Other weaves with other binaries such as masculine/feminine, mind/body, rational/irrational, abstract/corporeal' (1996: 327).

[62] The 'women's rights as human rights' dictum came to prominence in the 1990s by feminists seeking 'global gender justice' (McLaren 2017b: 110). In *Women's Rights, Human Rights*, Julie Peters and Andrea Wolper write that 'traditional human rights formulations are based on a "normative" male model and applied to women as an afterthought, if at all [and that] traditional human rights standards categorize violations in ways that exclude women, eliding critical issues' (1995: 2–3; Charlesworth 1995).

'colonial legacies and histories, and the neocolonial implementations of dominant "rights" discourses' (2017b: 108). In addition, she reminds us that 'feminists from the Global North have [paid] scant attention to economic concerns, which are fundamental for many women in the Global South' (McLaren 2017b: 108–9; Mohanty 2003). She proposes that for these reasons, 'transnational feminism would be better served by a social justice framework/approach that includes rights, while recognizing that they function ambivalently' (McLaren 2017b: 109). Contrary to a human rights framework, 'the social justice approach questions background conditions and addresses structural inequalities [emphasizing] economic, social, and cultural rights, [while also] question[ing] the theoretical origins of rights and their contemporary applications' (McLaren 2017b: 110).

Writing from a Subaltern-studies perspective, Upendra Baxi (2008) also underscores the need to consider the standpoints and the voices of the violated for a decolonized conceptualization of human rights.[63] Such narratives of suffering would 'oppose and supplement the rationalist mood of established scholarship' (Barreto 2012: 25). In considering the pain and trauma of (post-) colonized people, the contribution of emotions in knowledge production about human rights would be restored, thus undoing the 'strong split between emotion and reason' which forms a core 'part of the history of colonialism' (Chakrabarty 2002: 24). The purpose of this monograph is to illustrate the contribution of graphic life narrative for a decolonized understanding of human rights violations suffered by othered people.

In *Human Rights and Empire*, Costas Douzinas writes that 'one could write the history of human rights as the ongoing and always failing struggle to close the gap between the abstract man and the concrete citizen; to add flesh, blood and sex to the pale outline of the "human"' (2007: 54). Graphic life narratives depicting the distant suffering of othered people constantly enflesh the abstracted human of human rights. At the same time, they embed them in precarious geopolitical contexts, outside of a *polis* that would potentially protect them and respect their human rights. As I show in the subsequent chapters, in so doing, they critically expose the failures of human rights discourses, the global distribution of injustice, and the violence of the sovereign State and of modernity/coloniality.

---

[63] For instance, writing from a Latina Critical Legal theory standpoint, Elvia R. Arriola (2000) highlights the importance of personal narratives in exposing the structural violence of Western neoliberalism in Juarez and the human rights deprivations it causes for female workers of American factories established in the area. Legal scholar Adrien Katherine Wing (1997) follows a similar approach through the lens of a critical race feminism for the study of social justice. I follow a similar model in my approach to the texts concerning both Juarez and Mae Sot

Chapter overview and a note on myth

In Chapter 1, I focus on different forms of violence inflicted against women and girls. I look into rhetorical and figurative nuances of comics such as graphic metaphors, visual and verbal intertextual allusions, thematic and visual circularities, as well as the intra-diegetic presence of the Western humanitarian reporter/witness. Through a decolonized perspective on them and on the suffering they remediate, I show how Western, masculinist complicities, colonial pasts and neo-colonial presents produce and sustain particular kinds of violence against women and girls in Juarez, Mae Sot and Palestine. In Chapter 2, I introduce the concept of *graphic martyria* to refer to the ways in which notions of witnessing, testimony, torture, resistance and spectacle become connected with suffering and divine truth, and related to vulnerable and precarious masculinities displayed through the comics form. I also explicate the ambivalence of the selected texts' attempts to present the distant suffering of othered men and boys in Sri Lanka, Palestine and Burma.

In Chapter 3, I investigate thanatic photo/graphics, temporalities and tempos, as well as the role of dolls and animals in the mediation of death in Vietnam, Juarez and Palestine. I introduce the concept of graphic thanatopoetics, which refers to depictions of death through the comics form, as well as to their close examination, and I argue that it entails decolonized postcolonial potential.[64] In Chapter 4, I demonstrate that looking into space, place and the environment, in graphic life narrative nuances the understanding of how social injustices, which are always-already spatial, become distributed in Juarez, Sri Lanka and Palestine, as well as at European and Australian borderzones. I introduce the concept of graphic topopoetics to refer to the depictions of space and place and to the analytical approach that unpacks their rhetorical potential when it comes to aesthetically enriching, countering and critiquing the spatial and social injustices that become narratively structured. Lastly, in Chapter 5, I argue that depictions of monsters, icons of (in)justice and witnessing animals alongside the othered people who become configured into the living dead of Western borders, enrich the spectacle of border violence, and expose the pain of (neo-)colonial border policing regimes in Australia, Europe and beyond. The conclusion

---

[64] In this monograph, I use 'graphic' as defined in the *Oxford English Dictionary* to refer to something that is drawn or which relates to writing, painting or drawing, or 'pertaining to [...] the use of linear figures or symbolic curves'. (Simpson and Weiner 1989: np). Further to its form-related meanings, I use it in the sense of 'vividly descriptive, life-like', or explicit (Simpson and Weiner 1989: np). With the term 'poetics' I mean to point to 'the creative principles informing any literary, social or cultural production, [and] the theoretical study of these' (Simpson and Weiner 1989: np).

reiterates the findings of the main chapters and the contribution of the monograph.

In each of these chapters, I use a fragment from Greek myth as a metonymic explication for the contemporary forms of suffering, sovereign State violence and injustice that I explore in my primary corpus. I do so not because I mean to revert back to the canon or the roots of Western civilization. If anything, Ancient Greek culture has been influenced by and created via the contact between people from Greece, Africa and Asia, even if European philology's 'ideological protectionism [created] an image of a pure, classical Greece in splendid isolation' (Burkert 1995: 1). Rather, I use these texts in an attempt to point to the ways in which myth can help better understand what different forms of injustice, and sovereign State violence, have morphed into through the centuries.

Due to their lack of scientific knowledge, which in the modern/colonial schema is linked to rationality, people initially used myth – the unreal and the imaginary – to conceptualize, represent and understand social and natural phenomena. As myth gradually became relegated into the realm of the irrational, reason came to be the only legitimate source of knowledge. Michael Hauskeller, however, writes that 'what we commonly see as the progression from *mythos* to *logos*, story to argument, emotion and intuition to reason and rational thinking, and subjectivity to objectivity is not, and can never be, complete. Logos always remains firmly rooted in mythos, which gives logos its direction and purpose. In this sense, logos always points back at mythos' (2016: 4, emphasis in the original). In an attempt to speak back to the dichotomies and the hierarchies of modernity/coloniality, I hope that my turn to myth enriches my explication of the potentialities of graphic life narrative for the study of other people's distant suffering.

1

Precarious femininities and gendered inequalities

In this chapter, I investigate the extent to which comics can enable nuanced representations of violated femininities in graphic life narratives accounting for human rights deprivations occurring in Juarez, Burma and Palestine, namely *La Lucha* by John Sack, *Burma* and *Juarez*, the second and third volumes of *I Live Here*, which is edited by Mia Kirshner et al., and *Palestine* by Joe Sacco. I also examine how racially and religiously othered subjects navigate global post-colonies and how they become injured by neoliberal economy and modernity/coloniality, both of which largely determine the kinds of violence inflicted against women and girls. My argument is that these graphic life narratives illustrate how metaphors, intertextual allusions, thematic and visual circularities, as well as the intra-diegetic presence of the Western humanitarian reporter/witness, highlight the need for a decolonized perspective on women's rights. Such a perspective would take into consideration the ways in which Western, masculinist complicities, colonial pasts and neo-colonial presents produce and sustain particular kinds of violence against women and girls in the Global South.

Remediating the graphic tale of Philomela, (de)colonizing human rights

Contrary to its injurious implications, as reflected by the relegation of women and girls to the status of the silenced spectacle, the visual also has distinctly feminist rhetorical potential as Philomela's mythical tale illustrates – one that is linked to the undoing of forcefully imposed silences surrounding gendered sexual violence. As such, it can be used to re-produce objectifying, silencing takes on femininity, but also, and importantly, to question or subvert them. In Sophocles' lost play, *Tereus*, and as also recounted in Ovid's *Metamorphosis*, Philomela, Procne's sister, was raped by the latter's husband, who subsequently cut her tongue to ensure her silence. Philomela wove a piece of tapestry and showed it to her sister, thus delivering the visual testimony of her assault, which she was otherwise unable to articulate because of the further violence that was inflicted upon her after her rape, the gruesome removal of her tongue – of her ability to speak/testify (Hornblower and Spawforth 1999; March 2000).[1] Upon bearing witness to her sister's testimony, Procne became enraged and killed her son Itys to revenge her husband, whom she then deceived into eating his murdered child. The myth thus demonstrates how violence produces further, inter-generational harm in a vicious circle whereby suffering spreads across subjects in a multiplicity of ways.

Violence is therefore both contaminating and protean in that it transforms as it moves from one individual – both the victim and the perpetrator – to another. This aspect of violence also becomes illustrated in the graphic life narratives under investigation in this chapter. As it appears in different geo-, bio- and necro-political contexts, it is also shown to trigger the perpetuation of further and different forms of harm against women and girls from the micro-level of the family to the macro-level of the (inter-)nation. The visual/verbal hybridity of comics enables the structuring of temporal conflations, whereby past violence may surface, either implicitly or explicitly, in the diegetic present to injuriously influence women's and girls' lives in the midst of conflict, occupation, and industrialization. My aim is to investigate whether interactions between Anglophone artistic practitioners and violated female subjects, as displayed in the texts under investigation, enable the structuring of new, de-centred versions of Philomela's testimony, or if they result in the testifying subjects' further silencing and invisibilization.

For Philippe Codde, the myth of Philomela constitutes 'one of the earliest literary renditions of a traumatized mind [whereby it is] not by ordinary linguistic means, but via art [and] alternative semiotic, non-linguistic' channels that the female victim of abuse manages to bear witness to her trauma (2007: 246). While Codde highlights the value of iconicity and art for the

---

[1] For Elisabeth Krimmer, Philomela's story 'shows that the discourse of rape is not simply one of silence, but a complicated transaction where an irresistible desire to express oneself exists alongside different forms of silence, repression, and redeployment' (2015: 85).

expression of traumatic memories of sexual violence, Graham Huggan reads 'Philomela's story [as] a paradigm for the re-enactment of colonial encounter, for the articulation of a violent history of dispossession and deprivation which circumstances dictate must be told in another way' (2008: 155). The myth, he writes, provides postcolonial writers with 'an alternative framework for the expression of an otherwise repressed, or censored, history' and illustrates how 'non-verbal codes [can] subvert and/or replace [...] earlier, overdetermined narratives of colonial encounter in which the word is recognized to have played a crucial role in the production and maintenance of colonial hierarchies of power' (Huggan 2008: 155–6). In a more polemical vein, Martha J. Cutter interprets this myth as 'the archetypal rape narrative [and] the dominant master narrative of patriarchal culture itself: the silencing and objectifying of women and "others" as the basis for male subjectivity' (2000: 176).

Like these authors, I also hope to re-centre the feminist, postcolonial and decolonizing rhetorical implications of the visual in the graphic life narratives that account for the human rights violations suffered by women and girls in Juarez, Burma and Palestine. As I do so, I mean to counter the marginalization of the image in relation to the word in terms of its contribution to the understanding of the human rights deprivations endured by othered people. My analysis of the visual/verbal combinations of *La Lucha, Burma, Juarez,* and *Palestine,* highlights the need for an investigation of women's rights that moves beyond the Eurocentric, masculinist production of knowledge about human rights that privileges the male *logos* over the feminized image.

To foreground this potential, but to also point to the limitations of texts wherein othered women and girls are rendered further invisible and silenced precisely in and through the creative work itself, I pursue a decolonial feminist perspective. Via my use of brackets in '(de)colonizing human rights' in the heading of this section, I mean to point to the ambivalence that characterizes such artistic works, which at times uncritically reproduce the global, gendered hierarchies they seek to counter through the mediation of othered girls' and women's testimonies. In her introduction to *Decolonizing Feminism: Transnational Feminism and Globalisation,* Margaret A. McLaren writes that 'as a project concerned with multiple power structures, feminist theory must address the historical legacies of colonialism, postcolonialism, and more recently, decoloniality' (2017a: 15). For a decolonizing, feminist reconceptualization of human rights, she further explains, attention needs to be paid 'to both micro- and macro-political structures', and awareness must be acquired regarding 'the effects of colonization, not only as political, historical, and economic forces but also as effects on consciousness, theories, research practices, epistemological frameworks, and ways of knowing' (McLaren 2017a: 18–19). In analysing graphic displays of violence inflicted against othered women and girls in Juarez, Burma and Palestine, I consider each location's (neo-)colonial histories, and I illustrate the specific forms of diachronic and contemporary rights violations they cause, and the extent to which these are embedded within or remain outside the frame of representation.

The game of neoliberal economy and coloniality in Juarez

La Lucha and the *maquiladoras*

La Lucha, for instance, accounts for local feminist activism against the violation of women's and girls' rights in Mexico and embeds the femicides of Juarez in the context of global neoliberal economy, which produces specific kinds of gendered violence. As it does so, it highlights the contribution of modernity/coloniality in the production of an excessively precarious femininity in Juarez, that of the *maquiladora* worker.[2] In this account, the pinball game is used as a figurative means that metaphorically stages the neo-colonial, gendered implications of the violence of the *maquiladora* system (Figure 1.1). In displaying gendered human rights violations through this lens, this full-page graphic metaphor that presents the impact of the North American Free Trade Agreement (NAFTA) on Mexican lives also illustrates how profit ends in the United States and Canada, while Mexican workers are reduced to mere disposable parts of this economic game.

In in the upper part of the image, the word NAFTA renders an image of an indigenous man and a woman semi-visible, while the smiling faces of Bill Clinton, the US president and signatory of the agreement, and Carlos Salinas de

---

[2]   Legal scholar Adrien Katherine Wing (1997) writes the *maquiladora* system exposes mostly young women to excessive precarity through exploitation, abuse and forced contact with toxic substances. She also notes that the United States financially benefits from this structure that renders women's lives disposable given that 'U.S. labor, employment, and environmental laws do not apply in' this context (Wing 1997: 346). Likewise, Elvia R. Arriola describes a 'vast array of socio-economic and human rights problems that currently exist at the U.S.-Mexico border', underlining the importance of personal narratives as evidence in attempts to unveil 'the central role of the *maquiladoras* in perpetuating the systemic racial and sexual exploitation and abuse at the border that is legitimated by American law, public policy, and official conduct' (2000: 731–2).

Figure 1.1 Panel from page 6 of *La Lucha: The Story of Lucha Castro and Human Rights in Mexico*, by John Sack, © 2015, used with permission from Verso.

Gortari, the Mexican president and signatory, are foregrounded and positioned above numbers that account for the profit in US dollars deriving from their pact. A hybrid three-part flag at central position composed by US, Mexican and Canadian fragments metonymically captures the (financial) links established between the three countries, while two women and a man enter the bus, presumably, to the *maquiladoras*. The small size of the workers' visual embodiments contrary to the rest of the graphically displayed information is quite telling in regard to their significance in this state of affairs. This upper part of the pinball game further relates that a 'total trade [of] $500,000,000,000' takes place in Mexico (Sack 2015: 6). Importantly, this full-page metaphor is positioned at the beginning of *La Lucha*, prior to the first chapter and subsequently to the prologue, setting the scene for the gendered violence and activism that will be further narrated.

The pinball game is, in itself, a coin-operated machine. Money, in this sense, seems to trigger the activation of the NAFTA game in Mexico. A woman's face drawn on the ball that is located at the game's starting point illustrates her devaluation in this image that stages the violations and precarities she has to navigate through 'in the Free Trade Zone' (Sack 2015: 6). The ball/woman is about to be shot through a route inscribed with the phrase 'endless supply of cheap Mexican labour', which becomes predominantly feminized in this visual/ verbal combination (Sack 2015: 6). The word *maquiladoras* at central position is accompanied by factory chimneys and thick smoke in the visual register, and by labels of well-known US manufacturing brands. The human agent behind the activation of the game remains outside the frame of representation, apart from a small part of their hand. Subsequently to shooting the ball, they will score points based on how they manage the life of the female *maquiladora* worker that is drawn on it. The ball/woman has to move through tax-free raw materials, the profit of 'US manufacturing tanks' as described above, export profits, harassment, the absence of unions, and the non-existence of workers' rights (Sack 2015: 6). In this context, harassment and gendered rights violations become manifested, *inter alia*, by how when a woman is 'pregnant [she gets] sacked' (Sack 2015: 6).

In addition to the above, the game includes H. Ross Perot's famous statement against NAFTA, that upon its implementation US citizens would hear 'a giant sucking sound' (Sack 2015: 6). 'You implement [. . .] the Mexican trade agreement, where they pay people a dollar an hour, have no health care, no retirement, no pollution controls', Perot said during a presidential debate that took place in 1992, 'and you're going to hear a giant sucking sound of jobs being pulled out of this country' (quoted in Shaiken 2019: np). Through this intertextual reference,

La Lucha stages the devaluation of Mexican lives and the violation of workers' human rights alongside a statement that signals the emergence of negative stereotypes introducing Mexicans as thieves of American jobs (Wing 1997). The devaluation of female lives as sustained in this context is also displayed in Kirschner's narrative account of her visit in Juarez in the corresponding volume of *I Live Here*, where she explains that 40 per cent of the local population live in poverty and that the 'wage of a typical maquiladora worker [is] $1.50/hr', also noting that the 'estimated annual wholesale value of Mexico-US cocaine trade [is] $9 billion' (Kirschner 2008b: np). Further to the *maquiladoras*, Phoebe Gloeckner's (2008) depiction of female sex work in 'La Tristeza' (Sadness), her own contribution in *Juarez*, sheds light on another industry, which produces a different category of excessively precarious femininities and leads to the commodification and abuse of women and girls.

Sex work in 'La Tristeza'

In addition to its aforementioned bio- and necro-political attributes, Juarez has historically provided leisure in the form of prostitution and alcohol to the 'predominantly single, male [US] population' that has been stationed at the military base of El Paso and crossed the border into the city (Vila 2005: 113; 2000). Contemporarily, US citizens involved in Mexico's sex industry frequent Juarez for cheap services that place female sex workers in extremely precarious positions not only because of aggressive behaviour and harassment often directed against them, but also due to their higher exposure to STDs such as HIV (Nathan 1999; Risley 2010).[3] Elva Fabiola Orozco describes this type of tourism as masculine and explains that it is attracted to a 'leisure industry that commodifies women's bodies' (2019: 139).

In 'La Tristeza', Gloeckner turns her attention to the femicides occurring in the context of sex work and domestic violence. To represent her biographical subjects, she attached edited photographs of real people's faces to the bodies of dolls she had sewn, and then photographed, items that evoke the reduction of the female body to a mere (sexual) object (Michael 2014; Chute 2016).[4] As further mentioned in Chapter 3, the written captions that explicate the visually

---

[3] Steffanie Strathdee et al. write that a study concerning sex work in Juarez showed that 'US clients were more likely to have current STIs and to engage in higher-risk behaviors' (2008: 263).
[4] The symbolic implications of dolls are also discussed in Chapter 3.

depicted crimes are characterized by the ungrammaticality of earlier versions of Google Translate, which Gloeckner used to transform Hispanophone articles from Mexican newspapers into the Anglophone text we come across in her graphic novella (Gloeckner and Flores-Olivier 2011). It is only in the graphic narration of a sex worker's violation and murder that the caption becomes distinguished by its grammaticality because it was not taken from a local newspaper, but rather, from 'the discussion board of Mexico Sex Tourist' (Gloeckner 2008: np).

I read this section of 'La Tristeza' as manifesting both verbally and visually an injurious inter-national gendered encounter that becomes metonymically reflected through the physical contact between the American tourist and the Mexican sex worker (Figures 1.2a and 1.2b). I propose that, in this instance, Gloeckner implicitly stages the impact of coloniality on the devaluation of female Mexican life through an implied juxtaposition between (dark) sinful female sexuality as embodied through the figure of the sex worker, and ideal (white) virginal femininity, as embodied through the figure of the Virgin Mary of Guadalupe. In this sense, masculinist (neo-)colonial violence against Mexican femininity, as staged by Gloeckner in this excerpt, is both physical and ontological and its latter implications become manifested through the visual register of the narrative that adds further layers of meaning to the objectifying *logos* of the American tourist.

On the first page of this two-part vignette, a woman is shown wearing make-up and a short, tight, green dress, while walking alone at night in silence.[5] The space through which she walks is dark, apart from the light Gloeckner chose to shed on her figure, thus highlighting her status as a mute, voyeuristic spectacle. Discussing the precarity faced by female sex workers in Mexican borderzones, Katsulis et al. write that because of 'structural violence [...], the majority of [them] exercise their right to work in [...] hazardous conditions in the face of extreme limitations because of poverty, gender discrimination, and other forms of social inequality' (2010: 358; Farmer 2003). This structural violence is largely triggered and sustained by neoliberal economy that led to the transformation of Juarez into a Free Trade Zone. As such, further to US and Canadian profit made via the *maquiladoras*, where women's and girls' lives are devalued and rendered

[5]　Studies have shown that 'street-based' sex workers in Tijuana and Juarez frequently 'experience violent encounters while on the job' (Katsulis et al. 2010: 345). These include theft, and physical violence that causes serious injury, as well as harassment by the police, *inter alia* (Katsoulis et al. 2010; Wahab 2005).

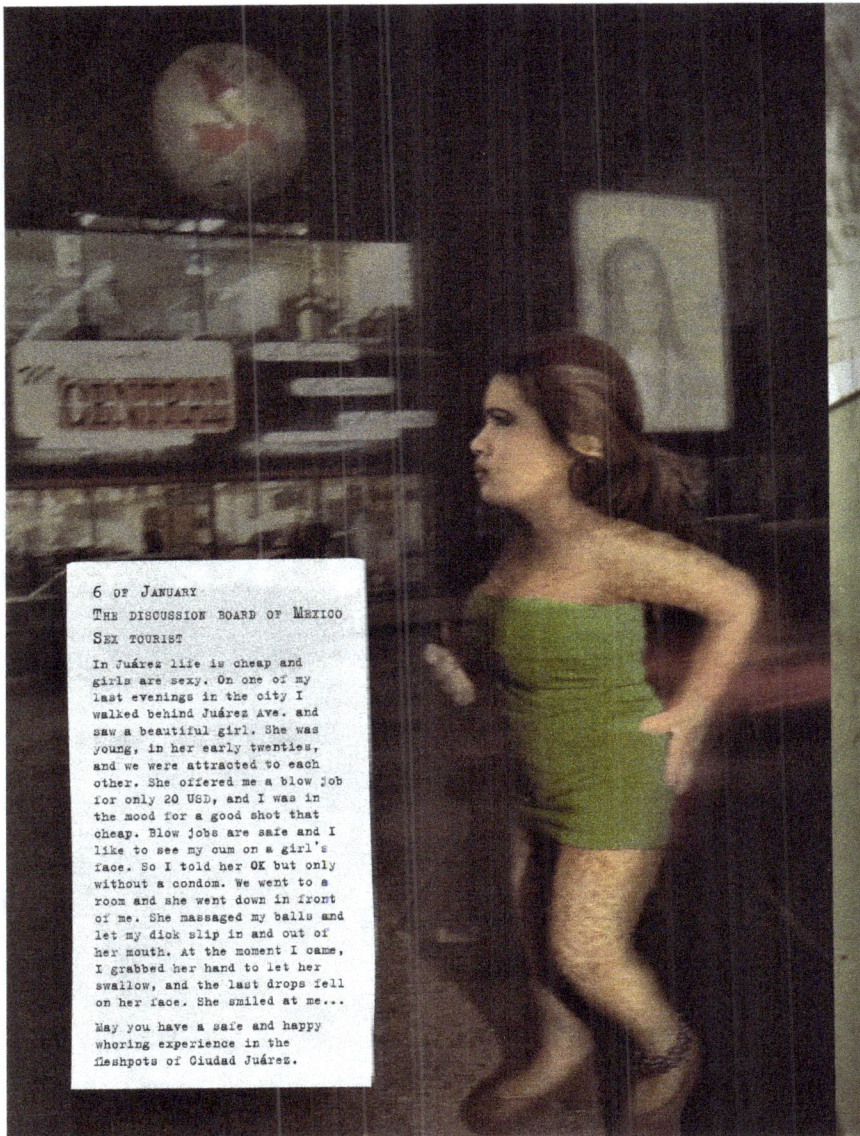

Figure 1.2a Sex worker (i), from 'La Tristeza' by Phoebe Gloeckner, © 2008, used with permission from Phoebe Gloeckner.

disposable, the city's sex industry is a different means through which local femininities become commodified in the service of (US) male clientele.

This commodification is reflected through the narrative caption that is positioned prior to the woman in the green dress, which accounts for the experiences of an American tourist in the city. After introducing Juarez as a place

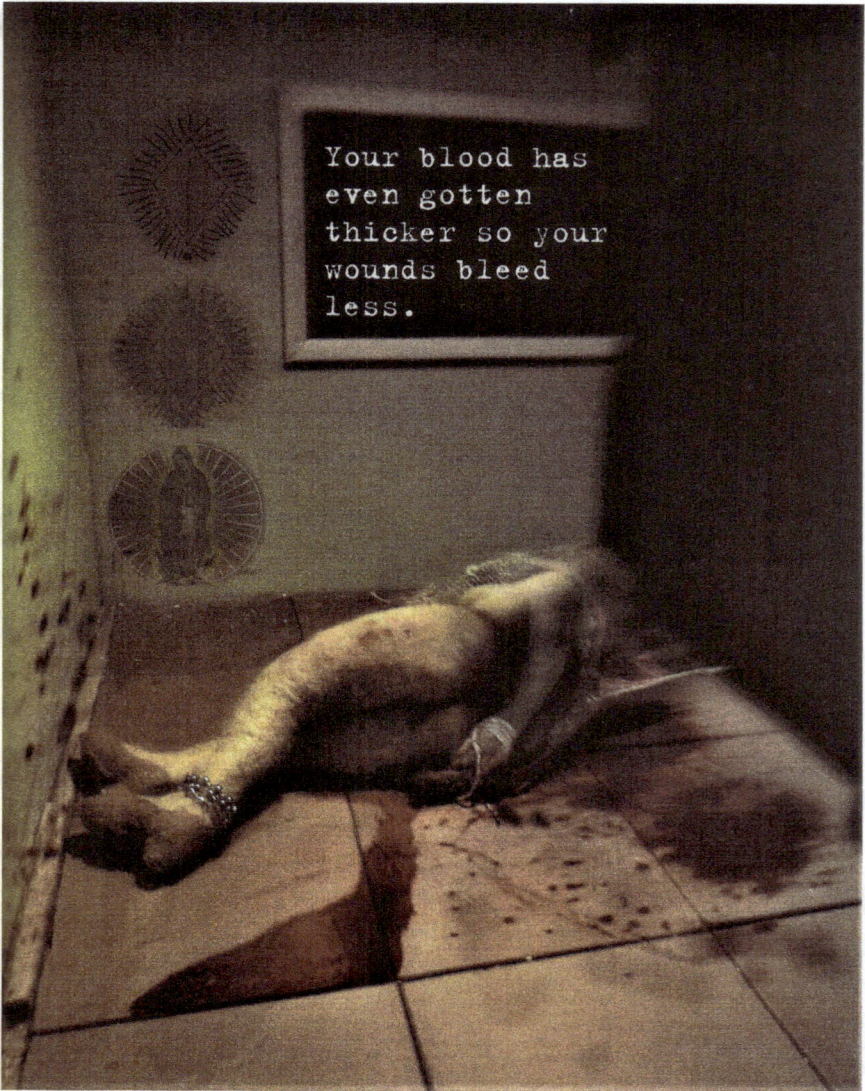

Figure 1.2b Sex worker (ii), from 'La Tristeza' by Phoebe Gloeckner, © 2008, used with permission from Phoebe Gloeckner.

where 'life is cheap and girls are sexy', the man relates how a 'beautiful girl [...] in her early twenties [...] offered [him] a blow job for only 20 USD', and explains that because 'blow jobs are safe' and he enjoys seeing his 'cum on a girl's face', he agreed to pay the amount provided that he would not use protection (Gloeckner 2008: np). Subsequently, he describes how the girl 'went down on' him, how he forced her to swallow his semen, and how 'she smiled at [him as he saw] the last drops fall[ing] on her face' (Gloeckner 2008: np). The man closes his entry wishing his readers 'a safe and happy whoring experience in the fleshpots of Ciudad Juárez' (Gloeckner 2008: np). In its demand that we see this young woman through the gaze of the American sex tourist, 'La Tristeza' presents an exoticizing, objectifying view of the female Mexican sex worker, and illustrates how the US exploitation of women and girls becomes manifested through this masculinist industry.

The subsequent page depicts the corpse of the woman, who is simultaneously excessively visible as described above, and invisible because her suffering, and eventual death, remain unseen and ignored due to her devalued gendered existence and her status as a racially othered sex worker. In her analysis of this artistic recreation of murder, Hillary Chute writes that 'in an act of informed but imagined witnessing, Gloeckner offers us hidden, unviewed moments – "hidden" from public eye because the victims are dead and cannot testify – and provokes us to build narratives backward and forward' (2010: 90). In provoking us to do so, she also invites us to consider the implications of the politics of the invisibilization of gendered suffering that is caused by US masculinist (neo-) colonial drives, which dehumanize women and girls, reducing them to commodities in the violent Free-Trade Zone of Juarez.

On this second page, the woman is naked, with her hands tied behind her back and what seems like a net covering her head that is turned to the wall, all of which point to gruesome torture and a violent death. She is lying on a floor that is stained by her blood, while a caption written in the second person explains that 'your blood has even gotten thicker so your wounds bleed less' (Gloeckner 2008: np). The red stains on the floor and the walls of this dark room seem to contradict what becomes verbally articulated through the narrator's caption, which is embedded in a frame hanging on the wall, next to a symbol that becomes repeated, albeit with differentiations, three times in an instance of visual intertextuality (Figure 1.2b).

In *The Pursuit of Signs: Semiotics, Literature, Deconstruction*, Jonathan Culler writes that through an intertextual lens, a given artwork 'has the meaning it does only because certain things have previously been written' (1981: 103). Mieke Bal defines intertextuality as referring 'to the readymade quality of signs [...] that the maker of images finds in earlier images and texts produced by a culture' (2004: 68). In such instances, the original meaning 'may have changed, but the new meaning that replaces it will carry the trace of its precursor. The latest artist may reject or reverse, ironize or deconstruct, pluralize or marginalize the meaning of the borrowed motif, but that meaning cannot be undone, ignored or cancelled out' (Bal 2004: 69).[6] It is precisely because of the rhetorical implications of Gloeckner's intertextual references that this narrative section on the sex worker's life and death illustrates a different, ontological kind of (neo-) colonial violence against Mexican femininity.

In its first iteration, the icon on the wall evokes vaginal imagery. While this is also true for its second repetition, there vaguely appears, in this instance, the figure of the Virgin Mary of Guadalupe. In the icon's third iteration, the vaginal imagery disappears from view and becomes completely replaced by the image of Virgin Mary, the Christian embodiment of ideal femininity that is marked by (white) sexual purity and innocence. In being positioned in this narrative fragment of 'La Tristeza', the vaginal icon that transforms into an image of the Virgin Mary of Guadalupe is placed in stark juxtaposition with the sex worker, whose life and death become graphically narrated. Through this arrangement, 'La Tristeza' stages such dichotomies as pure/impure, virgin/whore, clean/dirty, white/dark, which are mirrored in Christian doctrine through Mary and Eve. Importantly, however, the icon of Mary is positioned in such a way on this page so as to be understood as a transformation of a previous take on sacred femininity, inviting one to consider what this earlier conceptualization was and how it became manifested in Latin America, where Christianity was imposed through colonialism, alongside patriarchal understandings of gender and gender relations (Lugones 2007).

Ann E. Pearson describes 'the persistence of vaginal iconography in both religious and secular medieval iconography', further noting that 'in ancient times the vagina was a sacred sign of powerful creative forces associated with many different goddess figures' (2001: np). In polytheistic traditions, female deities were celebrated for their vaginal potency and sexual activity that were thought to bring 'the blessing of fertility to individuals, the land, [and] the animals', with its benefits extending 'to other realms of human culture' (Pearson 2001: 39). Patriarchal monotheism brought about the 'disappearance of sexuality from the realm of the divine [and] the combination of woman and power, especially power associated with women's sexuality, became suspect' (Pearson 2001: 42). In its understanding of female sexuality as dangerous, Christianity relegated it to the status of the sin, introducing as the sacred embodiment of ideal femininity,

---

6 For Bal, intertextuality is 'indifferent [...] to authorial intention' (2004: 68), and its identification depends on the reader's engagement with a given text.

Virgin Mary, with her immaculate conception, and the virgin birth of Jesus (Pearson 2001).[7]

The icon of the Virgin Mary of Guadalupe that is shown in 'La Tristeza' accompanied Mexican struggles of independence against colonial Spain in the nineteenth century and came to be understood as a symbol of national protection (Wolf 1958). According to myth, this image first appeared miraculously on the cloak of a Christianized Indian in 1531. Prior to this, Mary revealed to him that a church should be 'built in her honour on Tepeyac Hill, [, which] in pre-Hispanic times, [...] had housed a temple to the earth and fertility goddess Tonantzin, Our Lady Mother' (Wolf 1958: 35). Jennifer Colby explains that 'Guadalupe played an important role in the conversion of Meso-America to Catholicism in the 16th and 17th centuries and provided a symbol that allowed indigenous peoples to continue devotion to [the] mother goddesses of their own cosmology' (2019: 33).

With the imposition of Christianity, Tonantzin came to embody Virgin Mary's dark, '*bruja*-ized (witched) Other in colonial discourse' (Lara 2008: 100; Bartra 1992). Irene Lara discusses the 'virgin/whore dichotomy' that is embodied through Mary and Tonantzin and explains how traces of this pre-Hispanic Mother Goddess became transposed, with the defeat of the Mexican rebellion, onto 'La Malinche, the indigenous mistress of, and translator for, conqueror Hernan Cortes' – the woman who betrayed her people and became the cause of their colonization (2008: 109). As a result, Virgin Mary 'was crowned the Patron Saint of New Spain [...], while Malinche became known as *la Chingada* [...], the violated, "fucked" mother of the first mestizo' (Lara 2008: 99). Her sexuality, in this sense, became linked to betrayal and the colonial defeat of the Mexican nation, and thus Virgin Mary and Tonantzin/Malinche came to embody the virgin/whore dichotomy.[8] Such colonial myth making led to the production of an ideal for Mexican femininity that is embodied through 'Marianismo [whereby] the Virgin of Guadalupe [has constituted] the role model for womanhood which insists that the mother, nurturer, who endured pain and sorrow and is willing to serve, should be emulated by women serving their husbands and children' in the domestic sphere (Colby 2019: 38).

---

[7] Sigmund Freud's psychoanalytical take on Medusa's head and the monstrous vagina dentata also captures the patriarchal understanding of female sexuality as threatening (2001).

[8] Lara explains how Chicana feminists like Sandra Cisneros and Cherríe Moraga have deconstructed and decolonized this 'virgin/whore' division through their writings by fusing and en-fleshing these female deities. For instance, Moraga writes of the Virgin's 'burnt red flesh [and her] vagina openings [that] split into two thick thighs of female eruption' (quoted in Lara 2008: 121). In this sense, she revisions sacred femininity by restoring the female subject's flesh, sensuality and sexuality.

Female sex workers, and at a different level, women and girls abandoning the domestic sphere to work in the *maquiladoras* as those described in *Juarez*, do not fit into this ideal. In addition, they embody a shift in the understanding of traditional gender roles, which have relegated Mexican women in the domestic space. Gloeckner's artistic decision to place the vaginal turned virginal, Marian icon in the narrative section that accounts for the female sex worker's abusive contact with the American tourist and her subsequent murder, allows an interpretation of this incident that also points to a longer colonial history that has produced specific understandings of, and positions for, Mexican femininities. As it does so, it also illustrates how globalization constitutes a 'contemporary form of coloniality [that] structures relationships of race and gender in order to retain their usefulness to the global political economy' (Gamlin 2022: 513). As a result, globalisation also produces forms of human rights violations that are specific to the precarious othered femininities navigating Juarez.[9]

(Post-)colonial encounters and sex work in the journal entries of *Burma*

Like *Juarez*, the second volume of *I Live Here* also zooms in on another border city of the Global South. This one, however, is located in Southeast Asia, and separates Thailand from Burma (Myanmar). *Burma* tells the stories of adult and underage female sex workers and child soldiers. These people's gendered precarities, and the violations of their rights, emerge in the context of the Burmese/Karen conflict and related hostilities. In order to contextualize the testimonies of rights violations re-mediated in this volume, Kirschner provides a timeline accounting for the events leading to the contemporary crisis in her introductory note to the text. The earliest event mentioned in this timeline is temporally located in 1949, when 'six million Karen' people who constitute one of the 'one hundred thirty-five distinct ethnic groups' of Burma started 'fighting for an autonomous state' (Kirschner 2008a: np). Kirschner further refers to Burmese dictatorships, the authoritative change of the country's name from Burma to its equivalent, Myanmar, 'in the language of the country's largest ethnic

---

[9] Gamlin also writes that 'feminist historical research largely agrees that colonisers and subsequent postcolonial governments in Mexico, as in other parts of Latin America, saw women [as] minoritised and minimised, confined to the domestic sphere' (2022: 514). This process is described by Silvia Rivera Cusicanqui as the 'colonial seal of the exclusion of women' (2012: 106).

group', as well as to the aggressive suppression of protests by Burmese army and State authorities, and the prevention of 'access to food, funds, recruits, and information in areas of ethnic rebel resistance' (Kirschner 2008a: np). These factors, she explains, have caused huge refugee flows in the Karen community, many of which ended up in the border city of Mae Sot. She concludes by noting that 'it remains difficult to imagine manual labor, domestic work, or the sex trade in Thailand without the presence of refugees' (Kirschner 2008a: np).

The testimonies shared in this graphic life narrative exist alongside Kirschner's journal entries, which detail her reflections and feelings, as she navigates dark and dangerous spaces at the Burma/Thailand border. In this section, I focus on the entries that account for her encounter with a seventeen-year-old sex worker, and on Kamel Khélif's graphic novella, which narrates the life story of Mi-Su, a girl who also works in the sex industry of Mae Sot. My analysis foregrounds the potential, but also the limitations of these remediated gendered testimonies for a decolonized understanding of gendered human rights violations occurring in the context of female sex work in this border city. Importantly, like 'La Tristeza', *Burma* also includes religious allusions in its accounts of sex work and child soldiering. Unlike Gloeckner's intertextual references to sacred femininity, however, those made by Kirschner are charged with ambivalence, which lies in how they seem to reproduce associations between love, faith, humanitarianism and Christianity, without explicitly staging the injurious implications of the colonial imposition of this religion in Burma. This imposition has significantly contributed to the ethno-religious conflict between the Burmese and the Karen people that continues contemporarily and produces specific forms of gendered violence.

For this reason, the narrative context in which girls' and boys' testimonies appear is important for my analysis. Kirschner's biblical allusions take the form of paraphrasis and numeric directions to corresponding biblical excerpts. In one of her journal entries, she explains that 'a Karen woman who works for a local human rights organization' helped her gain access to an illegal brothel (Kirschner 2008a: np). As the narrative describes her entry into a sex worker's room and the locking of the door behind her, it is her own vulnerability that becomes foregrounded: 'It's hard not to feel vulnerable in a locked room', she mentions, 'I've been told to be careful – a Western man was shot in this brothel last week' (Kirschner 2008a: np). On the next page, a photograph of a girl alluringly looking at the reader is accompanied by a caption which explains that 'love is peace' and that 'while we are in this world if we have love, we will have peace – we will have God', concluding with the statement that 'if there is no love we will be in trouble [and that] God is love' (Kirschner 2008a: np). As such, on the one hand, the narrative stages Kirschner's Western origins, in addition to her gender, as what renders her excessively vulnerable in the brothels of Mae Sot. On the other hand, in being juxtaposed with what seems as a paraphrasis of an excerpt from First Corinthians about the value of (Christian) love for one's fellow human being, the information mentioned above suggests that Kirschner's precarious endeavour is one stemming from this kind of religiously prescribed love for an other.

A repetition with a differentiation of a similar excerpt from First Corinthians appears later in numeric form alongside one from Proverbs. The journal entry that accounts for Kirschner's illegal entry into a Karen-controlled area, where she would interview Burmese child soldiers, once again stresses her Western gendered precarity. In order to successfully cross into this area, she is introduced by her driver to a Karen soldier as a 'Christian missionary, convincing Thai youngsters to embrace the faith and find salvation through Jesus' (Kirschner 2008a: np). On the next page, a photograph shows a bridge connecting Burma and Thailand. An image of Jesus looking at the reader is collaged on this photograph and his chest is inscribed with the biblical references '1 Cor· 13:13' and 'Prov· 3:5–6' (Kirschner 2008a: np). In verses four to five in First Corinthians, Paul explains that 'Love is patient; love is kind. [Love] is not jealous; it does not brag; it is not arrogant. It is not rude; it does not seek its own interest; it does not become irritated; it does not reckon with wrong' (quoted in Fitzmyer 2008: 14). In verse thirteen, he concludes by noting that 'faith, hope, love remain, these three; but the greatest of these is love' (quoted in Fitzmyer 2008: 14). A link thus emerges between this excerpt and the paraphrasis that previously accompanied the exoticized girl's image.

The verses from Proverbs to which readers are directed, instruct us to 'trust in the Lord with all [our] heart, and rely not on [our] own understanding. In all that [we] do, [we should] hold him in mind, and he will keep [our] path smooth' (quoted in Fox 2009: 610). The way these biblical intertextual references about love, faith and trust in God become positioned in the narrative of Kirschner's endeavour to seek and share the testimonies of underage othered gendered subjects in Burma is charged with ambivalence. On the one hand, by juxtaposing the image of Jesus with her false presentation as a Christian missionary seeking to convert Thai youth to Christianity, the narrative may be seen as implicitly pointing to the instrumentalization of religion in Kirschner's humanitarian project of collecting otherwise untold stories about girls and boys suffering gendered violence.

On the other hand, Kirschner's biblical references can be interpreted as pointing to the driving force behind her humanitarian work, during which she places herself in precarious positions because of her femininity and her Western origins, as she relates in her journal entries. In such a case, they would seem to reproduce a neo-colonial approach to othered populations that need to be saved by a Western, ethically driven humanitarian, who is, in this case, also a woman. Further to these implications, however, these biblical allusions may be read as implicitly evoking the injurious impact of the colonial imposition of Christianity in Burma. Nevertheless, the fact that the introduction to *Burma* largely accounts for Burmese atrocities against Karen people and starts at the temporal point of 1949, when the latter started fighting for autonomy, omits the role of British colonial rule in the ethno-religious conflict created and sustained in the area.

According to Mikael Gravels, Burma has gained notoriety for the extreme violence used by its military regime [and] has long been in Amnesty International's spotlight', but its problems are not investigated through a postcolonial lens, and this gap limits the understanding of the factors leading to them (1999: 1). Mandy Sadan also underlines the need for 'deeper and more nuanced demographic and social insights into Burma's history of internal militarized conflict' (2013: 601). For Gravels, the 'explanation of Burma's present situation must be sought in the legacy of the colonial era, or rather in the nationalistic paranoia which was generated by developments following independence in 1948 – a politically orchestrated paranoia linking fear of the disintegration of both union and state with the foreign takeover of power and the disappearance of Burmese culture' (1999: 2). In her analysis of 'divide and conquer' colonial practices in Southeast Asia, Sarah Womack explains that 'in addition to finding and exploiting "warlike" peoples [there], the British had maximised the effectiveness of their control by manipulating tensions between different ethnic and religious groups' (2006: 108). In Burma, this manipulation escalated with the recruitment of Christianized Karen soldiers in the British army, which aggressively oppressed the Burmese population threatening its existence (Taylor 2006).

In accounting for cultural, religious and socio-political shifts brought about through British colonization, Gravels explains that 'whilst demanding total subjugation, [Christian] missionaries also began to reorganise everyday life and work [. . .]. This was followed by the teaching of European culture, from learning the English language to ideas on order and cleanliness' (1999: 23). As a result, 'Burman culture became synonymous with paganism and something less civilised, which was incompatible with Christian identity' (Gravels 1999: 23).

Sadan also refers to an unpreceded crisis brought about through the British colonial rule and to 'the anti-Burman colonial racial prejudice' of the British army, which Burmese nationalists took to challenge (2013: 602). As a result of these developments, 'anti-colonial struggle [transformed] into a fundamentalistic nationalism, and a struggle for survival which legitimised the use of violence' (Gravels 1999: 24).[10]

By omitting this information, and focusing on Burmese atrocities, while referring to Christian missionary work and presenting biblical references about love, faith and trust in God in the narrative account of sex work and child soldiering in Burma, the second volume of *I Live Here* presents a somewhat limited and limiting take on the Burmese/Karen conflict, casting a veil of silence over British colonial complicities in the perpetuation of harm and ethno-religious division. Thus, unlike Gloeckner's politically-charged references to sacred femininity, Kirschner's religious allusions seem to ambivalently reproduce hierarchies between the Western humanitarian self and her others.

At the same time as leaving histories of Western (neo-)colonial presence in Burma outside the frame of representation, the narrative also refrains from accounting for further factors that have shaped the geo- bio- and necro-political attributes of rural areas and led to urbanization, and of industrialized border areas like Mae Sot, which place female sex workers' lives in extremely precarious positions. Peter Munro explains that Mae Sot's borderland nature has rendered it a 'key trading hub' through the centuries, and a point where weapons, drugs and people have been trafficked (2012: 159, 172). This is 'a quasi-legal liminal space', where workers of all kinds, including those of the sex industry, become heavily exploited (Ciocchini and Greener 2021: 1622). Pablo Ciocchini and Joe Greener also note that 'police corruption, state-sanctioned violence and systemic flouting of labour laws are a core part of social life around Mae Sot revealing the complex interactions between official and unofficial state powers, imperative in creating conditions for the hyper-exploitation of labour' (2021: 1622). In its function as an Export Processing Zone (EPZ), Mae Sot, like Juarez, constitutes one of 'the central sites of global commodity production, [and] an embodiment of the core Global inequality between [centres] and peripheries [thus emerging as] one quintessence of the neo-colonial regime of corporate production' (Ciocchini and Greener 2021: 1622).

---

[10]   I am not attempting to justify contemporary Burmese violence, but rather to point to the causes of its emergence.

Gendered violence and harassment, corruption, environmental pollution and other injustices occurring in Mae Sot, as described by Ciocchini and Greener (2021), mirror those that become graphically mediated via the pinball game metaphor of *La Lucha*. As Ciocchini and Greener aptly point out, 'the legal and infrastructural permission for corporate activities is constructed differently in Global South and North contexts. In this sense, corporate regimes have a certain geography in terms of the degree of "permission" they are granted within different locations' (2021: 1622). Mae Sot is thus similar to Juarez in terms of how its border positionality renders it a point of illegal trading, a space where sex work and gendered violence prevail, and whose residents become exploited in different ways because of modernity/coloniality and neoliberal economy.[11] And while *Juarez* stages these implications through references to NAFTA, the *maquiladoras* and the drug wars impacting the city, *Burma* seems to cast a veil of silence on similar matters, thus foregrounding Burmese violence as the main cause of gendered suffering. Indeed, as early as on the book's cover page a monstrous hand threateningly approaches and encircles a Karen flag, while armed soldiers around it also threaten civilians, who are on the move while carrying their belongings. This visual arrangement implicitly guides readers to a particular direction in relation to their interpretation of the text, while also structuring a neat victim/perpetrator dichotomy.

For these reasons, the narrative context of Kirschner's journal entry, which describes her encounter with the seventeen-year-old sex worker in Mae Sot, and of Khélif's graphic novella entitled 'The Story of Mi-Su', is important for their interpretation. Further to the focus on Burmese military violence and its ambivalent religious allusions, Kirschner's attempt at triggering empathy and forging identificatory bonds through her journal writing seems to re-produce the problems of Western feminist thought as described by McLaren, by ignoring the differences relating to the factors leading to sex work and the violence suffered by female sex workers in the Global North and the Global South (Goldberg and Moore 2011). For instance, as she lies in her hotel room in Mae Sot, Kirschner's autobiographical subject remembers 'walking along Patpong Road' and seeing American tourists 'taking digital pictures of young girls standing outside karaoke booths, flirty, their wanting breasts on offer' (Kirschner 2008a: np). Like Gloeckner's reference to the American sex tourist in Juarez, this account invites us to see these girls from the perspective of the ignorant American tourist, which introduces them as commodified, exotic, sexual spectacles.

---

[11] On the similarities between Thai factories and Mexican *maquiladoras* see Lubeigt 2007.

Subsequently, the narrative shifts from Kirshner's (2008a: np) memories of the tourists to her own past, her 'first encounters with the sexual underworld [and] the illicit thrill of going to the sex shows and the strip clubs'. At the background, a two-page-spread photograph that zooms in on red nail-polished hands in a dimly lit space accompanies Kirschner's memories of her explorations of the Canadian sexual underworld, which she perceived during her youth as both thrilling and 'liberating [; as a] big fuck you to being a nice girl' (2008a: np). As the background picture shifts from the hands to a woman's face, which remains semi-visible given that it is cut through by the end of the page that keeps her eyes outside this representation, Kirschner explains that in the past, it had not occurred to her 'to wonder about women in the porn videos' (2008a: np). As it stages a transition from ignorance, presumably similar to that of the American tourists in Thailand, to awareness – to the autobiographical subject's *bildung* – the narrative reminds us, on the next page, that these women too 'have dignity' (Kirschner 2008a: np). By structuring Kirschner's exploration of Mae Sot's sex world in parallel to her memories of her youthful entry into the Canadian sexual underground, the journal entry is meant to imply a more mature and aware perspective on the workings of the sex industry. However, one is left wondering about the narrative function of the autobiographical subject's memories, which intervene in, and delay the story of the underage sex worker she met, and which she is supposed to recount for the reader.

Do these memories constitute attempts at shaping identificatory bonds between the present of the girls in Mae Sot and her own past as a university student who rejected the norms of proper femininity, or are they there to underscore the radically different gendered experiences of encountering the sexual underworlds of Thailand and Canada? At the final section of this journal entry, Kirschner explains that the sex worker she met 'is 17 and terrified. She wants me to know that she has just started working in the brothel and that she is a very good student' (2008a: np). The girl's request implies differences in relation to the factors that led each of them to the respective sexual underground, and her desire to be acknowledged as a good student comes to juxtaposition with the autobiographical subject's rejection of proper femininity. The visual register of the narrative is again predominantly dark. At the background, a female silhouette can be seen, but nothing specific about her can be deciphered. Her head is also turned away from the reader in an artistic attempt to visually hide her identity.

Mihaela Precup reads silhouettes in Nina Bunjevac's graphic memoir, *Fatherland*, as pointing to 'the blind spots of postmemory, a process that preserves the frames of events and contours of individuals through storytelling and photography, but through which access to the past is not complete' (2020: 125; Saltzman 2006). In *Burma*, the blind spots that become reflected in the girl's visual and verbal representation do not derive from, nor embody, a process whereby memory moves from one generation to the next, thus necessarily becoming porous in its transformation into postmemory. Rather, this gap in representation is caused, at least partly, by the positioning of the girl's experiences of sex work in Mae Sot alongside the autobiographical subject's experiences of the Canadian sexual underworld, and her own sexual suffering. As a result of this narrative framing, the girl remains elusive, and largely invisible in both the visual and the textual register.

'I recognize those eyes', Kirschner writes, 'eyelashes that protect you from seeing too much and keeping others from doing the same' (2008a: np). Then, she returns to her own memories and accounts for her own injurious experiences at the age of seventeen, which include illicit drug use and enforced sexual intercourse under its influence. 'There is nothing unusual about my story', she writes, 'but it was the last time, until now, that I examined things so closely' (Kirschner 2008a: np). An arrow directs the reader to the next page, which presents the sex worker's black silhouette. In this journal entry, however, Kirschner's own sexual trauma becomes narrated in ways that relegate her interlocutor's testimony to the margins of her own. While the text's objective is to trigger empathy and raise awareness about the gendered violence suffered by the unnamed underage sex worker in the brothel of Mae Sot, the reader remains unable to adequately witness her testimony. As such, despite their 'textual attempts at transnational feminist solidarity', *Burma*'s journal entries are characterized by a 'representational imbalance [that] is rooted in the flip approach to "first-world" as compared with "third-world" experiences of sexual violence by women' (Goldberg and Moore 2011: 246).

As a result of this approach, Kirschner's 'emphasis on a shared experience of gender and sex elides the dramatically different ways that patriarchal prescriptions around women's sexuality, the violation of women's bodies, and the sex industry that capitalizes on them operate in the cultural and economic contexts of the geopolitical spaces constructed in the text' (Goldberg and Moore 2011: 247). As Alexandra Popescu also writes, Kirschner's 'shift from compassion to a violent identification with the sex workers of Mae Sot', further shows how 'the humanitarian is sometimes obscured by Kirshner's own emotional profit' (2012: 66–7). But as James Dawes reminds us, humanitarian work is often marked by this paradox, since 'it is sometimes impossible to distinguish the desire to help others from the desire to amplify the self, to distinguish altruism from narcissism' (2007: 122). The tensions emerging from this attribute of Western humanitarian work mark Kirschner's creative attempts to speak on behalf of othered girls and women, and tend to marginalize their testimonies, limiting the text's potential for remediating Philomela's graphic testimony.

(Post-)colonial encounters and sex work in 'The Story of Mi-Su'

In another (almost forced) attempt of drawing connections between sex work in the Global North and the Global South, Khélif's graphic novella starts by explaining via a subheading under its title that 'these are the words of a sex worker in Mae Sot, who was interviewed using questions provided from a sex worker in Vancouver' (Khélif 2008: np). However, the image of Mi-Su, the girl who is about to narrate her story, next to the title, shows her directly facing the reader, demanding response-ability adress-ability. Intra-diegetically, this graphic narrative also provides more complex insights on the particularities of sex work in Mae Sot. For instance, Mi-Su explains how her parents were led to bankruptcy and unemployment in Rangoon, which caused fights and led to their divorce, further accounting for her mother's move to the 'Myawaddy army camp' when Mi-Su was six years old (Khélif 2008: np). In order for her and her daughter to survive, her mother sold Mi-Su to a family, and found work at a paddy field. After her father bought her back, he sent her to live with her sister, who worked at a bank and promised to provide for her. However, when she was eleven years old, her sister took her to a woman who initiated her into the sex industry of Mae Sot (Khélif 2008).

Unlike the attempts of forging identificatory bonds in terms of women's and girls' experiences of sex work and abuse in Canada and Thailand, Mi-Su's testimony illustrates stark juxtapositions between the reasons that led her and Kirschner's autobiographical subject into completely different sex worlds and corresponding experiences. Kirschner's journal entries, for instance, account for how she gave 'a hand-job to the guy who sat in the back of [her] Russian Lit class' (Kirschner 2008a: np), thus also evoking her privileged educational background, while relating how she became exposed to the thrilling dangers of the Canadian underworld, which, nevertheless, she could exit in relative safety upon wishing to do so. Mi-Su's experience of sex work is radically different. It took place when she was eleven, and it was caused by poverty, parental neglect and potentially, illiteracy, in the turbulent socio-, bio- and necro-political context of the border between Burma and Thailand. The black and white illustrations that accompany the girl's verbal testimony highlight these differences. Upon relating how she had to work at the age of eleven in order to survive, the verbal narrative stops, and a wordless two-page illustration presents the city landscape she is forced to navigate alone. Similarly to her initial visual depiction, in this case too, both her body and face are directed towards the reader and foregrounded in the image. That her account is presented in the first-person and her interlocutor does not appear in the text increase the degree of her visibility, even if her testimony is fictionalized by the creative practitioner.

After the wordless two-page illustration, the narrative further underscores Mi-Su's isolation, which was previously mediated through her positioning in the urban space, by describing her life as a sex worker. Mi-Su relates, for instance, how much her virginity was worth and how her payment was split between her and the brothel owner. In the visual register she is drawn nude, cleaning her vagina, and subsequently collecting the money left by her client. Unlike Gloeckner's depiction of the sex worker in Juarez, the sequential narrative of Mi-Su's daily life presents her commodification in the context of modernity/coloniality through her own perspective. Furthermore, contrary to the sex worker in 'La Tristeza', Mi-Su is not silent.

As the visual register shows her during intercourse with a client, she explains that she is 'happy when the client is happy' (Khélif 2008: np). She then relates that as she gets older she gets less work, wondering 'why they make a person cheaper like with old clothes' as time passes (Khélif 2008: np). She also mentions worrying about being contaminated with HIV, and that her fear of being infected has caused her to dislike her 'lower parts' (Khélif 2008: np). In the visual register, a sexual encounter ends and her client leaves, as she explains that through her income, she financially supports her family. The narrative concludes with a repetition of the phrase 'I am happy when the client is happy' (Khélif 2008: np), staging a causal link between customer satisfaction and her own. Further to this textual repetition, in the visual register of the narrative that describes her abandonment by her mother and her sex work, a teddy bear is often placed next to her, as a silent witness to her suffering, and a reminder of her young age.

Kevin Bales explains that the increase of child slavery in Thailand 'reflects the enormous changes [that have occurred] over the past fifty years as the country has gone through the great transformation of industrialization – the same process that tore Europe apart over a century ago' (2003: 233). While in the past 'daughters were sold in response to serious family financial crises, [contemporarily], the steadily growing market for prostitutes, [and] the loss of girls to HIV infection, [have created an] especially strong demand for younger and younger girls' in the local sex industry (Bales 2003: 233, 235). These factors need to be considered alongside the Burmese/Karen conflict in Mi-Su's story. Mae Sot's geo-, bio- and necro-political attributes have, as in the case of Juarez, provided criminals with the ability 'to operate with impunity and [...] everyday tourists [with the opportunity] to engage in criminal activity with little chance of recrimination' (Munro 2012: 174). The human rights violations suffered by girls and women there are produced and sustained by the gendered interactions enabled by (post-) colonial border zones, which sustain conditions of gendered precarity and fuel the global neoliberal economy at the expense of human lives in the Global South, and more so, those of the girls and women working in the sex industry.

In an instance of narrative circularity and visual repetition, one of the final panels of Khélif's graphic novella returns to the beginning, presenting Mi-Su sitting alone on the floor, with her teddy bear next to her, watching TV, and waiting for her next client. This visual depiction is also the one that initiates her story. While in the verbal register of the first panel an extra-diegetic narrative voice relates that she is waiting for her next client, in the repetition of this panel towards the end of the narrative, Mi-Su mentions 'a memory of her mother [she] can't forget' (Khélif 2008: np). The following panels show her standing nude in front of a mirror, as she describes this memory: 'I am young and we're swimming at Lake Lay. I can't swim and my mother dives in to save me' (Khélif 2008: np).[12] In the wordless panel following these statements, she uses the shower faucet to wash her genitals while still standing in front of the mirror. In the final panel, she explains that her mother's attempt to save her in her memory was a failed one because both ended up drowning.

In the visual register, dark liquid that resembles blood rather than water emanates from the faucet she holds in front of her genitals, onto the mirror, marring her reflection, in a pessimistic ending where both herself and her mother are doomed to destruction in this turbulent, poverty- and conflict-ridden context. Like Itys's murder by his mother Procne in Philomela's myth, Mi-Su's commodification through child labour that became initiated by her mother and then sustained by her sister may be interpreted as another illustration of how the violence a person may have suffered can cause its transformation in its intergenerational transmission. In this sense, what may be perceived as

---

[12] Her positioning in front of the mirror as she accounts for the memory of her mother evokes the latter's impact in the former's development and self-conceptualization as well as to Jacques Lacan's interconnected theory of the 'mirror stage'. Lacan explains that this stage 'manufactures for the subject, caught up in the lure of spatial identification, the succession of phantasies that extends from a fragmented body-image [...] to the assumption of the armour of an alienating identity, which will mark with its rigid structure the subject's entire mental development' (2001: 3).

monstrous maternal femininity as that also embodied in colonial myth-making through the figure of Tonantzin/La Malinche, becomes configured in Khélif's graphic novella as the product of the Burmese/Karen conflict, of modernity/coloniality, and of global neoliberal economy.

Spectacles of gendered violence in *Palestine*

Spectacles of violated femininities also appear in Sacco's *Palestine*, where girls and women navigate spaces marked by the Israeli/Palestinian conflict and by intra-communal patriarchal oppression. Sacco's graphic life narrative illustrates how Israeli and Palestinian masculinities, hegemonic, dominant or oppressed, inflict different forms of implicit or explicit violence against Palestinian female subjects. Specifically, it sheds light on gendered suffering in prison, and on abuse that occurs in domestic and public spaces, which at times goes hand in hand with the political visions of particular Intifada sectors. Wendy Kozol writes that at the same time as addressing the need 'to make human rights violations visible to international communities', *Palestine* also self-reflectively admits that such 'representations depend on gendered and racialized spectacles of violence for their commercial and humanitarian currency' (2011: 167). Thus, while Sacco shares the same goal with Kirschner, Gloeckner and Khélif, in terms of rendering gendered human rights violations visible in the West, his approach to it is very different. Instead of attempting to forge identificatory bonds with his interlocutors on the grounds of similar suffering, for instance, and as opposed to remaining outside the narrative frame, Sacco's autobiographical subject constantly highlights his positionality as a Western male reporter, and a privileged outsider in the Palestinian context. His interactions with, and accounts of, women and girls often include sexist comments and views, which reflect stereotypical, masculinist understandings of Palestinian femininity, both Western and local, thus leaving no room for the reader to perceive him as a sacrificial humanitarian hero.

He also frequently states his disinterest in, and at times boredom by, the stories of suffering he hears, given their repetitiveness and because they make no new contribution to his reportage. As such, he constantly reminds the reader that as a Western reporter, he too is necessarily involved in the commodification of racialized and gendered spectacles of violence. By thus foregrounding the problems linked to the 'gaze of western reportage' (Kozol 2011: 168), he casts a disillusioning perspective on the figure of the Western humanitarian who witnesses human rights violations in the Middle East. Kozol writes that the depiction of 'human rights crises through the gaze of an intermediary western figure is a representational convention used in human rights literature, advocacy groups' appeals to contributors and [...] Hollywood' (2011: 168). In these accounts there often appear 'sympathetic, mostly male, Americans who risk their lives to report on human rights crises resulting from state violence against its citizens' (Kozol 2011: 168; Goldberg 2007). A similar figure exists, for instance, in Kirschner's journal entries about gendered suffering in Burma. That her autobiographical subject is female often becomes presented as a factor that further contributes to the precarities she is exposed to through her humanitarian work. Contrarily, Sacco's sarcastic, self-deprecating autobiographical representation refrains from engaging in hagiography regarding the Western witness of the distant suffering of others (Whitlock 2017).

His work exists in juxtaposition with a large segment of Western reportage on the Middle East, particularly that which concerns veiled Muslim women. Ghazi-Walid Falah, for instance, writes that in American print media, 'Muslim women and their roles in society have been narrowly construed and projected' (2005: 300). In combination with written captions, images of veiled women in such representations 'reinforce images of Muslim society as the cultural, political, and moral "other" of the West' (Falah 2005: 302). In so doing, they manifest 'a direct link between societal racism, elite ideology, and the production of news' (Falah 2005: 304). In his analysis of how the press produces specific forms of racism, A. Teun van Dijk also explains that 'structures of headlines, leads, thematic organization, the presence of explanatory background information, style, and especially the overall selection of newsworthy topics [are] indirectly controlled by the societal context of power relations' (1991: 41).

But further to the sender of the message, its receiver also has a crucial role in identifying such depictions. As Kozol writes, Muslim women, and more so those who are veiled, have become 'a challenging subject to represent to American audiences [which have a] long history of Orientalist assumptions about Islamic attitudes toward gender and sexuality' (2011: 173). Consequently, visual depictions of Muslim women should be interpreted in the context of 'wider geopolitical discourses' (Falah 2005: 301).[13] *Palestine* performs such a

---

[13] Akbar S. Ahmed (1992) and Leila Ahmed (1992) discuss the negative implications deriving from representations of Muslim women in Western media and academic discourses. A different form of violation, which has not gained the corresponding visibility as such, regards veiled women's religious rights, and it becomes reflected through the veil bans that have occurred across a number of European countries (Brown 2012; Nicholson 2014; Margolis 2021).

historically and geopolitically contextualized approach to veiled as well as unveiled Palestinian women, and their suffering.

Sacco's work of 'slow [...] or stale journalism' (Whitlock 2017: 289), provides a nuanced and complex perspective on the women of Palestine, both the Muslim and the Christian. As the cartoonist accounts for different forms of violence they are exposed to, he does not remain silent about the harm caused by the constraints of a patriarchal conflict-ridden community. Hence, his gaze can deconstructively supplement (neo-)colonial depictions of Muslim women like those previously described. As Kozol points out, by 'using the narrator as the foil for western assumptions', Sacco effectively displays the injurious ignorance that lies behind them, while also staging the complexities that characterize Palestinian femininities, their agencies, and their suffering (2011: 173). As a result, his work provides detailed access to these otherwise silenced othered gendered spectacles.

Prison torture

For instance, it accounts for gendered torture in prison, which otherwise remains invisible, but becomes restaged through Sacco's 'act[s] of informed but imagined witnessing' (Chute 2010: 90). Chapter 4 of *Palestine* relates the testimony of a woman who was 'squealed on' by some of her male collaborators 'for underwriting nationalistic pamphlets', something 'she says she didn't do', Sacco's narrator explains (Sacco 2001: 97). Some of these men, the woman explains, 'were arrested in the morning and denounced me in the afternoon. Not only were their bodies weak, but their minds were weak, their commitment to the national cause was weak' (Sacco 2001: 97). This woman's testimony thus presents her collaborators' inability to endure suffering as damaging both for their gendered identities and their struggle.

Turning to her torture, Sacco's intra-diegetic self explains that 'she says' she has been locked up in a small dark box, where she had to stand up for half a day after she had 'undergone a liver biopsy', that she was forced to 'sit up straight with a metal bar pressing down the center of her back [and that she was] hit when she leaned against the wall' (Sacco 2001: 98). Further to bodily pain, she suffered mental strain due to her isolation in a 'cell, which was besmirched with filth [...], and where she was left without toilet paper and sanitary napkins' (Sacco 2001: 98). Because Sacco's other previously imprisoned interlocutors are predominantly male, the remediation of this woman's account adds an important feminine lens to Palestinian prison experiences.

Further to the psychic torture of her isolation, the taboo, shame and humiliation associated with menstrual blood when it is seen, point to how hygiene deprivation in prison can become particularly injurious for women. In addition, the remediation of her suffering illustrates how she became caught up within hierarchies of hegemonic, dominant and oppressed masculinities, which are directly connected to particular sides of the Israeli/Palestinian conflict. While sharing her testimony, she is shown smoking and looking at Sacco's autobiographical subject whose presence is only implied, and who is outside the frame of representation. Given that the reader is placed at the same position as his, as the woman looks at him, she also looks at us – the further removed secondary witness. Subsequently, Sacco's informed and imaginary witnessing offers visual access to the spaces of the Russian Compound, where she was imprisoned, presenting her from within the claustrophobic small box she was locked up in, and from inside her dirty cell. His decision to relate only in writing that she was deprived of sanitary towels and toilet paper, without visually capturing the consequences of this deprivation, preserves – through the visual register – this woman's dignity, which became attacked via an act of affectively charged gendered violence.

Sacco's narrator notes that 'the Shin Bet reckoned they could play the twin cards of gender and Arab culture against her [by explaining that] a long imprisonment would ruin her marriage prospects' (Sacco 2001: 98). In a statement that reflects a mono-dimensional perspective on Palestinian femininity, which does not consider the possibility that it may be embodied and performed in a plurality of ways, an officer mentions that they do not 'arrest girls', that they are aware 'of her situation as a girl in [her] society [and that] no one will marry' her because of her imprisonment (Sacco 2001: 98). This statement demonstrates that while time in prison is considered a core attribute of Palestinian masculinity, as further discussed in the following chapter, it becomes a source of disgrace for Palestinian femininities.

Upon responding that she does not care about her marriage prospects and the stigma of her imprisonment, threats against her become more aggressive. 'They threatened rape, she says … they accused her of using a trip overseas to find sexual partners', Sacco's narrator continues (Sacco 2001: 99). The frequent repetition of the phrase 'she says' in the remediation of her testimony reminds the reader that the words we read are her own, and that Sacco's narrator only repeats them. At the same time, it may imply that the narrator, who is also presumably trustworthy, cannot confirm their validity, leaving it up to the reader to determine their truthfulness, and thus, their testimonial value. As such, while refusing to relegate this woman to the position of the mute, helpless, passive victim, the repetition of 'she says' creates an ambivalent distance between Sacco's intra-diegetic self, the reader and this woman.

When she admitted to having indeed been abroad to find sexual partners because she 'wanted a change', and the Shin Bet realized 'they wouldn't intimidate her sexually', they released her, the narrator relates (Sacco 2001: 99). In the visual register, an Israeli officer tells her that 'if all the women we interrogate were like you, we'd have to close the Russian Compound', further commending her for her strength in a scene that stages an attempt to initiate a humanized interaction between the two interlocutors (Sacco 2001: 99). The woman, however, responds with suspicion and hostility to the officer's comments as she leaves, showing how the fear of further violence perpetration prevents such an interaction from taking place. In his description of this response, as well as in the initial presentation of this woman, Sacco's narrator describes her as a 'tough cookie' (Sacco 2001: 97, 99). In contrast, when he shares his own thoughts about enduring prison torture, he mentions that he would not cope for a long time 'getting the business behind a closed door' and describes himself as a first class 'pussy' (Sacco 2001: 97). Through his self-deprecating sarcasm, he unsettles the link between heroic masculinity and Western humanitarian witnessing, and by juxtaposing this image of himself with that of the woman, he foregrounds her own resilience and strength. At the same time, though, her descriptions as a 'tough cookie', and those of himself as a 'pussy', semantically maintain a sexist, masculinist attitude, which restores Sacco's ambivalent positioning within global gendered and racial inequalities.

Women's activism, shifting gender roles, male disability and polygamy

In addition to its staging of gendered torture in prison, *Palestine* also reports on the local women's movement and the hijab, presenting practicing Muslim women, who choose to wear it through various perspectives: through the views of the feminist members of the women's movement, via the Western, Orientalist, masculinist gaze of Sacco's autobiographical subject, and through the eyes – both literal and metaphorical – of Palestinian men. The graphic displays of these perspectives form a complex, multi-layered take on veiled women that foregrounds the discrimination and oppression they suffer, their agencies, and multiple reasons why they may choose to wear the hijab. In Chapter 5, Sacco's avatar discusses with members of the women's movement about their struggles, which span from offering legal advice on domestic abuse, to outreach programmes aiming to teach girls about 'self-sufficiency' and older women about 'their economic and legal status' (Sacco 2001: 134). One of the women he interviews distinguishes between 'the elite [and] the educated, who live in cities [and] are exposed to the women's movement' and those residing in villages, who perceive being equal to men as foreign and completely incomprehensible (Sacco 2001: 134). In the visual register, women in rural areas are dressed in traditional attire, they welcome the member of the women's movement in their home, but they appear unable to grasp the concept of gender equality, as illustrated by their welcoming, yet seemingly ignorant smiles.

A different interviewee, however, shares a more optimistic view on the condition of Palestinian women, and notes that 'slowly but surely women are taking on decision-making roles in their families, and if they work, they're more likely to keep their wages' (Sacco 2001: 134). The Israeli/Palestinian conflict has deeply influenced traditional gender roles, and while the father of the family has been perceived as its main provider, with the wounding and killing of many, women have been forced to move outside the domestic sphere and to search for jobs (Akesson 2014; Gokani et al. 2015). This may have indeed increased women's self-sufficiency in terms of providing both for themselves and their families, but it has also unsettled the image of Palestinian masculinity as connected to one's ability to protect and provide for his family (Gokani et al. 2015). As such, it has left people trying to survive conflict, at the same time as coping with changes in traditional gender roles. Disability is a further injurious factor for Palestinian masculinity because of how it can limit one's agency in the domestic and the public sphere, as further discussed in the following chapter. As such, it unavoidably affects gender roles and relations.

For instance, in the sub-section of chapter 5 that is entitled 'Still One of the Boys' to remind readers of Sacco's gendered positionality despite his conversations with Palestinian feminists, a blind man he meets in Jabalia apologizes for not offering him tea: 'I haven't even had breakfast', he explains, 'one of my wives is sick, the other is visiting her parents ... I suppose I'll have to go out and get another wife' (Sacco 2001: 141). At this point, the narrative zooms in on Sacco, his translator and the blind man's avatars. The background space becomes washed in black, and white circular shapes around their heads visually foreground the men bursting into laughter upon this joke (Figure 1.3). Their speech bubble also onomatopoetically communicates what we see in the visual register. Sacco then jokingly adds that 'if you marry her within the hour, maybe

Figure 1.3 Panels from page 141 of *Palestine* by Joe Sacco, © 2001, used with permission from Fantagraphics.

you can get lunch' (Sacco 2001: 141). The panel including this statement zooms in on his face, showing tears dripping from behind his glasses.

Crying out of laughter denotes the degree of a joke's success. The grotesquely large mouth that Sacco draws on his avatar's face, though, introduces this graphic display of masculinity that becomes manifested through sexist jokes about the blind man's wives, as both awkward and problematic.[14] At the same time as reproducing objectifying discourse on these women, and showing how sexism becomes sustained through humour, this excerpt may also suggest that the blind

---

[14] Prior to the depiction of this man and his jokes about his wives, one of the women discussing with Sacco explains that 'polygamy [...] can be curtailed by a strict reading of Islamic law' (Sacco 2001: 135).

man's joke functions as a compensating mechanism for his wounded, disabled masculinity in its devaluation of his wives. This joke is presented on the final page of the chapter that accounts for women's struggles, for different forms of domestic abuse that is also at times understood as inscribed in the Islamic Law and the Quran, and after descriptions of how the veil became a means through which women and girls were harassed during the Intifada by Palestinian boys.[15] In choosing to close this chapter in this way, Sacco reiterates his positionality, while sharing a Palestinian male perspective on local femininities.

The hijab, the Intifada and stone throwing

Unlike this man's wives, who remain outside the narrative frame, Sacco's narrator mentions the feminists: 'It's good to chat with' them, he explains, 'we've all got our university degrees, we're all on the same wave-length, sometimes we could even finish each other's sentences' (Sacco 2001: 137). Contrary to the educated feminists who make sense to him, he fails to understand the others – the 'Muslim women wearing the hijab' (Sacco 2001: 137), who are thus also structured as presumably uneducated, through his Orientalist assumptions, whereby the veil signifies oppression and lack of education. 'Let's face it, I'm from the West', he mentions, 'I've seen plenty of leg, orange hair, too, and other fashion statements ... But this get up, it's nondescript, I blank out most all the women who wear it, they're just shapes to me, ciphers, like pigeons moving along the sidewalk' (Sacco 2001: 137). The hijab thus renders these women invisible under his gaze.

In the visual register, Sacco's avatar is shown walking in the street and being surrounded by veiled women who have their backs turned against him and walk towards different directions in what seems like a conscious effort to avoid him. This visual depiction can be seen as a metaphorical representation of his inability to access and understand them, which is also verbally reflected in his descriptions of veiled women as blanked out shapes, ciphers and pigeons. By drawing parallels between fashion statements he has encountered in the West and the hijab in the textual register, the narrator also forms a simplistic alignment between the two. As such, he fails to embed this choice in the particular religious, social, cultural and political context of Palestine.

---

[15] The feminists that Sacco meets explain that 'Islam [...] grants women property rights, and Islamic law can be interpreted to the advantage of women', further noting that 'in theory Islam offers avenues by which women can press for their rights' (Sacco 2001: 135; Mernissi 1991; El Guindi 1999).

This ignorant, Orientalist, masculinist view, which seems linked to the autobiographical subject's inability to understand these women, evokes perspectives on veiled Muslim femininities as those discussed by Franz Fanon (1965) in his analysis of the French colonial civilizing project in Algeria, which was based on the unveiling of local women. This view, however, becomes unsettled in *Palestine* through Sacco's subsequent interactions with veiled women, which foreground their agencies, while also accounting for the various reasons why each one chose to wear the hijab, from showing modesty and faith, to respecting their families, to protecting themselves from male aggression in the street, *inter alia*. Indeed, the narrator ends up admitting that 'the hijab was more [his] problem' than anyone else's (Sacco 2001: 137), thus owning up to the limitations and prejudices of his gaze on these women and girls. When a woman tells him that she 'want[s] to believe strongly enough to wear the hijab always', he realizes that one of the reasons he cannot understand the decision to veil oneself is because he has 'forgotten what it's like to want to have faith' (Sacco 2001: 140). Through this woman's response, however, he is reminded that religion, faith and the embodied, material performance of both, can have a central position in a person's life, something that a secular, non-religious person may choose to ignore or be unable to comprehend.

In the Palestinian context, the hijab has also become connected to the Intifada in ways that show how women's rights became entangled within it. According to 'a non-practising Muslim [feminist,] at the beginning of the uprising the Unified Leadership – which includes the main PLO factions – called for traditional dress as a way of emphasizing Palestinian identity' (Sacco 2001: 135, 138; Litvak 1998).[16] Apart from the veil, the women depicted in the visual register wear long traditionally embellished dresses. Sacco's interlocutor further relates that 'Hamas, the extremist Islamic group which rivals PLO, then called for the compulsory wearing of the hijab [, and its] followers begun threatening women and sometimes beating them for going outside without a head covering' (Sacco 2001: 138). In 1990, when the 'conference on the social problems of Palestinian women declared women should have the right to choose whether to wear the hijab or not [...,] the Unified Leadership concurred with a leaflet and messages saying anyone who attacked a woman for not wearing the hijab was a traitor' (Sacco 2001: 138). In the visual register, we move from the panel depicting women in traditional dress, to one that shows a woman being beaten by Hamas members,

---

[16] Her description as a 'non-practising Muslim' is important because it foregrounds a particular ideological stance that comes against this imposition.

to another depicting a man writing a message on a wall regarding the acts of betrayal carried out by those beating women who refuse to wear the hijab.[17] Like the betrayal that led to the woman's imprisonment and suffering, the perpetration of gendered violence against women by Hamas members is presented as damaging for the Palestinian struggle.

In the context of veil impositions, stone throwing, a core symbol of Palestinian resistance against Israeli occupation that is connected to the struggles of Palestinian youth, transforms into a means used for intra-communal gendered oppression and violation. A veiled woman remembers, for instance, four boys throwing stones at a female physician while she was driving unveiled. In the visual register, she is shown in pain, with her head bleeding, while sitting in a car with shattered window glasses. Two boys yell at her to cover her head, and an older man in traditional attire angrily asks them to stop, informing them that she is Christian (Sacco 2001: 140). Rema Hammami writes that because of Hamas's instructions, 'young boys (between 8 and 12)' started harassing girls at school and elsewhere for not veiling themselves (1990: 26). She further points out that 'if there were no soldiers to throw stones at, women without headscarves made good targets. Politically unaffiliated shabab who felt left out found harassing these women a safe way to express nationalist sentiment. Simultaneously, soldiers were raiding homes and attacking women' (Hammami 1990: 26). Sacco's graphic life narrative introduces the reader to all these agents behind abuse inflicted against women and girls through its dense visual/verbal combinations, which demand a slow reading practice that enables the adequate witnessing of such suffering.

Honour killing

Another form of abuse Sacco's graphic life narrative stages emerges in the context of honour killing. Because a woman 'committed adultery with a collaborator' in wedlock, 'her family strangled her', Sacco's narrator mentions (Sacco 2001: 160). A male lawyer tells Sacco's avatar that 'the Islamic law [. . .] calls for death to adulterers', further noting that 'the Jewish and Christian traditions call for the same punishment' (Sacco 2001: 160), thus illustrating how sexual activity outside

---

[17] Hammami writes that the Hamas 'endowed the hijab with new meanings of piety and political affiliation. Women affiliated with the movement started to wear long, plain, tailored overcoats, known as shari'a dress, which have no real precedents in indigenous Palestinian dress. Supposed to represent a return to a more authentic Islamic tradition, it is in fact an "invented tradition" in both form and meaning' (1990: 25; El Guindi 1999).

wedlock becomes regulated and punished in these religious contexts. At this point, an asterisk under the lawyer's speech bubble directs readers to the relevant excerpt from Deuteronomy, which confirms this similarity between the three Abrahamic religions that call for the lethal punishment of adultery.[18]

In the visual register, a veiled woman is shown suffocating as her father tightens a rope around her neck and her mother bears witness to the murder while standing in the background. This killing is religiously justified, and it is perceived as caused by the shame brought onto the father, and to a different extent, the family and their honour, because of the daughter's act. Safdar Ahmed writes that in Islamic social systems there exists 'a notion of female shame, which is encompassed by the term *haya* [and that] because all notions of femininity and masculinity are imbricated in historical (social, cultural and political) settings, there can be no experience of shame which is not a product of these settings' (2013: 177, 188). This kind of gendered shame becomes prevented through veiling and sexual modesty, *inter alia*.

One of the most prominent Indian Islamists, Sayyid Abul A 'la Maududi, explains that "'the meaning of *haya* is *sharm* (shame/shyness/modesty) . . . which a wrongdoer experiences *before his own inherent nature (khud apni fitrah ke samne) and before his God*" (quoted in Ahmed 2013: 189, emphasis in the original). Gendered shame is thus experienced as a particular kind of visibility against oneself, their fellow human beings and God. Shame, as Sara Ahmed (2014) reminds us, is also contaminating and injurious, and it spreads from one family member to the other. In this incident, the shame caused by a woman's adultery leads to the provocation of honour killing, demonstrating the structural violence that emerges from within a strictly religious, patriarchal context and becomes embodied through a father's murder of his daughter.[19] The implicit violence of shame thus seems to trigger further injury as it spreads across gendered individuals and family members. Acts of violence against women that become visually displayed, close-ups to faces and bodies that charge the narrative with affective impact, and insights into a plurality of injurious gendered relations and hierarchies, embody a complex take on this matter in *Palestine*. In addition, they demonstrate how by adopting a feminist, social-justice perspective,

[18] Rather than alluding to Christian love, faith and trust in God like the biblical references of *Burma*, this excerpt evokes a particularly aggressive punishing act connected to Judeo-Christian perspectives on sexuality as manifested in Deuteronomy. For an explication of the punishment of adultery in this biblical text see Woods 2011.

[19] My aim is not to justify honour killings, but rather to present the religious dynamics that cause them as well as the centrality of shame in a faithful Muslim believer's life.

provincializing rights discourses, and paying attention to the feelings and stories of violated, gendered others, as well as to structural forms of injustice, can help expand our understanding of the limitations of human rights.

Colonialism

Further to the above, Sacco's text also embeds women's suffering within a longer history that includes British colonial complicities in the emergence of the Israeli/ Palestinian conflict. While the Arab Revolt that led to the Ottoman defeat in the First World War was expected to bring peace in the Middle East, 'Britain and France had struck a secret deal in 1916 to carve up the region between them' (Carr 2004: 39). In 1917, with Palestine under British control, Lord Balfour, the British foreign secretary, wrote to Lord Rothschild, the Zionist leader of the British Jewish community, that 'his Majesty's Government view with favour the establishment in Palestine of a national home for the Jewish people' (quoted in Carr 2004: 39). In one of the first pages of *Palestine*, Lord Balfour is drawn signing the declaration of the establishment of the State of Israel, in what was described as 'a land without a people for a people without a land' (Sacco 2001: 12). Above him, the figure of God is drawn – an old white man with a long beard. Next to his hand, a numeric biblical reference directs readers to 'Joshua 1:3', but this time, the relevant excerpt, which describes the land he had promised to Israeli people, is also repeated in God's speech bubble intra-diegetically (Sacco 2001: 12; Woudstra 1981).

The following page accounts for the uprooting of the Arabs living in Palestine, and for Balfour's statement that 'Zionism [. . .] is rooted in age-long tradition, in present needs, in future hopes, of far profounder import than the desire and prejudices of 700,000 Arabs who now inhabit that ancient land' (Sacco 2001: 13). The second panel presents Balfour drinking tea in his office and stating that the British do not desire to consult 'the wishes of the present inhabitants of the country' prior to the establishment of the State of Israel (Sacco 2001: 13). In the third panel, two Arab women in traditional attire stand out. The older one is being consoled by a man next to her, and the younger one is holding a baby in her arms. They are walking together with other people, as thick smoke emerges behind them. 'History follows', Sacco's narrator explains, 'but if it's been downhill for Palestinians ever since, Israelis have sored to greater heights' (Sacco 2001: 13). While pointing out the sufferings of both peoples, this excerpt illustrates how, due to Orientalist views on the Arabs of Palestine, and colonial interests in the Middle East, 'Britain left behind two communities in bitter dispute [and] set in motion the long years of Arab-Israeli conflict' (Carr 2004: 40). Thus, in addition to its detailed accounts of intra-communal gendered violence against women, unlike *Burma*, *Palestine* importantly reminds readers of how Britain's colonial project in the Middle East continues to have injurious implications today, which affect Palestinian women and girls in particular ways. Contrary to Kirschner's biblical references, those made in Sacco's graphic life narrative foreground the ways in which the three Abrahamic religions have enabled structural and other forms of violence to constitute core parts of gendered life in Palestine.

Coda

From the *maquiladoras* and the sex industries of Juarez and Burma to Palestine, the graphic life narratives examined in this chapter present spectacles of violated othered femininities through a plurality of perspectives, and via a number of aesthetic choices and artistic decisions. Sacko's game metaphor presents the ways in which neoliberal economy renders the female *maquiladora* workers' lives excessively precarious. Gloeckner's take on US sex tourism, and her visually mediated intertextual reference to sacred femininity, evoke injurious (neo-) colonial influences in Juarez, both past and present. In contrast, Kirschner's journal entries present an ambivalent attempt at forging identificatory bonds through shared experiences with a seventeen-year-old sex worker in Mae Sot. Lastly, Khélif's graphic novella provides a glimpse into the life of another equally young sex worker through a different lens that points to multiple factors contributing to the girl's suffering in the sex industry of the city. Overall, *Burma* neither explicitly relates the impact of modernity/coloniality on Mae Sot, nor the role of the British colonial project in the contemporary Burmese/Karen conflict, which is presented as the core factor for the devaluation of female life. *Palestine*, on the other hand, accounts for human rights violations suffered by Palestinian women and girls in prison, at home and in the public sphere, while constantly reminding readers of the Western reporter's privileged gendered and racial positionality. As it does so, it foregrounds structural forms of oppression, and a hierarchy of hegemonic, dominant and oppressed masculinities that are linked to the Israeli/Palestinian conflict, to religious oppression, to the British colonial project in the Middle East and to global gender inequalities, which become reflected in the production and consumption of human rights narratives.

As such, the texts examined in this chapter illustrate the potential of comics and decolonized postcolonial reading acts for exposing nuanced articulations of the violations of women's and girls' rights and of the injustices they suffer across different geo-, bio-, and necro-political contexts. Thus, they show that comics can indeed constitute a fertile ground for the remediation of new versions of Philomela's visual testimony. Simultaneously, though, they also illustrate that visual/verbal forms can be utilized in ways that re-silence postcolonial gendered testimonies and keep the complexities that lie behind the contemporary perpetration of gendered violence outside the frame of representation. As Goldberg and Moore write, the potential lying in such ambivalent texts 'in terms of both transnational feminist praxis and women's human rights' concerns the 'possible invocation of a reader or spectator who is unsatisfied by the text[s'] stated aims of exposure and unmasking, by the gap between [their] critique of capitalism and [their] performance of a capitalist status quo' (2011: 250). This reader 'may then be moved through the process of consumption to a space beyond consumption, to an active re-engagement with the shared conditions through which the encounter with – and, thus, the responsibility to – suffering emerges' (Goldberg and Moore 2011: 250). It is precisely by invoking this kind of engagement that such texts can trigger a decolonial understanding of women's rights, which can only emerge because of, but outside the narrative itself.

2

Graphic martyria and male suffering

In this chapter, I examine graphic representations of the injustices suffered by othered men and boys in the Israeli/Palestinian, the Tamil/Sinhala and the Burmese/Karen conflicts. Through the discussion that follows, I mean to trigger a reconsideration of preconceptions and stereotypes relating to male otherness, monstrosity and aggression. I explore how violence becomes displayed in graphic life narratives depicting male suffering, and how the spectacle of the violated – both explicitly and implicitly – adult and underage male body becomes represented. In my analysis, I take into consideration the interconnected meanings of the terms μάρτυς/*martys*, μαρτύριον/*martyrion* and μαρτυρία/*martyria*, which conflate notions of witnessing, testimony, torture, resistance and spectacle with suffering and divine truth, and I relate those to vulnerable and precarious masculinities displayed through the comics form, via what I introduce as *graphic martyria*. While examining aesthetic choices in artistic representations of violated male subjects, I also investigate the ways in which their vulnerabilities and precarities emerge and how they critically foreground the wounds caused by conflicting hierarchies of masculinity. I further explore the potentialities offered by comics in relation to unsettling the monstrosity that often accompanies the figure of the male other, and with regard to displaying him beyond it, as well as outside the limitations of extreme victimhood in the selected texts.

Hierarchies of masculinity, male suffering and *graphic martyria*

Graphic life narratives that negotiate gendered injustices are populated by wounded and psychologically or physically tortured men and boys, thus calling for an exploration of the aesthetic choices made for such depictions, which may unsettle monolithic, neo-colonial perceptions related to non-white non-Western male people.[1] Further to adult men, boys – the child soldiers found in *Burma*, the second volume of *I Live Here*, and in *Vanni: A Family's Struggle through the Sri Lankan Conflict*, by Benjamin Dix and Lindsey Pollock, as well as those who fought in the Intifada, as shown in Joe Sacco's *Palestine* – constitute particularly vulnerable and ambivalent masculinity categories.[2] My aim is to demonstrate how these graphic life narratives unveil the particularities that become hidden under quantitative presentations of male vulnerabilities to death, and to physical as well as psychological injury, through the nuances of comics. The analysis that follows demonstrates the usefulness of these texts as tools for the display and critique of gendered injustices suffered by men and adolescent boys, since they are often marginalized, in relation to women and younger children, within humanitarian discourses as well as laws, treatises and migration policies can offer them protection, as explained in the Introduction.

Taking an intersectional approach in their analysis of power relations between men, Ann-Dorte Christensen and Sune Qvotrup Jensen describe 'dominant masculinities' as those that may prevail in particular social contexts over masculinities that are 'non-normative' (2014: 63). They also refer to 'dominating masculinities' that function oppressively in relation to 'other masculinities' in ways that are 'overt, explicit, or brute', and to 'hegemonic masculinities' that dominate social groups 'through cultural and discursive consensus as opposed to overt use of raw force, physical coercion, etc.', thus also legitimizing 'patriarchal gender relations' (Christensen and Jensen 2014: 63; Messerschmidt 2010). Raewyn W. Connell also points out that because gender intersects with class, race, 'nationality and position in the world order [...,] white men's masculinities are constructed not only in relation to white women', and women of colour, 'but also in relation to black men' (1995: 75). Sexuality and age also influence how gendered subjectivities become distributed across different positions of power or lack thereof as reflected, for instance, by male

---

[1] Regarding the Israeli/Palestinian conflict, according to the United Nations Office for the Coordination of Humanitarian Affairs (2007: np), 'the overwhelming majority' of those killed between 2000 and 2007 were men, reaching up to 69 per cent for Israeli and 94 per cent for Palestinian deaths. A similar tendency is reflected in children's casualties, whereby '87% of Palestinian children killed [...] were boys and 13% were girls' (UN OCHA 2007: np). Michelle Dukich and Tarak Shah (2019) identify a 69 per cent of male deaths in the context of the Sri Lankan war with 12 per cent of data listed in their death records lacking gender identification.
[2] Krug et al. (2002) estimate the global number of child soldiers to be 300,000, pointing out, however, that due to limitations in the process of data collection this number is significantly underestimated. In their analysis, they account in detail for the psychological and physical injuries these children suffer due to child soldiering.

vulnerabilities embodied through the figure of the child soldier. In this chapter, I investigate how adult and underage masculinities navigate different geopolitical contexts and the questions I seek to respond to are as follows: How do forms of visible/physical and invisible/mental wounding suffered by male prisoners, child soldiers and underage Intifada fighters become graphically displayed in the aforementioned narrative contexts? What are the artistic choices cartoonists make to mediate such suffering? How do male in/visibilities become depicted? How do instances of *graphic martyria* (in the multiple senses of the word *martyria* referring to witnessing, resistance, undergoing torture, providing testimony, and rendering one remembered as explained below) become played out?

In *The Novel of Human Rights*, James Dawes asks 'what turns men into monsters' (2018: 175; 2013) and mentions Belinda Luscombe's (2007) description of child soldiers as the sexiest among other victims of war. This description introduces child soldiers as vested in ambivalence because they spectacularize the victimhood that accompanies one's enforced transformation into a perpetrator, which causes public attention to them. The vulnerability and presumed innocence and unawareness that comes along with their age, underscores their victimization through the monstrosity that becomes involuntarily cast upon them. Unlike them, adult male perpetrators 'are less frequently the subject of analysis in human rights work than one would expect' (Dawes 2018: 168).

The monstrosity and inhumanity of an actual, and I would add, of one imagined as a potential perpetrator is embodied in media, legal, migration and humanitarian discourses that produce unknowable, othered, threatening male subjects. The unsettling of the perpetrator's otherness can be achieved, Dawes proposes, through the 'aesthetic contradictions and wrenching moral paradoxes' that are characteristic of the American 'human rights novel' (2018: 202). In the conclusion of his book, he writes that 'we live in a world of compromised options and unforeseen consequences' and that 'justice urgently calls us to decisive action' (Dawes 2018: 202). These closing remarks are aptly ambiguous. On the one hand, they refer to the impact of one's decision to become a perpetrator in contexts of perceived injustice, where the available options are limited in the face of the urgent need to defend one's nation, family and self. On the other, they invite readers to ethically engage with the literary or otherwise figure of the monstrous male perpetrator – both the actual and the one who is stereotypically imagined as such. Through the analysis that follows, I foreground the contribution of graphic life narratives in complicating and enriching life stories related to this figure, and in supplementing media, humanitarian, legal and migration policy discourses regarding the male other.[3]

The monstrosity of the male perpetrator – both the real one and that who is imagined as such – is connected to the visual given that the Latin verb 'mōnstrāre' means 'to show, to be an object of note [or] to demonstrate' (Glare 2012: 1244). In this chapter, I investigate what forms of audibility and visibility are enabled by comics, and to what extent these unsettle the monstrosity that accompanies the othered male subject in his discursive formations as an oppressor, a terrorist and a religious extremist – formations that ignore and erase his vulnerabilities and precarities. If refugees, and more so male ones, in addition to further categories of evil male others, are 'dehumanized and demonized' becoming compared to this era's 'privileged monsters', as Penny Crofts and Anthea Vogl (2019: 29) suggest, then how can this form of otherness be challenged and how can their humanity be restored via one's engagement with graphic displays of their suffering?[4] If being forced to become a perpetrator is in itself a form of victimhood, why is it difficult to (re-)consider the causes that might have led men and boys to such positions, which may lie in the West itself? To what extent can graphic life narratives present such responsibilities as well as visibilities of male otherness that move beyond inaudible monstrosities? How do witnessing and *graphic martyria* become negotiated in such texts?

The term 'martyr' is contemporarily understood first and foremost as associated with the figure of the suicide bomber – the iconic othered male perpetrator. A 'μάρτυρ'/*martyr* in Ancient Greek is 'a witness of truth', but also 'a confessor of faith' (Montanari 2016: 1283). The Arabic equivalent of the term, the 'shaheed', refers to the witness, to the one who is 'always alive' and to someone 'killed in the name of God' (Ghanim 2008: 78). Honaida Ghanim explains that in its earliest uses, this term was 'one of God's names, literally meaning "witness"' (2008: 78). Later, specifically in the Palestinian context, the term became secularized 'to refer to anyone killed by the occupation, militant or civilian, directly or indirectly, without regard to his religion' (Ghanim 2008: 78). The verb 'μαρτυρέω'/*martyreo* in Ancient Greek means 'to give testimony, to act as witness, to attest' (Montanari 2016: 1283). It also means 'to give testimony of faith' and 'to suffer martyrdom' (Montanari 2016: 1283). The 'μαρτυρούμενος'

---

[3] For a detailed analysis on the graphic narrativization of the male perpetrator see Michael 2022a.

[4] The critics draw from Michel Foucault's analysis of abnormality and monstrosity. Foucault sees 'the monster as a juridical rather than a medical notion' and notes that 'monstrosity requires a transgression of the natural limit' or 'to fall under, or at any rate challenge, an interdiction of civil and religious or divine law' (2003a: 63). In this sense, the monster is understood as existing beyond the law, and as not being a citizen as most stateless, refugees and asylum seekers are.

/*martyroumenos* is the one who 'is remembered', while 'μαρτύριον'/*martyrion* like 'μαρτυρία'/*martyria*, refers to 'testimony, proof, evidence' as well as to suffering or torture (Montanari 2016: 1283). This overview highlights the ways in which notions of witnessing, delivering testimony, undergoing torture and literally as well as metaphorically seeing truth become interchangeable and linked to memory. In this chapter, I argue for the suitability of comics for nuanced depictions of what I would describe as the *graphic martyria* of gendered trauma and injustice. If martyrdom is often associated with the one-dimensional spectacle of the male terrorist, by taking into consideration the multi-dimensional implications of *martyria*, I investigate how the male other becomes re-membered in ways that can re-invest him with, or run the risk of further depriving him of, dignity and humanity via how his testimony and suffering become artistically remediated. Hence, I use the term *martyria* as indicative of the artistic risk of causing the other further but subtler (neo-)colonial wounding through their aesthetic (mis-)representation, which may lead to their artistic dehumanization.

At the same time as bearing witness to the sufferings, the vulnerabilities and precarities of othered male people in order to render such individuals *martyroumenoi*/remembered/witnessed, Anglophone cartoonists also become charged with the responsibility to provide an ethical and just mediation of the testimonies they are entrusted with. The spectacle of embodied suffering they display through their art can encounter voyeuristic consumption, responsible witnessing, or reactions oscillating between the two.[5] In his analysis of the suffering of Jesus, Jacques Derrida refers to the Romeo-Christian connotations of the term 'passion' and mentions its relevance to the 'experience of love, [which is] inseparable from [...] confessional testimony and from truthfulness' (2000: 27). Passion also denotes 'an engagement that is assumed in pain and suffering', otherwise known as 'martyrdom, that is – as its name indicates – testimony. A passion', Derrida writes, 'always testifies', primarily through the martyr's body; consequently, it can never be fully reduced to narrative (2000: 27–8). From the photographic records of torture of prisoners in the Abu Ghraib prisons in Iraq, to video-recorded and publicly released ISIS executions and rapes, the spectacle of suffering is one that shocks and disturbs at the same time as triggering voyeuristic curiosity.[6] The understanding of grotesque bodily

---

5 Frances Guerin and Roger Hallas also explain in their introduction to *The Image and the Witness* (2007: 13–14), that 'the task of visualising the corporeal consequences of trauma is forever fraught with the risk of dehumanisation'.

6 For analyses of the pornography of Jihadism, see Simon Cottee (2019) and for a typology of ISIS online death videos, see Lilie Chouliaraki and Angelos Kissas (2018).

suffering through *martyrion*/torture as a public spectacle available for consumption is not new. It has also been common, for instance, in Ancient Athens, where citizens were privileged via their exclusion from it, in contrast to slaves and aliens, who were subject to State-initiated torture in juridical proceedings that were open for male spectators.

In such contexts, torture was, as it still is, albeit in different ways, in line with Western 'democracy's policies of exclusion, scapegoating, ostracism, physical cruelty and violence' (DuBois 1991: 37). This history of torture spans from the slave trade, to colonial projects beyond the West at the time of Enlightenment and Humanism, to contemporary neo-colonial (semi-)visible enactments of torture outside and within Western borders, while concurrent public narratives repetitively reproduce the male other as the one capable of monstrosities (Comaroff and Comaroff 2012; Lentin 2008; Mbembe 2019b). As Costas Douzinas remarks in relation to the misconception that the West has not been capable of atrocities, which it tends to cast upon its others, 'humanity started committing crimes against itself in the 1930s when the Germans, this philosophical embodiment of humanity, acted atrociously against its own' (2007: 74). These crimes 'were appropriately called crimes against humanity because only the West is endowed with full humanity and can become the proper victim of atrocity. Humanity offends against herself in the West and against sub-humans in the South', he explains (Douzinas 2007: 74).[7] While examining male vulnerabilities to suffering and hierarchies of masculinity in Palestine, Sri Lanka and Burma, it is important to bear in mind that such contemporary tensions have not emerged at the present moment, but rather, they constitute outcomes of past colonial projects, and of modernity/coloniality, which is always-already oppressively hegemonic and patriarchal as explained in the Introduction. While the West's crimes against the sub-humans of the South have remained invisible, the spectacle of the tortured male body that is caused by extra-legal sovereign State violence has had a significant position in Western mythology and the arts across the centuries as shown via the figure of Prometheus.[8] Through the analysis that follows, I situate graphic life narratives depicting such suffering alongside this tradition.

[7] Contrary to Douzinas, for a discussion on the racialization of and discrimination against Jews that led to the Holocaust see *Decolonial Judaism: Triumphant Failures of Barbaric Thinking* (Slabodsky 2014).
[8] In *That the World May Know: Bearing Witness to Atrocity*, Dawes refers to Aeschylus's *Prometheus Bound* as 'one of the most enduring Western texts about tyranny and torture' (2007: 219).

Tortured male bodies, (graphic) art and literature

In Aeschylus's *Prometheus Bound*, itself based on the corresponding myth from Hesiod's *Works and Days*, the Titan was punished for giving fire to humans, enraging Zeus by offering them the opportunity to grow (Grene 2013). His punishment was delivered through his sinking beneath the earth and his subsequent re-emergence to its surface, only to be bound to a rock on mount Caucasus and to have his forever-growing liver continuously eaten by an eagle. Because of his reaction against Zeus's wishes, during the Romantic period, Prometheus's story became 'a parable of human revolt against autocracy and established religion' (Grene 2013: 68). In the play, autocracy and established religion become embodied through Κράτος/Kratos (might), Βία/Via (force), and Zeus. 'Via' stands for violence and force, and while one of the connotations of 'Kratos' is indeed might (Grene 2013), the term also refers to 'sovereign power [,] dominion' and to the State (Montanari 2016: 1173). As such, Kratos in the sense of the sovereign power of the State, Via, that is, its forceful violence, and Zeus, as the divine power overseeing both, become the causes of Prometheus's *martyrion*/martyrdom. Because of his actions, Prometheus became 'the symbol for man himself', contrary to 'Zeus [. . .], Kratos and Bia, the figures of a power so absolute that it lies beyond justice and understanding' (Vernant 2006: 271). Similarly to the oppressive sovereign power displayed in *Prometheus Bound*, the graphic life narratives examined in this chapter present instances of State-initiated, religiously informed, incomprehensible and extra-juridical violence inflicted against othered men and boys, which causes further violence perpetration as also explained in the previous chapter. I therefore situate these texts within the lineage of *Prometheus Bound*.

The mythical narrative of Prometheus's torture was remediated by Aeschylus in the fifth century BC as a theatrical spectacle (Ruffell 2012) and negotiated in Peter Paul Rupens painting between 1611 and 1612, among other artistic and literary negotiations.[9] In 1918, Franz Kafka also wrote a condensed version of the myth in a short story that relates four legends about Prometheus. In the first one, the Titan is punished because of his hubris, he is tied on a rock and eagles eat his ever-growing liver. In the second, he presses 'himself deeper and deeper into the rock until he [becomes] one with it' because he cannot tolerate the pain caused by the birds (Kafka 1983: 475). In the third, his transgression becomes

---

[9] For the painting, see: https://artsandculture.google.com/asset/prometheus-bound/sAGbhKGi1-phAg?hl=en-GB.

'forgotten in the course of thousands of years, forgotten by the gods, the eagles, forgotten by himself', and in the fourth and last one, everyone, including the gods and the eagles, grows 'weary of the meaningless affair' (Kafka 1983: 475). There only remained, Kafka's narrator concludes, an 'inexplicable mass of rock', which 'the legend' tried to explain (Kafka 1983: 476). The tortured male body thus becomes erased both by how Prometheus literally fuses with, and consequently becomes one with the rock, and by how the whole matter sinks into oblivion. As a result, the witnessing of his martyrion becomes disrupted, and it can no longer be rendered *martyroumenon*/witnessed/remembered.

Kafka's short story illustrates a contradiction 'between the timelessness of myth and the power of history and time to obliterate the past' (Gray et al. 2005: 231). As it foregrounds the use of imagination and myth to explain natural phenomena, Kafka's tale highlights history's ability to keep specific hi-stories unseen. Thus, it may urge one to reflect upon the role of myth, the arts and literature in producing counter-narratives to such historical erasures, unsettling the invisibility of certain narratives, facilitating their witnessing and their subsequent remembering, rendering them, therefore, *martyroumena*. In this chapter, I show that graphic life narratives accounting for injustices suffered by othered men and boys share the same potential. In addition, I perceive the spectacle of the tortured male body that is inextricably linked to State sovereignty (Kratos), its violence (Via) and divine power (Zeus) in *Prometheus Bound* as particularly apt and relevant to artistic representations of contemporary State-initiated torture and human rights deprivations against those discursively formed as the monstrous male others of the West. In referring to visual and textual representations of Prometheus's resistance to extra-juridical, violent and incomprehensible sovereignty, and to his torture, I mean to point to how the *graphic martyria* of othered male subjects can articulate similarly nuanced depictions of embodied male suffering. Furthermore, I examine whether graphic life narrative can constitute a counter-discourse that resists legal, humanitarian, migration policy, and media discursive formations of the male other as a threatening monster, by preserving the testimonies of the subjects whose human rights have either been denied or grossly violated, as both respectfully witnessed and remembered.

Male suffering off-scene in *Palestine*

The wounding implications of bodily torture are deeply gendered, as already explained in the previous chapter, and they cause specific forms of humiliation.

Palestine and *Vanni* display instances of genital torture, forced nudity and verbal harassment suffered by Palestinian men in Israeli prisons, and Tamil soldiers in the Sri Lankan war, respectively. The depiction of such suffering in graphic life narratives is highly complex because of the visuality of comics. In *Graphic Women: Life Narrative and Contemporary Comics*, Hillary Chute (2010) discusses the censorship of Phoebe Gloeckner's graphic memoirs, noting a resistance to visual depictions of rape, that is not the same for written accounts. This resistance is linked to the risk of representation Gloeckner took in presenting her autobiographical avatar's sexual suffering through explicit scenes of sexual contact, and in ways that do not delineate her as an ideal, innocent, pure victim (Chute 2010). In *Palestine* and *Vanni*, the suffering that is graphically depicted does not concern the female self, but rather, othered male objects of representation. In addition, it does not take the form of rape. Contrarily, as mentioned, it is expressed through acts of genital torture, verbal harassment and forced nudity. Unlike the risk taken by Gloeckner in *A Child's and Other Stories* (2000) and *The Diary of A Teenage Girl: An Account in Words and Pictures* (2002), that which was taken by Sacco on the one hand, and Dix and Pollock on the other, is related to how male suffering of this kind is less frequently exposed in literary and graphic life narrative. It does not concern the autobiographical subject, but rather, the other, whose testimony is remediated and who becomes the object of representation, and the hierarchical relations in which Western artists and their racially and religiously othered subjects are embedded. As such, the risk of representation described by Chute becomes complicated in graphic life narratives that concern the suffering of racially and religiously othered men and boys.

Garay Menicucci writes that 'sexual torture against Arab and Muslim detainees' is frequently used 'as a routine psychological technique' to derive information 'or to shame prisoners in a manner that manipulates perceived notions of authentic Arab/Muslim masculine identity' (2005: 18; Butler 2009). Torture inflicted upon men and older boys during incarceration often occurs on the grounds of its shaming impact that leads to its silencing and subsequent unspeakability. In the context of the Israeli/Palestinian conflict, violence has been commonly used against Palestinian detainees 'even though Israel has ratified the UN Convention Against Torture (1986/1991), prohibited the use of several forms of torture (1999), and promulgated national laws against (sexual) harassment and abuse' (Weishut 2015: 71). Daniel J. N. Weishut explains that 'Israeli authorities admit interrogators employ "exceptional" interrogation methods and "physical pressure" in "ticking bomb" situations but claim that this is done out of "necessity" and do not call these methods "torture"' (2015: 71). Weishut's comment importantly highlights how words veil, through renaming processes, the enactment of torture. In *Palestine*, textual references to 'moderate pressure' as those existing in official Israeli narratives become accompanied by graphic depictions illustrative of it, which deeply unsettle their definition as a mild form of disciplinary non-torture (Sacco 2001: 93, 102).

Torture that ranges between verbal harassment and forced nudity to 'severe genital violence, such as squeezing the scrotum, rape, genital mutilation and castration' grossly violates victims' sexual rights (Weishut 2015: 72). The consequences of such abuse include severe psychological and at times sexual damage, as well as PTSD symptoms, which frequently remain untreated exacerbating gendered psychological injury because of related gendered shame and taboo (Weishut 2015). Forced nudity, for instance, which becomes displayed in *Palestine* and *Vanni*, 'strips a person of his/her identity and puts him/her in a shameful position and at risk of assault' (Weishut 2015: 78). Gendered chastity, modesty and morality have a crucial role in Arab and Muslim life, as explained in Chapter 1, while 'honour [is core] in social life in much of the Muslim world' (Weishut 2015: 78). As such, the impact of different forms of such violence against Arab men can be severe since it is charged with 'long-lasting [and] humiliating consequences [that are] often based on dynamics of emasculation, feminization and/or homosexualization' (Weishut 2015: 78). The 'social stigma [and] relative silence in discourse about sexuality' in Muslim communities render the 'sexual torture of men extra painful and difficult to resolve', requiring significant 'efforts to bring it into the open' (Weishut 2015: 79). While graphic life narratives depicting similar forms of torture may function as an attempt to bring such suffering into the open by rendering it visible, they also precariously expose the humiliation it is designed to cause. However, in exposing it, cartoonists can make aesthetic choices that introduce their subjects respectfully *martyroumenoi/* remembered/witnessed.

In *Palestine*, for instance, Sacco's narrator contextualizes torture in the mass incarceration of Palestinian men and boys when he explains that 'it's all but impossible not to sit beside a prison or jail story' while in Palestine, given that only 'in the first four years' of the Intifada, there were '90,000 arrests' (Sacco 2001: 81). Because of the ordinariness of imprisonment, what draws his attention 'is a male in his mid-twenties who hasn't been arrested' (Sacco 2001: 81). In this verbal account, Sacco's narrator provides numbers, which he then proceeds to briefly contextualize historically and politically. Subsequently, he delves further into this information by graphically illustrating the impact of torture on his interviewees, as shown by the displays of their testimonies. In his structuring of Palestinian men's suffering, Sacco does not introduce his avatar in the narrative realm to stress his morality, which would presumably stem from bearing witness to their testimonies – from being the heroic Western humanitarian in charge of speaking on behalf of those perceived as less than human, as monstrous, in/visible and inaudible others. Rather, at the same time as stressing the distance between himself (as well as the implied reader), and the Palestinian men he interviews, he highlights his own cynicism and cowardice in the face of the ordinariness of imprisonment and torture they undergo. His autobiographical subject's physical, emotional and verbal responses to the testimonies he bears witness to effectively foreground this distance, which introduces Palestinian men and boys in a position of extreme precarity and vulnerability to violence, contrary to him – the Western outsider who can step in and out of their world as he pleases.

When he asks Abu Akram how he was beaten during incarceration, the latter chooses to enact the scene of torture with Sacco in the position of the detainee because he cannot otherwise explain how torture occurred. The delivery of this testimony, then, becomes staged as a theatrical spectacle, parodically illustrating that claims of potential identification between Sacco, the Western journalist, and the Palestinian men are futile and doomed to fail. Abu asks Sacco to sit on a chair, forcibly pushing his chest and demanding that he remains still without having his back supported by the backrest. The latter laughs, remarking that 'this is [a] highly irregular' form of abuse (Sacco 2001: 94). In the following panel, Abu is shown aggressively directing his fist towards the autobiographical avatar's genitals. An arrow links the first and the second panel, directing the reader's gaze to the fright shown in his face, his grotesquely drawn open mouth, and the sweat emanating from his forehead. 'Don't worry', the narrator then tells us, 'he stops short … he doesn't do it … he spares me' (Sacco 2001: 94). From his initial reaction as shown through his laughter at what he describes as an irregular form of abuse, to his terrified response at the potential of an attack, Sacco's avatar is subsequently drawn crouched in fear next to a threatening visual representation of Abu, with sweat still dripping from his head. As such, any element of heroism attached to the Western journalist reporting on Palestinian suffering collapses in this disillusioning spectacle.

After re-enacting this scene, Abu tells him that in cases of torture during detention, 'the door closes, and the world cannot see' (Sacco 2001: 94). This happens because torture occurs literally behind closed doors and thus it remains unseen, because its particularities become veiled under quantitative accounts which may also be imprecise, because it becomes discursively disguised by, and thus hidden under, euphemistic expressions presenting it otherwise, and lastly, because it tends to remain silenced due to shame. By visually displaying it and presenting its physical and affective impact on the survivors, however, *Palestine* unsettles this silence and undoes Palestinian men's in/visibilities.

One of Sacco's interviewees, for instance, mentions that Israeli officers forced him to take his clothes off and kept him tied to a roof in the rain for four hours. Another relates how they threatened to 'fuck' and 'kill' his 'mother and sisters', showing how the relationality of gendered sexual shame becomes a tool for torture (Sacco 2001: 94). As they share their testimonies, the men's eyes mediate their weariness, rage and psychic wounding. While speaking, they either look towards Sacco's avatar, whose presence is implied by the direction of their gaze, even when he is absent from the frame, or elsewhere, thus avoiding his eyes, and those of the readers, possibly as a result of their shame. As Abid delivers his testimony and looks away, the narrative temporally moves to the past, and presents him in his cell, alongside a verbal summary of *The Landau Report*, which was commissioned by the Israeli State in its investigation of crimes during Palestinian people's imprisonment.[10] Sacco's authorial intervention, at this instance, is marked by his ironic commentary on this official script. His remarks also concern the men's stories, which are, as he notes, 'stylistically speaking, disappointing' and they consist of 'vulgar stuff for behind the shed' (Sacco 2001: 95). Sacco thus reminds the reader that the men's testimonies have been selected and edited in order to be transformed into an artistic commodity that will circulate in the Western market in search for readers.

As an artist, Sacco gets to decide which stories to include in his book, necessarily leaving things unsaid, (slightly) modified or incomplete. Immediately after this comment, he explains that even though *Palestine* does not explicitly show what happens 'behind the shed', this does not mean that 'interrogations themselves aren't effective', because 'Abid, for example, who whispered how he'd been left naked in cold cells, who was beaten with clubs and strangled, who had his balls stomped, he signed a confession' (Sacco 2001: 95). Abid's whispered account of the humiliations he suffered becomes verbally mediated in small narrative captions on the left side of the page (Figure 2.1). The first of the three panels on the same page visually presents him when signing the false confession.

---

[10] The *Landau Commission Report*, which becomes briefly summarized and commented upon by Sacco in *Palestine*, states that 'under the provisions of the necessity defence, the exertion of a moderate measure of physical pressure is both justifiable and permissible in the interrogation of persons suspected of hostile terrorist activity' (Kremnitzer 1989: 217).

Figure 2.1 Panels from page 95 of *Palestine* by Joe Sacco, © 2001, used with permission from Fantagraphics.

In so doing, it critically displays the otherwise presumed truthfulness of this document, contrary to the fictionalized testimony that is rejected in legal contexts but becomes presented in *Palestine* as a counter-narrative to the official Israeli script, constituting an alternative jurisdiction. The black-and-white contrast that distinguishes Abid from the guards in the background of this panel highlights the affective impact of his act, the signing of a false confession, through which he betrayed his fellow-Palestinians. The intended humiliation caused via verbal harassment, torture, nudity and genital violence is therefore underscored by the one he experiences because of betraying his people.

In this graphic account, Sacco chooses not to visibly present the bodily torture Abid suffered, or to display him completely naked, artistically staging an act of respectful witness. By noting that Abid had whispered his testimony, Sacco's narrator points to this man's trauma and shame, which also become expressed through the aversion of his gaze from his interlocutor, and consequently, from the implied reader. The narrator's captions relate how Abid later 'retracted his confession in court', and how 'the Shin Bet denied touching him', saying instead that they had served him coffee and tea (Sacco 2001: 95). From the post-torture signing of a false confession in the first panel, to the Shin Bet officer's version of the unseen prison events as accounted for in front of the judge in the Israeli court in the second, the narrative moves, in the third one, to a depiction of Abid in his cell during his subsequent fifteen-year imprisonment. The textual supplement on the right side of the page accounts for the official Israeli take on the events. In what seems like an encyclopaedia entry, Sacco mentions that Israel, which is thought to be 'the Middle East's only democracy', became troubled by events like the one shared by Abid, and remediated by the cartoonist himself (Sacco 2001: 95).

For this reason, the Israeli government commissioned a report in 1987, which was prepared by Justice Moshe Landau. Landau concluded 'that Shin Bet officers had consistently lied in court by denying they'd extracted confessions through physical force' proposing that 'no charges be brought against those responsible' because they were 'defending Israel from "terrorist activity"' (Sacco 2001: 95). For these reasons, according to the report, excerpts from which Sacco quotes in this narrative fragment, 'some means of "non-violent psychological pressure" and "moderate . . . physical pressure"' were allowed during interrogation (Sacco 2001: 95; Kremnitzer 1989). Landau, Sacco writes, 'got the Israel prize and Israel goes on being "the Middle East's only democracy"', while 'Palestinians go on being interrogated, though now within secret guidelines, subject to who-knows-what interpretations', which have also been legitimized (2001: 95).

As such, a single page in *Palestine* presents the interconnectedness of Kratos and Via as embodied through instances of extra-legal sexual and other forms of torture, as well as democracy's invisible links to such practices. It verbally relates Abid's affectively charged testimony and his shame, through the narrator's captions on the left margin of the page. It visually presents, via three panels that take up most of the space of the page, the result of his torture as reflected in the signing of a false confession, as well as the court's rejection of its retraction, and Abid's subsequent imprisonment. Lastly, it reiterates the official Israeli version of the events textually, on the right margin of the page, which becomes self-consciously filtered through Sacco's political positioning and solidarity towards his Palestinian interviewees. Thus, what remains unspoken in the official Israeli script of the events becomes exposed. In this way, the contents of the report become questioned and criticized in *Palestine*'s narrative context, both visually and textually. This *graphic martyria* therefore presents what is framed through Sacco's perspective as the incomprehensible, violent sovereign-State oppression beyond the law, which becomes embodied, in *Prometheus Bound*, through Zeus, Kratos and Via.

Commenting upon depictions of sexual violence in Sacco's *Safe Area Goražde* and *Journalism*, Sandra Cox writes that these texts show how 'when enacted against specific individual bodies, [this kind of torture] becomes an exercise in cultural violence. Because rape is visually linked to Islamophobia, his renderings of the Muslim body's vulnerability to assault is key to the ways in which conflicts between' Muslims and non-Muslims 'are framed as sites of ethnosexual power, exerted through objectification' (Cox 2018: 196). Cox explains that Sacco's graphic depiction of State-sanctioned violence against male as well as female Muslim populations becomes filtered through his 'subjective truth' (2018: 197). Torture against detained Palestinian men and boys is also presented and contextualized, as explained above, through the same perspective in *Palestine*.

Indeed, Sacco explains that the graphic journalism he practises 'signals to the reader that [it] is a process with seams and imperfections practiced by a human being' who learns a lot from his interactions with other people (2012a: xi). The journalist must investigate all the versions of events to 'get to the bottom of a contested account independently of those making their claims', he writes in his preface to *Journalism* (Sacco 2012a: xii). In addition, he admits to having chosen the stories he wants to share and explains that through his choices he means to make his political standing clear. He further points out that due to their 'inherently interpretive' nature, comics do not allow him to remain confined within the limitations of conventional journalism; rather, they have forced him to take and express a particular stance (Sacco 2012a: xii). What Sacco's comics foreground, then, concerns the ideological standpoint of a journalist, or an artist, who has the responsibility to mediate through his or her work, conflict and other people's suffering, the impact their contact with others may have had on them, and the subsequent impossibility of journalistic or artistic objectivity in such frameworks. As he proposes, rather than attempting to eliminate our prejudices, it is important to acknowledge them, as he does in his own work (Sacco 2012a).

As Pramod Nayar also points out, when admitting to having seen/perceived Israelis from the Palestinian standpoint in *Palestine*, therefore mainly as settlers and soldiers, Sacco confirms and owns up to 'the limitations of the "objective observer" perspective' (2021: 122). This approach may very well be valid not only for journalists, but also for artists and spectators as well as readers engaging with graphic or other narratives of conflict and human rights violations, because it highlights the importance of one's positionality in choosing how to listen/bear witness to the testimonies of others, how to frame and remediate them, or how to consume/interpret them as a further removed secondary witness. 'Moderate Pressure: Part One' from *Palestine*, which structures Palestinian men's testimonies of suffering during incarceration, and the subsequent impunity and silencing surrounding such practices via euphemistic naming procedures illustrates, in three pages, all the attributes of graphic journalism described by Sacco in his manifesto.[11] At the same time as commenting on the ethics of (Sacco's) journalistic work, *Palestine* also illustrates how torture can be presented in ways that render the predominantly inaudible, in/visible Palestinian man respectfully witnessed and remembered by displaying his *graphic martyria*.

Spectacles of male suffering in *Vanni*

State-initiated sexual torture against men has also occurred during the Sri Lankan conflict. Richard Traunmüller et al. (2019) have explained the factors leading to statistical unreliability, which causes the invisibility of sexual violence in this context, while also noting the heightened vulnerability of Tamil

---

[11] The sexual torture of Bosnian Muslim men in 'The War Crime Trials', the first chapter of *Journalism*, is also displayed in a similar mode to that described above in *Palestine*. While torture is verbally present, visually it is strongly suggested but once again remains off-scene (Sacco 2012b: 2–8).

men or those considered as their potential collaborators to this form of suffering. Harry Apperley writes that 'more than a fifth of Sri Lankan Tamil men detained in the conflict report being sexually abused', at the same time as explaining that these men are very often 'silent victims, even compared to women' because of the gendered shame that comes with being sexually violated, and that, at times, they 'are socially discouraged from vocalizing their emotions, or lack the vocabulary to do so, for fear of breaching some masculine code' (2015: 93, 97). Because of this, and due to governmental restriction of access to relevant data, very little is known about sexual violence in the Sri Lankan conflict (Traunmüller et al. 2019). Like *Palestine*, Dix and Pollock's *Vanni* sheds light on nudity as a core aspect of torture, further highlighting the affective violence that comes with the rendering of such suffering a visual (in the sense of video-recorded and graphically reproduced) spectacle.

Like Sacco's view on graphic journalism, Dix and Pollock are preoccupied with the vexed notion of objectivity and, similarly to Sacco's journalistic project, core in their own work is the fictionalization of the testimonies they collect, as explained in the Introduction. This is necessary for the protection of the survivors they work with from further precarity, which lies in sharing information that places responsibility on particular actors for their suffering. The fictionalization of testimonies regarding sexual torture in particular also prevents survivors' further exposure and the potential shaming impact that may come along with it. At the same time as rendering this aspect of the Tamil/Sinhala conflict visible, *Vanni*, like *Palestine*, presents an attempt of depicting the human rights violations suffered by othered men ethically and respectfully. Unlike Sacco's aesthetic choice to present genital torture and nudity off-scene in the visual register, in the interactive collaborative work that preceded the completion of *Vanni*, Dix and Pollock, together with their interviewees/collaborators, chose to place two nude male spectacles explicitly on-scene.

Different forms of violence become contextualized peritextually as well as in the *mise-en-scène* realm of the book. In his Introduction to *Vanni*, Dix refers to the social structures of Sri Lanka prior to colonization, which were based on a deep-rooted caste system that reflected 'the linguistic and historical identities of the island's various kingdoms' (Dix 2019a: 6). He then explains how upon their arrival, British colonizers divided 'the population based on language, religion, custom and clothing' and sought 'to formalize these cultural differences' by making the new categories they created 'the basis for political representation, thus "rewriting" the history of Sri Lanka in racial terms' and planting the seeds of Sinhala and Tamil nationalisms (Dix 2019a: 6).

While in the struggle for decolonization Sinhala, Muslim and Tamil communities were united, subsequently each followed their own nationalist agendas.

The imposition of Sinhala as the island's official language, for instance, prompted an 'ethno-linguistic crisis' in Sri Lanka because it denied 'non-Sinhala speakers access to civil service and, therefore, access to economic and political power' (Dix 2019a: 6). This led to calls for the formation of separate ethnic States and later escalated into a violent Tamil/Sinhala conflict, the peak of which is narrated in *Vanni*. Similarly to Sacco, albeit peritextually, Dix also provides quantitative information about the dead in conflicts across the second half of the twentieth century and the first two decades of the twenty-first, noting the damage each of the two sides has inflicted on the other, which became exacerbated because of the international community's indifference. He also dedicates *Vanni* 'to friends and colleagues lost in the Sri Lankan conflict and to all those who survived but continue to live in a world that has failed to acknowledge their basic human rights' (Dix and Pollock 2019: 8). By embedding the contemporary conflict within this trajectory, Dix unearths deeper causes that often remain ignored. In mediating Antoni, its fictionalized Tamil protagonist's experiences of the conflict's escalation through these years, *Vanni* counters hostile perceptions on Tamil men at the same time as highlighting their precarities, vulnerabilities, emotional ties and traumas, which remain largely ignored in Western mainstream media and migration policies that often prolong their trauma.

Vanni is filled with mutilated, disabled, dead and otherwise violated bodies. As Antoni's family tries to escape death, hunger and persecution, an account of torture suffered by his brother Radjan is given. Radjan, a soldier in the Tamil Tigers, carries his wounded friend Segar among corpses covered by flies that underscore the grotesqueness and inhumanity of the spectacle of death. In a failed attempt to remain unseen by Sinhala soldiers, they decide to pass as civilians by removing their military uniform and wearing plain clothes they find abandoned among the dead. Their arrest by Sinhala soldiers is presented through a fly-on-the-wall perspective (Figure 2.2). Radjan is wounded and blood is dripping from his mouth, both he and Segar are forced to kneel, and they have their clothes forcibly removed at the same time as being verbally insulted.

The narrative displays their capture, the removal of their clothes, the tying of their hands behind their backs and the covering of their eyes, all of which seem purposefully staged for the unseen fly-on-the-wall observer – the implied reader whose gaze may oscillate between voyeurism and adequate witnessing. The visual angle on the events interchangeably zooms in and out of scenes showing

Figure 2.2 Panels from page 212 of *Vanni: A Family's Struggle through the Sri Lankan Conflict* by Benjamin Dix and Lindsay Pollock, Oxford: The New Internationalist, © 2019, used with permission from Benjamin Dix and Lindsay Pollock.

both the Sinhala soldiers' aggression towards Radjan and Segar, and the two captives' fear and humiliation, the latter of which becomes heightened by how their nude bodies become exposed to the readerly gaze. In other words, *Vanni* presents the reader with an aesthetically arranged spectacle of male torture that is caused by the shaming implications of nudity and bodily pain. Contrary to Sacco's intra-diegetic theatrical re-enactment of torture in *Palestine*, this is neither parodic nor unthreatening.

Rajan and Segar are on their knees, their bodies face the reader, and the soldiers behind them mock them because of their fear, as such further attacking their dignities and already wounded masculinities in a graphic depiction that clearly demarcates extremely precarious and hegemonic masculinity positions. The visual register that moves back and forth between distant and close-up takes on the captured men's faces mediates both their horror and their hopelessness, which may have remained unseen/unobserved had the narrative's depictions remained limited at a particular distance. Radjan then listens to a gun shot and realizes that his friend is killed right next to him. A long-distance take on the scene shows Segar's nude body fallen on the ground with his hands still tied behind his back and blood flowing from his head. One of the soldiers laughs and another tells Radjan that his 'little friend is dead' (Dix and Pollock 2019: 213). Radjan remains exposed to the unseen observer/implied reader, with his position as a nude, wounded spectacle remaining marked, since in addition to the reader's intrusive gaze, the soldiers also decide to video-record his approaching execution.

A close-up take on him shows blood still dripping from his mouth and a tear on his cheek as they prepare to carry out and record his execution. The narrative's perspective then turns to the soldier holding his mobile phone, going from the 'menu' to the 'camera' and then to the 'video' function of his device (Dix and Pollock 2019: 213). When he is ready to start the recording, another soldier prepares to shoot Radjan and the visual angle changes once again, providing access to him from the viewpoint of the soldier holding his phone about to record the killing. A panel then zooms in on Radjan's face from behind the soldier's back, and a second one presents a distant view, placing the reader behind the recording device, allowing them to share the position of the perpetrator as he keeps a visual record of the murder.

The spectacle of Radjan's torture and execution thus becomes doubly remediated. In the next panel, a flock of birds is shown flying, suggesting that the sound of the unseen shooting has caused their abrupt flight. The soldiers then abandon the corpses in an identical position. Despite not constituting an instance of rape, this spectacle highlights a case of ethnosexual, in Cox's terms, violence that is posthumously preserved in how the violated male bodies become situated in a positioning that visually evokes the sexual, gendered humiliation that is intended through it and the victims' exposed nudity. These overtones are put in use for wounding the two men, and to a different extent, the Tamil community.[12] In freezing and mediating each of the moments of Radjan's suffering, *Vanni* slows the pace of the narrative down allowing an affectively charged engagement with the nude spectacle of torture. At the same time, its *graphic martyria* underscores the reader's and Radjan's awareness of the traumatic impact of being video recorded. By drawing the reader's attention to the soldier who keeps a visual record of the execution, this narrative fragment shows how the captive's pain becomes intensified precisely through the spectacularization of his suffering.

Unlike Sacco's decision to keep Palestinian men's nudity and genital torture off-scene, Dix and Pollock chose to expose and highlight nudity, forcing the

---

[12] Achille Mbembe refers to 'the masculinization of power' that becomes 'reinforced by the context of war,' leading to the 'substitutability between the phallus and the gun' (2006: 328).

reader to bear witness to a difficult spectacle unfolding in slow tempo and minute detail. In contrast to video displays of torture, which are characterized by the fast movement of frames (Mulvey 2006), in reading comics, one needs to pause and engage with each moment that becomes graphically depicted in each panel – each still narrative frame. At the same time as highlighting the two men's gendered pain, in staging this case of torture as such, *Vanni* also foregrounds the inhuman atrocity that prevails in armed ethnic conflict. And while the perpetrators' bodies and speech bubbles mediate the violence of physical and verbal abuse against their Tamil captives, their eyes and facial expressions do not indicate aggression, but rather, perplexity. At times, the soldiers also seem scared, thus unsettling the brutality that becomes verbally mediated. As such, *Vanni* casts the male perpetrator/victim binary via an ambivalent take on perpetrators, monstrosities, vulnerabilities and precarities existing alongside hierarchies of Tamil and Sinhalese masculinities in the context of the Sri Lankan conflict.

In so doing, it unsettles Western romanticized touristy views of Sri Lanka as an eartly island paradise as those expressed in Antoni's taxi in London at the beginning of the narrative.[13] By forcing the reader to engage with the video-recorded staging of violated male bodies, *Vanni* also asks that we consider the injurious impact of, and the ethical issues emerging from, the graphic remediation of such extreme forms of human rights violations. In their effort to maintain Radjan's and Sagar's dignity, however, to treat them with aesthetic justice, and to preserve them as respectfully witnessed and remembered in their work, Dix and Pollock artistically intervene in the narrative to hide the two men's genitals with black rectangles in a clearly marked editing act. In choosing to bring this instance of bodily torture to centre stage, they effectively and affectively mediate its horror. As such, despite the risk entailed in its explicit visual exposure, Radjan's and Segar's suffering becomes adequately witnessed in *Vanni*.

In his Afterword to the book, Dix refers to the international community's failure 'to investigate and hold to account, the crimes committed in Sri Lanka during the war' (Dix 2019b: 260). Evoking Britain's (neo-)colonial links to Sri Lanka, he also explains that in his role 'as head of the Commonwealth', Prince Charles awarded the Sri Lankan president, Mahinda Rajapaska, with 'the title of Commonwealth Chairman-in-Office' in 2013 (Dix 2019b: 260). In this sense, *Vanni* functions similarly to *Palestine*, which refers to the Western

---

[13] A detailed analysis regarding this perspective can be found in Chapter 4.

celebration of Israel as Middle East's only democracy, thus failing to acknowledge the human rights violations the Israeli State inflicts against Palestinian people, which become graphically displayed in the book. By peritextually zooming out of the atrocities that have occurred during the 2009 Sri Lankan war, and by graphically zooming in on them in the *mise-en-scène* realm, *Vanni* unsettles official narratives enabling impunity and the erasure of collective trauma, linking the contemporary conflict to the British colonial project, and illustrating the impact of modernity/coloniality on the island and its people both within and outside its borders.

As such, this graphic life narrative foregrounds diachronic, Western (neo-) colonial complicities in human rights violations that contemporarily occur elsewhere, forcing people to seek asylum in the Global North. Dix writes that Sri Lankans who sought refuge in the West 'found themselves contending with a hostile media and government policies intended to discourage people from' doing so (Dix 2019b: 261–2). Tamil people were treated with suspicion, often being 'accused of exaggerating the horror of the conflict and the risks they faced if returned to Sri Lanka' (Dix 2019b: 262).[14] Many had their asylum claims rejected, they 'were forcibly repatriated and subsequently disappeared or suffered further torture, discrimination and exploitation', living in fear for their lives, with the relatives of those who had disappeared 'terrified to question or challenge the authorities', he further points out (Dix 2019b: 262). As such, the Introduction's flash back to the British colonial rule in Sri Lanka and the Afterword's flash forward to the Western hostile treatment and suspicion against Tamil asylum seekers effectively contextualize the gendered suffering taking place in *Vanni*.

The child soldiers of Sri Lanka and Burma

Further to adult men's torture, *Vanni* and *Burma* negotiate the human rights violations suffered by boys in contexts of conflict and persecution. According to the *Convention on the Rights of the Child* (United Nations General Assembly 1989) and the Department for the Execution of Judgements of the European Court of Human Rights (2021: 2), among the most basic rights of children are 'their right to freedom from ill-treatment and servitude, their right to liberty and security, access to a court, family life, return proceedings in abduction cases and

---

[14] The hostile reception of Sri Lankan refugees in the Australian context is accounted for in Safdar Ahmed's 'Villawood' (2015).

freedom from discrimination in family law, inheritance matters and education'. However, the rights of racially othered children become grossly violated across the globe in multiple ways, among which are trafficking, the deprivation of their own and their families' safety, and their enforced army recruitment.[15] Liisa Malkki (2010) refers to the child soldier as a figure that destabilizes international perceptions of childhood innocence. She points out that 'the international moral shock about the child soldier may derive its significance from the generalized, universalizing expectation of children's innocence, the expectation that children are beings not yet caught up in history or politics' (Malkki 2010: 63). Nevertheless, *Vanni, Burma*, as well as *Palestine*, as discussed in the following section, illustrate how and why boys become unavoidably caught up in conflict, thus being deprived of their rights, and consequently being positioned on the margins of the category of the innocent child, who is seen as worthy of being saved.

Malkki writes that contrary to being referred to as children in the press, child soldiers, and boys who took part in the Palestinian Intifada, are 'often categorized [...] as "youths"' because it is easier to invest younger children with innocence, since older ones 'become more "tainted" and less worthy of special treatment' (2010: 64). The stories of child soldiers in Burma and Sri Lanka, and of boys recruited to fight for the Intifada in Palestine, become displayed in graphic life narratives attempting to shed light on their ambivalent existence in the midst of conflict and violence.[16] In *The Mind of the Child: Child Development, Science, and Medicine*, Sally Shattleworth refers to the idea that 'children should be seen and not heard', which often results in their exile 'to a metaphorical dark corner' (2010: 1). In this chapter, I am interested in the extent to which the othered boy speaks and becomes heard and seen in the selected graphic life narratives, and what their *graphic martyria* (torture, testimonies and remembering) says about their positionalities in contexts of conflict and their relationalities within hierarchies of masculinity. The comics form, I argue, allows

---

[15] For gendered statistics on human trafficking and for the types of trafficking men, women, boys and girls suffer see the *World Migration Report 2022* (IOM: 2022a). The numbers reported are, however, questionable, since many cases remain, by nature, unreported.

[16] Burma is one among the countries with the highest percentage of child soldiers. The Burmese National Army recruits children as young as eleven years old by force. The Human Rights Watch (2002: 2) relates that 'these children are subject to beatings and systematic humiliation during training. Once employed they must engage in combat, participate in human rights abuses among civilians, and are frequently beaten and abused by their commanders and cheated of their wages. Refused contact with their families and facing severe reprisals if they try to escape, these children endure a harsh and isolated existence'. Similar processes are described in the Human Rights Watch Report (2004) *Living in Fear: Child Soldiers and Tamil Tigers in Sri Lanka*.

one to see, observe and respectfully witness children's remediated testimonies, enabling an affectively informed understanding of their stories that may lift them from the dark corner of invisible and inaudible otherness.

In *Vanni*, for instance, Radjan enrolls as a Tamil Tiger child soldier because of his guilt and feelings of responsibility for his father's death, which was caused by a bomb in Colombo where the latter took the former for medical purposes when he was significantly younger (Dix and Pollock 2019).[17] In this sense, the Tamil/ Sinhala conflict is introduced as having caused loss and trauma throughout Radjan's childhood and adulthood, and as having predetermined his life choices. The text thus embeds a person's participation in contemporary conflict as a perpetrator of violence within a longer trajectory of trauma and suffering that can explain a decision which may otherwise seem incomprehensible, and it does so by resorting both to affect via visual spectacles of pain, and to reason via factual and historical information.

As he explains Radjan's decision to enlist as a child soldier to his wife, Antoni holds a photograph of his brother. The graphically reproduced photograph, which appears later in the narrative as well, highlights the ambivalence of the figure of the child soldier (Figure 2.3). Later, Antoni, together with his family and their neighbours, gather to pay respects and lay candles and flowers for those who died defending the Tamil community on the Martyrs' Day. Nelani, his next-door neighbour, realizes when looking at the martyrs' photographs, that most of them were 'just kids', a piece of information that the reader may also access through the visual register (Dix and Pollock 2019: 22). Further to illustrating how children can get caught up in conflict, *Vanni* also demonstrates how ideologies that sustain inter-communal hatred and violence become transmitted from one generation to the next, even from a very young age, through the boys' attitudes towards the war and the Sinhalese community.[18]

Jaga, Nelani's son, also joined the Tamil Tigers. During his visit to his family home for the Martyrs' Day, his brother Bala, a toddler, wears his boots and sings that 'our stolen Tamil land will be redeemed by our troops', describing

---

[17] Daya Somasundaram explains that Tamil children's continuous 'exposure to war trauma', such as 'shelling, helicopter strafing, round ups, cordon and search operations, deaths, injury, destruction, mass arrests, detention, shootings, grenade explosions, and landmines' has severe 'psychological sequelae' often functioning as a 'push factor', leading to their enrolment as child soldiers (2002: 1268).

[18] In *Ethics in the Gutter: Empathy and Historical Fiction in Comics* and her investigation of 'historio-metagraphics', graphic narratives that 'seek to present some measure of historical reality, but do so from a fictional vantage point', questioning, at the same time, how such realities become represented, Kate Polak mentions the 'possibility that there is a noncultural transfer of memory', and consequently, of trauma and aversion 'across generations', which facilitates the preservation and continuity of conflict (2017: 5, 147).

Tamil Tigers as 'uncontrollable human spinning bombs [...,] righteous and unafraid' of death (Dix and Pollock 2019: 21). His eerie singing becomes interrupted by his mother, whose speech bubble literally obscures the wording of his song by being drawn over his own bubble. His singing while wearing his brother's oversized boots foregrounds his unawareness about the impact of his song, which seems configured into a means of entertainment for him. Bala then pretends to be a Tiger soldier in a game of war, and later, the narrative returns to Antoni's house, presenting Radjan's photograph once again, which then becomes positioned in-between other family photographs, and prior to a panel showing Antoni's children sleeping (Figure 2.3). In this instance of braiding, and via this visual arrangement of the photographs of martyrs alongside those of Radjan, and of other members of Antoni's family, prior to the panel that shows the bodies of his boys as they sleep, *Vanni* silently stages an uncanny juxtaposition between the dead, the precariously living and those who are about to die in battle.[19] In so doing, it subtly foregrounds the inescapability of suffering, and stresses the excessive vulnerability of these boys to violence.

At the same time, through their families' conversations, it presents the worries and pride stemming from romanticized views on being recruited to fight for one's community, which subsequently becomes undone. As the narrative progresses, such views on becoming a Tamil soldier and a martyr collapse as Radjan becomes tortured and humiliated prior to being executed, and Tamil

Figure 2.3 Panels from page 25 of *Vanni: A Family's Struggle through the Sri Lankan Conflict* by Benjamin Dix and Lindsay Pollock, Oxford: The New Internationalist, © 2019, used with permission from Benjamin Dix and Lindsay Pollock.

---

[19] Braiding refers to an aspect of comics that demands 'synchronic' and 'diachronic' readings (Groensteen 2012: 147). Thierry Groensteen explains that synchronically the reader's focus is on 'the co-presence of panels on the surface of the same page; and diachronically [it produces] a recollection or an echo of an anterior term' (2012: 147). Via braiding, a narrative fragment in a comics text enters 'a potential, if not actual, relation with every other, leading to a densification of detail that charges the layout with meaning' (Horstkotte and Pedri 2012: 336).

soldiers attempt to forcibly recruit Bala when he is twelve years old (Dix and Pollock 2019). As the two families move from one place to another to escape natural disasters and persecution, the narrator explains that Tamil Tiger patrols occasionally went to camps 'seeking more recruits as the fighting escalated', taking 'young people' and 'older children' by force (Dix and Pollock 2019: 89). This brutal reality comes to contradiction with the image of the Tamil army Bala mediated through his singing. *Vanni* thus stages, through its graphic displays, the impact of the remnants of British colonialism in Sri Lanka on the lives of boys and on their familial relationalities, foregrounding their suffering, and their vulnerabilities.

In *Burma*, male child soldiers are depicted outside their familial contexts, after having been forcibly recruited by, and then escaped the Burmese army. Kirschner's experiences and affectively charged interaction with her interlocutors become quite clear across the four volumes of *I Live Here*. Elizabeth Swanson Goldberg and Alexandra Schultheis Moore identify in this four-volume project 'three spheres of identity, identification, and desire for recognition' (2011: 248). These spheres consist of

> the desire to be recognized as a person who is aware of and cares about global human rights, and who envisions a different, more just world [;] the desire to be recognized and to participate in a global community of women familiar with the shared exigencies (and brutalities) of gendered experience; and the desire to recognize and to identify with the pain of others around the world, a pain that may either affirm or minimize one's own sense of experiencing emotional or physical pain.
>
> Goldberg and Moore 2011: 248

As such, Goldberg and Moore introduce the causes and drives that lie behind *I Live Here*, while focusing primarily on the suffering of women and girls. However, further to trafficking and sexual violence, which was explored in the previous chapter, *Burma* also concerns, as mentioned, the precarious masculinities of child soldiers, which become negotiated alongside Kirshner's narrative presence, showing how gendered hierarchies of humanity become reproduced in this humanitarian project.

Kirschner's approach in terms of authorial standing is different from that of Dix and Pollock, who remain outside the narrative realm, and similar to Sacco's whose intra-diegetic presence and contact with his interlocutors are marked and core in the plot development of *Palestine*. However, her project dangerously oscillates between ethically mediating the *graphic martyria* of others and overshadowing it in its display of her autobiographical subject's emotions and personal as well as familial accounts. The stories of Burmese child soldiers who found refuge in the Karen community are presented in the form of transcribed interviews or otherwise, collaged together by J. B. MacKinnon, with accompanying images created by Tara Hach.

The Burmese child soldiers' testimonies are preceded, as explained, by Kirschner's journal entry, which relates how she and her driver got stopped by Thai soldiers on their way to meet the boys and got asked to present all their documents. In this narrative fragment, Kirschner's narrator mediates her own gendered precarity in a foreign militarized context, where she is also unaware of the language, explaining that she felt she had to 'push [her] bra strap underneath [her] blouse and roll down [her] shorts' when they got stopped (Kirschner 2008a: np). As mentioned, if read through a decolonized, postcolonial lens, her fake presentation as a Christian missionary can implicitly be linked to colonial crimes justified precisely through the enforced Christianization of the Burmese population. In the page that includes a picture of Jesus attached to the photograph of a bridge that links Burma and Thailand, as well as references to excerpts from the Bible, which were discussed in the previous chapter, the words of a child soldier are also transcribed, expressing his dream of 'living quietly and peacefully with [his] parents and [his] brothers again' (Kirschner 2008a: np).

Like the identities of characters in *Palestine* and *Vanni*, those of the child soldiers in *Burma* also remain unknown because 'if they return to Burma, they risk arrest for desertion' (Kirschner 2008a: np). Kirschner's narrator explains that 'there are approximately 380,000 soldiers within the Burmese army', and that '1 in 5 is under 16 years of age' (Kirschner 2008a: np). *Burma*'s pages include typewritten testimonies shared by boys, accounting for their kidnapping, enforced recruitment, beatings and sufferings while in training. Visually, the narrative presents photographs of boys, whose eyes are hidden by what seem like pieces of black fabric, as well as pictures drawn by some of them. The narrator's caption, which refers to the number of underage soldiers in the Burmese army, is written on a piece of paper tape collaged at the bottom of a digitally reproduced close-up image of a boy in darkness, whose torso is facing the reader but whose face and hidden gaze, since his eyes are covered, are directed elsewhere. In this sense, the number – one in five of the 380,000 soldiers – becomes a particular person, who nevertheless remains semi-visible in Kirschner's attempt to hide his identity. The aversion of his gaze from the reader may imply fear, shame, as well as the impossibility of artistically mediating his demand for response-ability and address-ability in this context.

On the following page, which is also marked by its darkness, an excerpt from the boy's responses to his interlocutor's questions hauntingly floats over a piece of paper on which a part of his testimony is transcribed, illustrating his loss of childhood innocence. 'I am not afraid of anything. I don't feel anything, I don't have any dreams, I don't want anything', the boy declares (Kirschner 2008a: np). The translator intervenes in the transcribed conversation to explain that the boy 'really believes this. He believes in his statements' (Kirschner 2008a: np) as if to confirm the validity of the minor's statements. Subsequently, a child's painting of 'a truck that kidnapped [him] for army duty' is shown, and the narrator mentions that the boy who drew this image 'couldn't read or write and shook when he told his story' (Kirschner 2008a: np). The underage testifying subject accounts for his torture during training, his exhaustion caused by having to carry sacks of rice to the top of a mountain through the day, the beatings he suffered when he got tired, and his escape. When asked if he liked to use guns, he responds affirmatively, also explaining that he made friends with whom they shared plans of escaping, and that given that they were abused by the Burmese and saved by the Karen, they 'would kill [their] abusers with a knife or a gun' because they could not 'forgive them' (Kirschner 2008a: np). The boy's narrative concludes by explaining that 'if we don't die, we would like to meet our parents again' (Kirschner 2008a: np).

On this narrative section's final page, a papercut picture of a child soldier and his commander, drawn by a child with a pencil, is attached to a darker paper surface. The figure of the child is embodied through a collage and from his waist-down a coloured piece cut from a magazine or a photograph shows a realistic version of a boy's legs, one of which is artificial. These visual/verbal arrangements thus illustrate both the physical and the psychic traumas these children are burdened with, at the same time as staging their radical otherness. Their presumed monstrosity seems rooted in how they simultaneously embody the perpetrator's drive to kill and the child's trauma and desire for parental intimacy and protection. In its depiction of child soldiers alongside the ambivalent account of Western humanitarianism, then, unlike *Vanni*, *Burma* highlights the abject otherness of child soldiers, without explicitly delving into the historical factors that have led to the contemporary conflict and involve, as in the case of Sri Lanka, the British colonial project in the East. In its arrangement of the gazes on and of the other, this narrative reproduces an unbreachable distance between the Western humanitarian artist, as well as the intended reader, and the semi-visible underage male other it attempts to render audible and visible, but who nevertheless still remains restricted in the dark corner of representation.

The Palestinian Shebab

The stories of similarly ambivalent figures to the child soldiers of Sri Lanka and Burma, those of the Palestinian Shebab who fought in the Intifada, are accounted for in Sacco's *Palestine*. John Collins describes 'the *atfāl al-hijāra* ("children of the stones") [as] political caricatures about whom we know surprisingly little. The assumption', he continues, 'seems to be that the actions of the "intifada generation" speak for themselves, thus obviating the need for a closer look at the particular kinds of consciousness and social analysis they undoubtedly possess' (2004: 11). In his book, Collins seeks to go 'against the grain of this assumption, and to do so in a way that treats young people as the truly multidimensional human beings they are. This means soliciting their ideas as well as their stories, and it means respecting them enough to engage [with] their testimony critically' (2004: 12).

In his graphic journalism, Sacco approaches these boys and their accounts from a similar standpoint. In *Palestine*, most of chapter seven is devoted to the testimonies of boys who partook in the Intifada. The first page of 'The Boys: Part One', visually introduces readers to the eighteen-year-old Mohammed, a member of Fateh, as indicated by the black colour of his keffiyeh, who had been 'shot three times in clashes', and to the twenty-year-old Husein, member of the Popular Front as indicated by his red keffiyeh, who had been imprisoned for six months in the notorious Ansar III prison (Sacco 2001: 190). Mohammed has his head covered with his keffiyeh, visually performing his political stance and resistance to Israeli occupation. Like Husein's, his avatar does not mediate his age difference from Sacco and his translator. Rather, the autobiographical avatar's distance from the boys is visually marked both by how he is situated away from them as they walk, and by how his eyes are covered by his glasses, that prevent access to that facial part, which is a significant indicator of emotions and affective reactions in *Palestine*. People's eyes are those that mediate both the invisible psychic trauma and the weariness that comes with living under occupation in Palestine.

Sacco's narrator explains that 'it is kids like this – the shebab – who've spearheaded the Intifada' (Sacco 2001: 190). However, those described as kids become visually embodied as tired men. Their verbal descriptions as boys and their visual embodiments thus mediate a marked juxtaposition between what is said and what is seen. The Arabic term 'shebab' refers to 'Palestinian activist youth', who only get to speak 'through the ritual of shahada (martyrdom)' (Pitcher 1998: 8–9). Recalling Malkki's analysis of why this naming, as opposed to 'children', matters, it is important to note Sacco's decision to refer to the Shebab as kids in a narrative that, like *Vanni*, deconstructs the romanticized perception of their martyrdom at the same time as highlighting these boys contribution to Palestinian resistance and the consequences this has had for their gendered subjectivities.

In the second part of 'The Boys', adolescents gather around a table as Sacco's avatar asks questions while facing Mohammed and Husein. Unlike the transcribed, typewritten interviews collaged and digitally reproduced in the pages of *Burma*, the graphic display of these boys allows access to non-verbal information that enriches their narrative. Husein's face, for instance, shows his rage for what he perceives as the injustice of the occupation, while Mohammed looks weary and tired. When Sacco asks why they throw stones given that this action does not have significant impact, Husein explains that despite knowing that there is not 'much chance of injuring the soldiers', they feel the need 'to show what is inside' them (Sacco 2001: 195). Contrarily, in a response that indicates disillusionment, Mohammed explains that this is now mostly 'a habit', further mentioning that contrary to 'everyone else', he has never been imprisoned (Sacco 2001: 195). In situating the implied reader in Sacco's position, who is faced by the two boys, the narrative offers access to two juxtaposing attitudes that become visually and verbally expressed: that of enraged resistance and that of weariness. While at this point he does not intervene to comment on their responses, when they leave, Sameh, Sacco's translator, informs him that Mohammed is ashamed of not having been incarcerated. The narrative thus introduces imprisonment as an element that is core in the structuring and maintenance of Palestinian masculinity. This is indicated both by Sameh's supplementary comment on Mohammed's testimony, and by the affective implications of his visual embodiment.

In part three of 'The Boys', Firas, a fifteen-year-old, explains that he was approached by his neighbour at age thirteen 'to work for the Popular Front', since it was decided that he 'might be the right man' for the job (Sacco 2001: 196). He then relates how he moved from 'spray paint[ing] slogans on the wall and giv[ing] out leaflets' to warning collaborators and then beating them in cases when they did not comply (Sacco 2001: 197). Firas is well-informed in terms of politics and seems clear and firm about his political standing in relation to the resistance. In his maturity, he illustrates how notions of childhood innocence, as lack of knowledge leading to the absence of agency and the inability to decide for oneself, are culturally and geographically bound. As he describes having been shot 'once and arrested three times', as well as having his eyes covered and being beaten, he also notes that as a minor, he does not 'have to go to jail if [his] parents pay a $300 dollar fine' (Sacco 2001: 198). While this demarcates a distinction in the Israeli treatment of Palestinian men and boys, the visual depictions of Israeli force against them re-establishes violent hierarchies between Israeli and Palestinian masculinities.

When Firas's interview concludes, Sameh once again supplements the information Sacco gathers by placing responsibility for the boys' excessive vulnerability to Israeli violence on the Palestinian leadership, which deprived them of other interests, forcing them to only 'think about the struggle', making the Intifada the only meaningful thing in their lives (Sacco 2001: 198). In further explaining how every home 'has someone who is imprisoned, who has died, [or] is wounded' (Sacco 2001: 198), and that Israeli soldiers continuously harass Palestinians, Sameh sketches the context in which Palestinian boys grow up, as well as the factors that have led them to spearhead the Intifada and to expose themselves to torture and death. The final part of 'The Boys' further underscores the harm that arises from conflict within the Palestinian resistance factions as it mediates the seventeen-year-old Rifat's testimony of how he got shot by men in Arabic attire and was then dragged in the street with his 'intestines hanging out' (Sacco 2001: 203). This grotesque graphic depiction of Rifat's suffering re-orients the reader's gaze in relation to the perpetrators of violence against underage Palestinian boys by highlighting their vulnerability to dominant masculinities within the Palestinian community.[20] Rifat refers to the surgeries he underwent, and to his complete and subsequently partial inability to move his legs, further mentioning that he undergoes physiotherapy and that he is no longer able to work as he used to.

His testimony becomes supplemented with information Sacco had previously gathered from 'the head of the YMCA Rehabilitation Programme [, which] works with young wounded Palestinians' to help them deal with the difficulties surrounding their integration in the community (Sacco 2001: 204). The man who leads this programme explains that initially, 'injured boys ... feel like heroes [...] but when a boy starts living with his injury, he might not feel the support of others' (Sacco 2001: 205). In the visual register, a boy is shown pushing his wheelchair across a rocky road (Figure 2.4). This image may be read as a visual metaphor depicting the obstacles he has to overcome due to his disability,

---

[20] At the same time, by relating that the men who beat him were dressed in Arabic clothes, as opposed to having been Arabs, Rifat's testimony may be read as suggesting that these men were Israelis in disguise.

which further wounds his masculinity. After the verbal contextualization of Rifat's disability, Sacco's drawing style changes to fragmenting and containing his visual depictions in three images that zoom in on the boy's torso and face. In being drawn as such, they decontextualize his presence from the community of men around him, and to a different extent, they stress his isolation. 'How do you fit in the community now that you're partially paralyzed?', Sacco asks in the first panel (Sacco 2001: 205). In the second, before the boy manages to speak, another man's speech bubble enters the panel explaining that the community respects him, something that Rifat then repeats in the third panel (Figure 2.4).

Sameh does not make a comment at the end of this interview. Rather, as he walks away with Sacco's avatar, the latter wonders what the boy could say in the

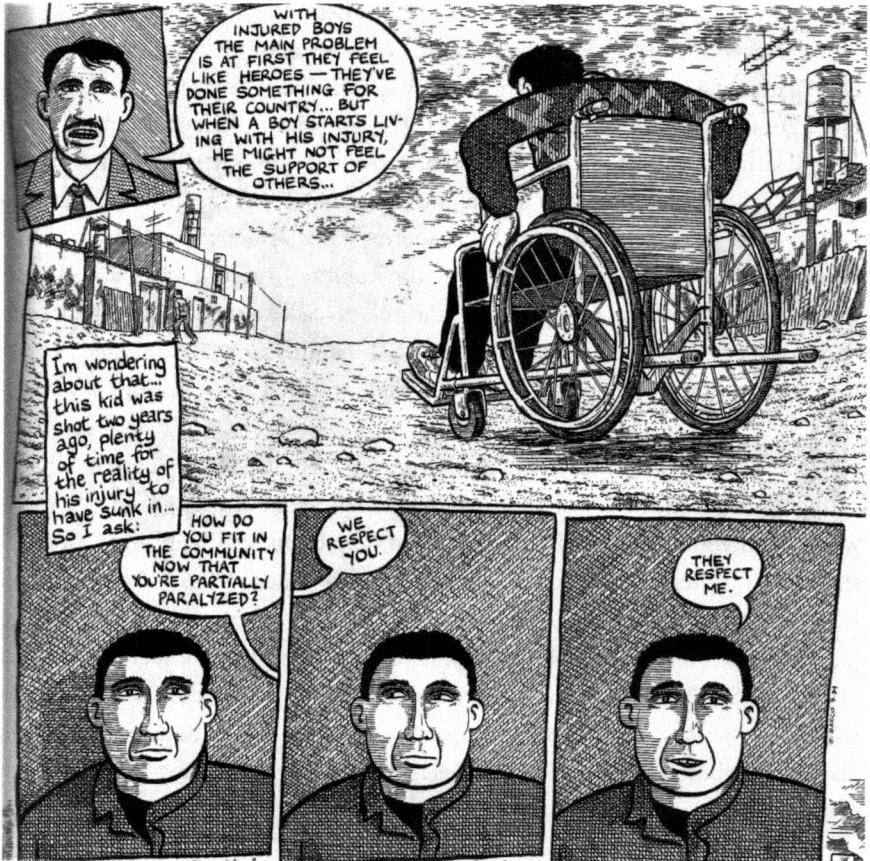

Figure 2.4 Panels from page 205 of *Palestine* by Joe Sacco, © 2001, used with permission from Fantagraphics.

presence of all the men around him, thus noting the limitations of his response. His comment, like the rest of the section devoted to Intifada's boys, illustrates how hierarchies and relationalities among different masculinities, as well as gendered expectations connected to the performance of boys' struggle for the Palestinian cause, can shape and at times limit both their testimonies and their futures. In this sense, the three panels that zoom in on Rifat's face mediate the boy's silenced isolation within the Palestinian community, deconstructing romanticized views of shahada/martyrdom. What this narrative fragment shows, then, is that despite making Sacco's preferences and political positioning clear in relation to the Israeli/Palestinian conflict, and while presenting events as filtered through his subjective truth, which aligns with the Palestinian cause, *Palestine* does not shy away from exposing the responsibilities lying within the leadership of the Palestinian resistance for the trauma, both physical and psychic, and the human rights violations suffered by the Shebab – the contested youth, the ambivalent boys of the Intifada. At the same time, as explicated in the previous chapter, it also does not refrain from illustrating how the boys themselves transform into perpetrators of gendered violence and harassment against Palestinian women and girls in the same context.

Resistance

According to Christine Hong, 'to read human rights-themed comics is to grapple with implicitly hierarchical conceptions of humanity, which [also] structure their form' (2016: 194). As they offer Western readers windows to distant suffering and misery, these texts re-produce hierarchical geopolitical divisions as they place the reader from the Global North at a necessarily central position in the consumption of human rights narratives concerning the suffering of others in the Global South (Hong 2016).

The comics examined above negotiate hierarchies of humanity and masculinity. *Palestine* and *Vanni* offer the Western reader access to the suffering of Palestinian men during incarceration in the context of the Israeli/Palestinian conflict and of Tamil people in the Sri Lankan war, lucidly illustrating how nudity, genital violence, verbal harassment and video recording can be used as tools for the humiliation of the men captured in these contexts. *Burma* turns the Western reader's attention to the human rights violations suffered by child soldiers, while *Vanni* also zooms in on the factors leading to voluntary army enrolment. Both texts also show how being forcibly recruited as a child soldier transforms one into an ambivalent perpetrator figure. Further to adult male suffering, *Palestine* also remediates the testimonies of boys, the Shebab, the ambivalent martyrs of the Intifada.

In addition to exposing the precarities and vulnerabilities of the men and boys who remain marginalized within legal, migration policy, media and humanitarian discourses, there are instances when these texts depict them beyond utter victimhood. While their bodies, like that of Prometheus, become wounded and tortured, there are times when, in displaying their agencies, these graphic life narratives show how these men and boys survive and move beyond the incomprehensible extra-juridical State-initiated and at times religiously informed violence that targets them. In *Palestine*, for instance, Firas unsettles mono-dimensional Western perspectives on the Palestinian Shebab by displaying his politically informed decision to join the resistance. In addition, among graphic displays of torture and humiliation, the men and boys incarcerated in Ansar III organize what Sacco sarcastically describes as 'edifying activities' consisting of lectures on 'ecology, philosophy, Einstein, the break-up of the Soviet Union [. . .], the Israeli peace movement', as well as language courses in Hebrew and English (2001: 87).

In showing how the thousands of men held in the largest Israeli prison organized themselves and educated one another, *Palestine* displays how dignity and humanity can be restored in the context of incarceration. Further to their educational activities, the detainees of Ansar III also stage a theatrical play dramatizing 'the death of a Palestinian in custody', at the end of which spectators applaud and Israeli soldiers fire tear gas (Sacco 2001: 87). In a Hamletian act, the men show resistance against State-initiated violence by exposing it through a theatrical play within the space of incarceration, highlighting the political impact of art in mediating the violence suffered by the Palestinian prisoners. Sacco does not present an excerpt from the play in the visual register of the narrative at this instance. Rather, he chooses to mediate the moment after its completion and the throwing of tear gas, which results in excruciating pain and tears in the prisoners' eyes and in the repression of their resistance. Through his choice, he focuses on and illustrates how the sovereign State's oppressive force becomes activated precisely because of the theatrical spectacle that remediates it, underscoring the political power of art.

Coda

In displaying the *graphic martyria* of these men and boys, and by rendering them adequately witnessed and remembered, like the visual and literary representations of Prometheus, the graphic life narratives examined in this chapter show embodied acts of resistance against the violent oppression of Kratos and Via and highlight how 'witnessing is the key process in the rebuilding of subjectivity after the confinement, torture and dehumanization' (Nayar 2016: 72). Like Kafka's short story on the Prometheus legends, they illustrate the value of art in rendering the *martyria*/testimony/suffering of othered men and boys remembered. Nevertheless, such graphic life narratives also run the risk of presenting mono-dimensional versions of the male other, of highlighting inequalities between the Western humanitarian and the non-Western victim, and of 'studiously [placing] the spectacle of the West as violence' beyond the representational frame and, thus, beyond view (Hong 2016: 202).[21] In addition, they may fall into the trap of treating the male other with aesthetic injustice that results in their 'narrative dehumanization' (Nayar 2016: 4), which becomes even more explicit in graphic life narratives because of the form's biocularity. In all their complexity and the aesthetic risk they take, by negotiating the lives of othered men and boys, and their precarities in conflict and incarceration, these narratives also demonstrate how comics 'both imbue our contemporary culture, and are themselves imbued, with the concerns of [. . .] justice', and they illustrate 'the vast breadth of potential' they have for the mediation of 'perspectives on international rights, law and justice' (Giddens 2015a: np).

[21] Randall Williams also describes the 'the narrow calculus of imperialist interest that [. . .] regulates the in/visibility of conditions of violence outside the West' (2010: 45).

3

Graphic thanatopoetics and the in/visible spectacle of death

In *Digging for the Disappeared: Forensic Science After Atrocity*, Adam Rosenblatt asks whether 'the *dead* have human rights' (2015: 153, emphasis in the original). He then explains that dead bodies are objects of mourning, research and political deliberations, but that they rarely benefit from forensic activities in relation to human rights, which can only apply for citizens living within a society that protects them and acknowledges individual claims for rights (Rosenblatt 2015; Arendt 1976). Thus, forensically, one cannot claim with certainty that the dead have human rights; rather, what they do have is the potential to reveal the workings and the limitations of human rights discourses (Rosenblatt 2015). In this chapter, I examine the rhetorical potential of θάνατος/*thanatos* – death – in relation to the human rights violations suffered by othered people in graphic life narratives about the Vietnam war, the industrialization and the femicides of Juarez, and the Israeli/Palestinian conflict. The thanatic representations I examine illustrate that while the dead are not active members of a given society, their posthumous existence is relational from the micro-level of the family to the macro-level of the inter-national community. For this reason, I investigate what dead bodies and their treatment can say about how injustice becomes distributed across individuals and nations.[1] To refer to embodiments of death through the comics form, as well as to their close examination, I use the term graphic thanatopoetics, which entails the potential for unveiling the Western framing of particular deaths as invisible by rendering their particularities visible.[2]

---

[1] Ernesto Schwartz-Marin and Arely Cruz-Santiago (2016: 483–4) define 'the moral and political challenges that come with attempts to manage death in anomalous circumstances, and [...] to connect the bodies of the dead with their social relationships and identities [as] "thanato-citizenship"'.

[2] Elizabeth el Refaie (2012: 51–2) introduces 'embodiment [as the] active, cultural process of rendering the body meaningful', further noting that 'pictorial embodiment' refers to how comics artists engage with their identity 'through multiple self-portraits' in autobiographical comics. The graphic narratives under investigation in this monograph primarily refer to the lives of others, and I am using embodiment to also refer to visual depictions of the dead.

Thanatopolitics, graphic life narrative and the meditation on death

Michel Foucault writes that '*meletē thanatou* [or the] meditation on death' enables a retrospective look at the past and the 'evaluative memorization of life' (2005: 480).[3] Stuart J. Murrey situates Foucault's analysis of the consideration of death within the context of caring for oneself and clarifies that such a relation to the self constitutes 'an attitude toward both self and world, an embodied relation in the *Lebenswelt*, a social, political, and historical exercise [*askēsis*], an ethic and an aesthetic' (2006: 210, emphasis in the original). Thinking about death can foreground the ways in which it 'is constitutive of the subject' (Murrey 2006: 210).[4] In Ancient Greek mythology, *Melete* (Practice), *Mneme* (Memory) and *Aoide* (Song) were the three original muses (Vernant 2006). Their mother, the Titan daughter of Gaea and Uranus, Mnemosyne, 'presided over the poetic function' (Vernant 2006: 140).[5] In this sense, *meletē thanatou* or the 'thought of death' becomes connected to poetics (Foucault 2005: 480).

As linked to a critical remembering, reflections upon death and its impact on life can become recorded in and remembered through literary or visual poetics and aesthetics.[6] In today's sociopolitical context, political *bios* is informed by death as shown by how 'in the name of life' certain deaths are rendered 'nameless and innumerable, obscure and obscured' (Murrey 2006: 192). The analysis that follows is based on this premise, and it seeks to demonstrate whether comics may expose in/visible or obscured deaths and their causes, thus foregrounding the political potential of the spectacle of death in the graphic narration of othered lives. My analysis draws from Murrey's theorization on the politics of death or thanatopolitics, which 'stands in opposition to biopolitics and its affirmative instantiations of [life, and constitutes a] resistant rhetorical counterpart to the dialectics and reductive ontologies of biopolitical life' (2018:

---

[3] The Greek traveller and geographer Pausanias, who lived during the second century AD, defines '*meletē* [as] the practice of a mental exercise, a training in memory necessary for an apprenticeship in the poetic technique' (Vernant 2006: 140).

[4] In *The Force of Nonviolence*, Judith Butler (2020) explains how Sigmund Freud moves beyond the field of sexuality, to apply the co-existence of *Eros* (love) and *Thanatos* (death) within the broader sphere of (inter)national and (inter)racial human relations. Thanatos appears in Freud's 'Civilization and Its Discontents' as a destructive human instinct that exists alongside 'Eros' and its investigation has significant impact on the understanding of human life (Freud 1961: 117–18).

[5] Further to its mythological implications, mnemosyne refers to 'memory, [or] record' (Montanari 2016: 1355).

[6] Aesthetics is used to broadly refer to 'the distinctive underlying principles of a work of art or a genre, the works of an artist, the arts of a culture' (Simpson and Weiner 1989: np).

718). A thanatopolitical perspective entails 'reckoning with the dead [in an attempt] to account for our own complicity in a regime that delivers death to some in the name of prosperity and life for others [, exposing] the fault-lines of biopolitical logics [and foregrounding] the rhetorical conditions in which the dead, the dying, and the dispossessed might rise up and speak' (Murrey 2018: 719). In this chapter, I take a thanatopolitcal perspective to investigate how the necropower,[7] necroviolence[8] and grievability[9] that are related to the figure of the other in different bio-, geo- and necro-political contexts, become depicted through comics. Graphic thanatopoetics, therefore, refers to the comics form, its thanatic content, and the examination of both.

The analysis that follows examines how graphic depictions of death can inform and critically complicate related quantitative data. The questions I seek to respond to are the following: What is the rhetorical function of photographs of death in graphic life narratives? What are the particularities of death when it takes the form of femicide in Juarez? How does it occur within the context of the Vietnam war and the Palestinian/Israeli conflict? How do artists choose to represent the dead in relation to the living, and how do comics enable different rhetorical articulations of *thanatos* from that found in Alan Kurdi's photograph, for example, through their visual/verbal hybridity and their 'proliferation of frames' (Chute 2016: 16)?[10]

The relationship between death and photography has been addressed by Roland Barthes in *Camera Lucida*, where he contemplates upon the impact of his dead mother's childhood photographs on him. Through the photograph he mentions, which is characterized by 'a strange stasis [...], Time's immobilization assumes [...] an excessive, monstrous mode' which aligns with death (Barthes 1982: 91). Kurdi's photograph visually captures both the monstrous stillness of

---

[7] Drawing from Foucault's work on biopolitics and sovereignty's 'power to "make" live or to "let" die' (2003b: 241), Achille Mbembe also examines 'contemporary forms of subjugating life to the power of death', and introduces 'necropolitics, or necropower to account for the various ways in which [...] death-worlds' are created (2019b: 92).

[8] Necroviolence is defined as 'violence performed and produced through the specific treatment of corpses that is perceived to be offensive, sacrilegious, or inhumane by the perpetrator, the victim (and her or his cultural group), or both. Unlike Mbembe's necropolitics, which centers on the capacity to "kill or let live" associated with modernity and the exercise of sovereignty, necroviolence is specifically about corporeal mistreatment and its generative capacity for violence' (De León 2015: 69).

[9] Butler writes that our and other people's vulnerability to injury and death causes 'both fear and grief' (2004: xii). She then proceeds to clarify that 'certain forms of grief become nationally recognized and amplified, whereas other losses become unthinkable and ungrievable' (Butler 2004: xiv).

[10] This photograph depicts the body of the dead toddler that was washed ashore in Bodrum, Turkey, in 2015. I return to it in the concluding chapter.

time and the monstrosity of his death. This capturing is achieved through the photographic still frame and via the shocking depiction of *thanatos* that is visually embodied through the corpse of the toddler. Nevertheless, the factors leading to this death, as well as to others, remain outside the frame of representation, and beyond the temporality of the monstrous still thanatic moment that was captured through the photographer's click. In this chapter, I am concerned with what comics can do differently from photography in relation to the representation of death given how this form enables the emplacement of individual moments within longer narrative trajectories.

I argue that the analysis of graphic and photo/graphic depictions of death can expose injustices suffered by others, both the dead and the living, and the limitations of human rights discourses. For Barthes, the photographed person or object is 'a kind of little simulacrum [an] *eidolon* [or] the *Spectrum* of the Photograph' (Barthes 1982: 9). In a different context, drawing from Katherine Verdery's (2004: 305) analysis of the 'political lives of dead bodies', Alexandra Délano Alonso and Benjamin Nienass point out that the dead 'remain present as spectres, arousing feelings of awe that [. . .] are part of their political and symbolic efficacy' (2016: 436).[11] While Barthes refers to the ghostly dimension of the photographically depicted person at a time that was but no longer is, for Délano Alonso and Nienass this spectral dimension concerns the symbolic posthumous existence of the dead, which may also become embodied through their photographs. Indeed, photographs of the dead are often used in post-war contexts in demand for accountability, retribution and justice. For Barthes, in contrast to painting, which mediates 'a memory, an imagination, a reconstitution' of the past, photography presents 'reality in a past state [and seems as if] it was not made by the hand of man [– as if it were] *acheiropoietos*' (1982: 82, emphasis in the original).[12] Together with the depicted stillness of time that was but no longer is, the supposed lack of human agency behind the photograph constitutes the grounds on which photography's connection to death and the non-human

---

[11] In Ancient Greek, '*Eidolon*'/'εἴδωλον' refers to an 'apparition, specter, [or] phantasm', and extends to 'simulacrum [. . .,] image' or 'figure', as well as to the 'image of a god [,or] false god' (Montanari 2016: 599). '*Spectrum*' is the term's Latin equivalent (Glare 2012: 1986). A quality beyond the human, and the living, which reaches the realm of the ghostly and the eternal as co-existing with visuality is implied in the Ancient Greek and Latin terms, and it re-surfaces in Barthes' discussion on photographed people and objects, as well as in Délano Alonso and Nienass' examination of the posthumous lives of the dead.

[12] The adjective '*Acheiropoietos*'/'ἀχειροποίητος' refers to that which is 'not built or operated by human hands' (Montanari 2016: 363), and it is often used in the context of religious discourse.

emerges, but as Nancy Pedri points out, photography only hides 'the hand of its maker' (2015a: 7).[13]

In this chapter, I am interested in the rhetorical potential of the photo/graphically captured stillness of time in relation to the spectre of death, and I use 'spectre' in its dual sense that points to the ghostly/eternal existence of photo/graphically depicted thanatic embodiments, at the same time as highlighting its connection to visuality.[14] Deviating from Barthes' understanding of the link between death and photography, I argue for a political graphically structured ghostliness/spectrality of *thanatos* that becomes displayed in graphic life narratives accounting for the injustices suffered by othered people. What is it that the returning spectres of the dead tell us in the context of the graphic – as in visual/verbal and explicit – spectacle of *thanatos*, and how is their return displayed through the comics form? How does the sequential nature of comics influence the depiction of this spectacle and how does it trigger a meditation on death that can point to global inequalities and injustices differently from a photograph or a painting read outside a given narrative context?

Comics exist in-between writing and painting, the moving and the still image. This invests the form with an important potentiality: it can present a pause on and the exaggeration of the spectre of *thanatos*, as such causing a meditation on death that can point to in/visible injustices and human rights violations suffered by othered people. In the analysis that follows, I examine how comics enable thanatic representations that can trigger resistance against human rights violations highlighting the relational, political life of the dead. I further look into how they can point to the responsibilities of individuals or State authorities for depriving people of their grievability by exposing them to necropower and necroviolence, and how they may, at times, re-silence the dead.

As opposed to insisting on what distinguishes photography from other visual artforms such as painting, film, as well as comics, in this chapter I am interested in the interweaving of comics and photography in graphic life narratives depicting the death of othered people. Like Pedri, I perceive 'photography not as

---

[13] The supposed limited human agency behind the taking of a photograph has also been challenged by Butler (2009) in *Frames of War*, where she explains how particular choices are made in relation to what gets to enter the frame and what is left outside in the context of war photography, and regarding how photographed persons and objects become staged for political reasons. Such reasons may concern, for instance, the visual recording of the enemy's humiliation, or the justification of neo-imperial US attacks in the name of protecting women's human rights elsewhere. To a different extent, technological advances have increased the degree of the photographer's intervention in how something is photographically presented through editing processes.

[14] The term 'photo/graphic' means to refer to the incorporation via digital reproduction, re-drawing or otherwise of photographs in graphic life narrative.

'a discrete medium," but rather as pertaining to "a pictorial continuum," as participating in an artistic tradition that extends beyond its medium specific qualities' (Pedri 2015a: 4). The inclusion of photographs in graphic memoirs has been interpreted as documentary evidence and a form of intertextuality (Miller 2007; El Refaie 2012). For Pedri, however, it has 'a narrative, story-based (and not a referential, reality-based) function that blurs boundaries separating the documentary and the aesthetic' (Pedri 2015a: 8). Thi Bui's *The Best We Could Do*, John Sack's *La Lucha: The Story of Lucha Castro and Human Rights in Mexico* and vol. 3 of *I Live Here: Juarez* that includes Phoebe Gloeckner's graphic novella 'La Tristeza', contain photographs of the dead that are either digitally reproduced in their original form, or become drawn. These may form part of a panel's contents or of a hybrid fabric-art collage, or they may constitute full-page visual images.

Such photographs may be held or viewed by characters, they illustrate how people's ungrievability becomes exaggerated in the precarious death-worlds they navigate, and they point to acts of necroviolence. At times, such photo/graphic depictions may unsettle Western framings of distant places and in/visible othered people, or they may illustrate how those who lost their loved ones perform their agonistic mourning and their survival, thus moving beyond silenced victimhood.[15] My analysis seeks to illustrate whether thanatic photo/graphics can trigger a meditation on death that leads to the acknowledgement of the political, ethical and aesthetic injustices suffered both by the dead and the living.

The Saigon Execution photograph in Thi Bui's *The Best We Could Do*

Bui's *The Best We Could Do* tells of her family's past in cold-war Vietnam, which constitutes of short intervals of peace, extended periods of war and persecution, and their journey to, and life in, the United States. In the preface, Bui explains

---

[15] Olga Taxidou writes that 'mourning comprises a discursive *topos* that examines the function of the law, the citizen, gender and the power over the dead and the past in the new democratic *polis*' (2004: 187, emphasis in the original). In her analysis of Women in Black, a transnational, antimilitaristic, feminist movement, Athena Athanasiou explains how 'the group brings forth the political restlessness and promise at the heart of mourning those socially instituted as impossible to mourn within the biopolitical archives of territory, nation, and war' as such enacting 'agonistic mourning' (2017: 1).

that her book is based on an academic project she had to complete as a graduate student in art education, which consisted of 'photographs and some art, but mostly writing' (2018a: np). This was, she explains, an unsuccessful attempt of solving 'the storytelling problem of how to present a story in a way that is human and relatable but not oversimplified' (Bui 2018a: np). In order to solve this problem, Bui decided to tell her family's life story through a graphic life narrative after having learned how to draw comics. And while for her, photographs and written text were inadequate for this task, the comics form seems to have done the trick as indicated by the reception of the book.[16] In addition to depictions of persecution, trauma and border crossings, Bui's representations of death and, specifically, her repetitions with differentiations of the Saigon Execution photograph in the chapter of this familial life story entitled 'The Chessboard', effectively illustrates the political impact of the framing of death at national, international as well as the personal level.[17]

This's father, Bo, tells her that he moved to South Vietnam with his grandfather through the 'American Evacuation' process because their lives were in danger during the land reforms in the communist north, which took place in the 1950s and aimed at 'reorganizing society' (Bui 2018b: 171, 169). Subsequent panels visually stage the torture and murders that occurred in the context of this reorganization. This, Bo explains, 'was the work of Trường Chinh, a leader in the Workers' Party, who copied Mao's reforms in China' (Bui 2018b: 169). A sequence of three panels illustrates a scene of torture, a portrait of the Workers' Party leader and a pile of skulls. A caption over the skulls explains that 'in a short time, the land reformers killed 220 000 people' (Bui 2018b: 169). In this instance, then, the massive number of deaths is depicted through a case of graphic metonymy. And while Bo had left Lợi Đông through what was advertised as a 'passage to freedom', death was also a common occurrence in South Vietnam because, as the narrator explains, by 1965 'the chess pieces of the Vietnam War had already been set [...]. American troops arrived by the tens of thousands [and] American planes carpet-bombed a country dependent on agriculture with Napalm and the defoliant Agent Orange' (Bui 2018b: 200).[18]

---

[16] *The Best We Could Do* is the recipient of the American Book Award, *inter alia* (see Christiansen 2018).
[17] For the photograph see: http://100photos.time.com/photos/eddie-adams-saigon-execution.
[18] This excerpt and the following pages describe a case similar to what Mbembe introduces as 'infrastructural warfare' in the context of the Israeli/Palestinian conflict, which eradicates Palestinian people's means of survival and leads them to slow death (2019b: 82, 44). In *The Best We Could Do*, this is caused by the destruction of agricultural production, the black market, unemployment, inflation and excessive surveillance.

It is in the unfolding of the chess game of the Vietnam war that the Saigon Execution photograph appears three times. The metaphor whereby the chessboard refers to the actual *topos* of Vietnam, and the chess pieces to the war participants, introduces the war as a game of strategy.[19] This metaphorical representation that highlights strategic political movements, defeats and victories, becomes informed by the personal trauma and loss that are narrated alongside it, as well as by the implications of the Saigon Execution photograph that was taken by the Associated Press photographer Eddie Adams. The information the narrative includes in this chapter is presented through the perspective of Bui's father.[20] The Saigon Execution photograph, which mediated to the American people the horrors of the war, becomes contextualized in *The Best We Could Do* in ways that unsettle its photographic framing of history, complicating the US gaze on the Vietnam war as mediated through it (Gusain and Jha 2020).

Thi's father tells her that the photograph was broadcast around the globe by the American media, and presented a negative view of South Vietnam, 'but no one talks about how that same Việt Cộng [who was being shot], just hours before, had murdered an entire family in their home' (Bui 2018b: 206). Bo's comment points to how one man came to represent a whole population for Western audiences, triggering stereotypical takes on the South Vietnamese, at the same time as underlining the photograph's partiality. James Jeffrey also explains that what remains outside this photographic frame is the fact that Nguyễn Văn Lém, the man depicted just when Nguyễn Ngọc Loan's bullet is about to kill him, 'was believed to have murdered the wife and six children of one of [his executioner's] colleagues' (2018: np). The photo, Jeffrey continues, 'did not – could not – fully explain the circumstances on the streets of Saigon on 1 February 1968, two days after the forces of the People's Army of Vietnam and the Viet Cong launched the Tet Offensive' (2018: np).

Maggie Astor writes in *The New York Times* of the iconic impact of the photograph that made Americans think about the morality of their cause in the Vietnam war since 'a police chief had fired a bullet, point-blank, into the head of a handcuffed man, in likely violation of the Geneva Conventions. And the official

---

[19] Game-play metaphors also mediate invisible aspects of mental illness in graphic memoirs (see el Refaie 2014; Pedri and Staveley 2018).

[20] In graphic memoirs, Pedri (2015b) tells us, visual narration is based on the cognitive (what a character thinks of particular subjects) and visual (what a character sees) framing of information. While the two have been distinguished, like Pedri, I also perceive 'ocularization' (the images presenting what one sees) as part of focalization (the images presenting how a character sees and perceives information), through point-of-view, or shot-reverse-shot perspectives (Pedri 2015b: 9).

was not a Communist, but a member of South Vietnam's government, the ally of the United States' (2018: np). And while her comment introduces a presupposed binary division between the good Americans and their allies and the evil communists and their allies, Bui's graphic life narrative illustrates the brutalities of both sides.

As her father relates his opinion on the Saigon execution and its photographic framing, Thi tries to make sense of his ideological stance, but her attempt ends up in failure. 'The contradictions in my father's stories troubled me for a long time', she explains, as her autobiographical avatar reads through her notebook, thinking about her notes in a panel that offers meta-commentary on the intergenerational transmission of Vietnam and her family's hi-stories (Bui 2018b: 207). Further to the contradictions in her father's account, Thi also becomes perplexed by the 'oversimplifications and stereotypes in the American versions of the Vietnam War' (Bui 2018b 207). The graphic memoir visually mediates these oversimplifications. The US 'good guys' – soldiers posing for a group photograph in their army uniforms, looking at the implied camera and readers; the 'bad guys' – 'the Việt Cộng (communist front in the South)', who are, as she explains, 'very hard to see' in a panel that obscures the depiction of a man hidden behind trees, and the South Vietnamese, who are referred to as 'bar girls and hookers, corrupt leaders, kids looking for handouts, Papa-san [and] small effete men' (Bui 2018b: 207). These verbally mediated stereotypes become visually represented through a small Vietnamese soldier standing next to an American one, who is significantly taller than him and who pets him on the head while smiling alongside other visual depictions. As such, Bui juxtaposes the distanced and misinformed context in which the Saigon Execution photograph was received by the US public with her father's understanding of it, which is shaped by his personal experiences of the war.

She then turns to the photographer himself and relates her surprise at how he 'won the Pulitzer Prize in 1969' for this photograph (Bui 2018b: 208). 'Like my father', she explains, 'Adams knew of the context of the shooting and that was absent from the photograph itself. Regretting the damage that his photograph did to the general . . . [, he] located him many years later in America. The former general, like my parents and so many immigrants, was in a state fallen from grace – working behind the counter in a pizzeria in Virginia', she further points out (Bui 2018b: 208). Jeffrey also refers to how the photograph came back to 'haunt Adams' despite the praise he received in the United States for it (2018: np). Adams himself also admitted to having received money and having been perceived as a hero for a photograph that showed two lives being destroyed

(Jeffrey 2018). The problem that Adams himself acknowledges regarding the photograph becomes reiterated by Thi's father in *The Best We Could Do*: the photographer framed Loan as a cruel murderer by capturing through his camera a particular moment that decontextualizes his act, thus exaggerating the moment of the killing and creating a neat distinction between the victim and the perpetrator of murder.

When Loan arrived in the United States, Adams was approached by the US Immigration and Nationalization Services to testify against him so as to ensure his deportation, but he refused to do so. The two became friends but Loan's past, as framed through the photograph, followed him in the United States, in the form of discrimination, insults and threats that forced him to early retirement (Jeffrey 2018). Following his death in 1998, Adams stated that 'two people died in that photograph [. . .]. The general killed the Viet Cong; I killed the general with my camera' (quoted in Jeffrey 2018: np). Adams thus underscores the ethical issues emerging from war photography that not only concern the Western gaze on and framing of the other in the context of war, but also the power of the photographic medium itself to form international opinions on a particular person that by extent may come to stand for a nation. Bui also graphically structures these implications in 'The Chessboard', at the same time as embedding them in her own family's trauma narrative.

When the narrator refers to how Adams also knew of the context of the execution, a repetition with a differentiation of the photograph occurs. A panel presents a perspective behind the photographer himself as he was about to capture the shooting, thus visually highlighting the partiality and fragmentariness of the photographic representation. The subsequent panels move temporally forward in the future of the executioner in the United States and of Bui's parents' retrospective take on the events. The photograph, Thi notes, 'is credited for turning popular opinion in America against the war [but] a lot of Americans forget that for the Vietnamese … the war continued, whether America was involved or not' (Bui 2018b: 209).

At this point, Bui chooses to repeat, for a third time, a photo/graphic take on the Saigon execution: unlike its first graphic remediation, which captures more or less the take of the actual photograph, and the second, which becomes a further-removed intra-diegetic take on the photographer himself capturing the scene, in this third instance the panel depicts a perspective that zooms in on the hand holding the gun and the executed man (Figure 3.1). As such, Loan remains outside the photographic frame. A red stain – blood – emanates from Lem's head visually capturing the passing of milliseconds from before to after the bullet

Figure 3.1 Panel from page 209 of *The Best We Could Do* by Thi Bui, copyright © 2018 Thi Bui, used by permission of Abrams ComicArts®, an imprint of ABRAMS, New York.

killed him. The red stain exceeds the panel's frame and becomes fractured by the end of the page in a depiction that implies its uncontainability not only in the panel, but also in the book itself as a material object.

The subsequent panels show the Vietnamese people's resistance to the war, and the American soldiers' return home to peace signs and flowers. Thi explains that back in Vietnam, 'there was a rocket that barely missed [her parents'] house … and killed a neighbour [,] best friends and students [were] killed in combat [, there were] frequent periods of separation [,] constant stress of money [, and a] baby that died in [her mother's] womb', all of which were followed by her own birth 'three months before South Việt Nam lost the war' (Bui 2018b: 209–10). As such, while it was the Saigon Execution photograph and the spectre of the executed man that triggered US public reaction to the war, in *The Best We Could Do* it becomes repeated, reconfigured and surrounded by other deaths in an instance of braiding to mediate private and public trauma, and to humanize impersonal and stereotypical Western perspectives on the Vietnamese people and on the war. Amidst the proliferation of death, Thi's birth seems to have marked the beginning of a more hopeful and safer future for her family, and *The Best We Could Do* stands as an artistic performance of Bui's agonistic mourning for the Vietnamese dead.

Femicide, social justice activism and photographs of the dead in *La Lucha*

Graphically reproduced photographs of the dead also have an important role in terms of intra-diegetically displaying agonistic mourning in Sack's *La Lucha*, which tells the story of the Mexican human-rights activist Lucha Castro, and of the social-justice struggles of Mexican women and their families in the border city of Juarez that constitutes 'the "necropolis" to El Paso's "metropolis"' (Davies 2020: 392).[21] As previously discussed, the contact between the United States and Mexico illustrates how 'the spaces of rights-based politics within the nation-state are predicated on the production of their exception, just as

---

[21] In their introduction to *Johannesburg: The Elusive Metropolis*, Mbembe and Sarah Nuttall write that 'there is no metropolis without a necropolis. Just as the metropolis is closely linked to monuments, artifacts, technological novelty, an architecture of light and advertising, the phantasmagoria of selling, and a cornucopia of commodities, so is it produced by what lies below the surface' (Mbembe and Nuttall 2008: 21). In using this term to define Juarez in relation to El Paso, Davies highlights how the United States benefits from the configuration of this city as a necropolis, a place where the lives of people are rendered precarious and ungrievable.

the smooth functioning of the neoliberal economy and the circulation of financial assets and commodities are predicated on the immobilization and containment of certain human bodies' (Davies 2020: 392). This division between those who do and those who do not have rights, and between those who benefit from and those who are harmed by neoliberal economy, forms excessively precarious death-worlds in the border territories of Mexico. In this sense, the geographical positioning of Juarez as an 'extraterritorial' border zone comes to deprive 'its inhabitants [of] "the right to have rights"' (Davies 2020: 389; Bourdeaux 2016).

While Davies writes that in his explorations of 'these extralegal territories' Sack does not attend as much 'to the dead' as he does 'to the living' (2020: 395), I would argue that through its thanatic photo/graphics, *La Lucha* equally attends to both by illustrating the political afterlife of the dead and their relationality with the living. In *La Lucha*, the resistance of the living is structured around and triggered by the deaths of girls and women, and it frequently becomes performed via their photographs. In this sense, the spectres of the dead seem to accompany the activist struggles and the agonistic mourning of the living. This mourning, in turn, becomes displayed in the graphic life narrative itself, which acknowledges the struggles of the living and the injustices suffered both by them and the dead.

Sack's intra-diegetic presence and role are much more marginal than Bui's in *The Best We Could Do*. His role as a mediator of the stories he collects in Juarez is clear, but his presence remains largely minor at the margins of activist women's stories, which are brought to central position to demonstrate their survival beyond victimhood, and their agency in claiming human rights, as well as truth and accountability for the girls who were killed. Apart from the introduction and the epilogue, each of *La Lucha*'s chapters is titled after the name of an activist woman Sack meets in Juarez and elsewhere. At the same time as acknowledging the living, however, as early as in the contents page of this text, the presence of the dead is also marked. An image that also becomes intra-diegetically repeated depicts a street in Juarez, wherein a billboard sign becomes foregrounded. This sign includes the missing-person photograph of Viviana Rayas, whose gaze is directed towards the reader in what seems to be a spectral demand for response-ability and address-ability. On the side of her photograph the word 'feminicidio' clarifies the context in which she disappeared in 2003 and a telephone number is also provided for those who may have seen her.

While young women often remain invisible in their precarity and disposability, Rayas' photographic portrait seems to introduce a demand for her to be seen through her returning gaze.[22] In his analysis of the 'self-reflexive layering' of the narrative, Davies refers to 'a forensic practice' that is organized by the women at Castro's Centre for the Human Rights of Women, which becomes 'oriented toward the reclamation and recovery of human rights', noting that the book attempts to 'repeat this rights-based *forensics* through its framing of activist lives' (2020: 397–8, emphasis in the original). Further to this, La Lucha foregrounds the photographs of the missing and dead girls as means of remembrance, resistance and agonistic mourning.

For instance, the titlepage of the chapter devoted to the familial narrative of Marisela Escobedo, who was killed during her struggle for the arrest of her daughter's murderer, is quite telling in relation to the activist use of photographs. In the titlepage, Marisela is facing readers while pushing a carrycot, wherein her daughter's baby lies. Most of the baby's body is covered by a poster showing a photograph of her mother with the captions 'donde esta mi mami?' (where is my mommy) and 'pena maxima' (maximum penalty) written on it (Sack 2015: 31). Prior to her own death, Marisela herself is drawn in all her activist struggles with a photograph of her daughter attached to her body. As her son, Juan, who was arrested at the US/Mexico border after having fled to escape murder, explains, his mother 'at times only wore a photo of Rubi on marches' (Sack 2015: 39). Rubi's face, as depicted in the photograph, invests the dead girl with humanity, of which she was deprived through her murder and the posthumous acts of necroviolence her body became exposed to.

Juan explains that when Rubi's boyfriend and murderer was arrested, he directed them to the place where her remains were: 'We were able to recover one third of her body, which was dumped among pig bones and set on fire. The rest of it', he continues, 'was eaten by animals [and hence] at this point we thought [the man responsible for the crime] would be charged with homicide' (Sack 2015: 36). The landscape where the bones were found becomes focalized through Juan's perspective, while a shot-reverse-shot take also illustrates his shock in the spectacle he faces, which displays the violation of Rubi's corpse. That it was dumped among pig bones, burnt and left to be devoured by animals illustrates an exaggerated form of necroviolence that Jason de León (2015) identifies in border-crossing routes from Mexico to the United States through the Arizona desert.

---

[22] El Refaie (2012) explains that one means through which readers become affectively involved in a comics life narrative is through the visual avatars' turn of their gaze to them. This is common in the thanatic photo/graphics of La Lucha and Juarez, where dead girls are repeatedly depicted looking at readers as such demanding address-ability and response-ability.

In his analysis of 'the complex intermingling of animals, insects, humans, and environmental processes that occurs once a body stops pumping blood', de León unpacks the factors that may influence the decomposition of a human corpse (2015: 73). Forms of necroviolence that become outsourced to nature and the environment of the desert, for instance, or to animals, as in Rubi's case, are linked with human or State agency or indifference.[23] In the case of the Juarez femicides, and in particular, in Rubi's murder, necroviolence is not only linked to the murderer's agency, but also to police and governmental corruption and indifference that enable this practice, which becomes a performative act that reiterates the reduction of women's lives to nothingness (Zebedúa-Yañez 2005). Rubi's photo/graphic spectre, however, resists her dehumanization. That her mother holds on to her photograph invests it with political meaning.

When Juan mentions that his sister's murderer was released by the police due to lack of evidence, Rubi's face appears in the narrative looking at readers in a smiling pose. The photograph that is digitally reproduced in its original form, in-between her graphically reproduced ones, is that of her boyfriend and murderer, Sergio Rafael, in what seems as a call for justice that renders the graphic life narrative itself a locus of 'alternative jurisdiction' (Gilmore 2001a: 134). Juan explains that the juridical decision to release the murderer 'killed Rubi for a second time' (Sack 2015: 38). Her haunting photo/graphic presence, however, repeatedly disrupts this extra-juridical violence as well as her invisibility. Her posthumous relationality, as mirrored by how her mother renders Rubi's photograph an essential part of her bodily stylization, only becomes interrupted when Marisela also dies.

As the narrative explains that the police could not touch Rubi's murderer because he was a member of a drug cartel, and that her mother had information proving his guilt and police involvement in his impunity, a long-distance shot captured in a full-page panel shows Marisela, wearing her daughter's photograph while protesting 'in front of the capitol building in Chihuahua' with other people (Sack 2015: 42). On the next page, two panels display Marisela's murder after the protest (Figure 3.2). The first one depicts her murderer holding a gun behind her. At the background there are white crosses – emblematic femicide memorials – that, as explained in the following chapter, spatially mark the continuity of femicides. In this visual arrangement, only a small part of Marisela's head is

---

[23] In the case of the Arizona desert deaths, De León (2015: 73) argues that necroviolence is 'intimately tied to Prevention Through Deterrence, territorial sovereignty, and the exceptional (i.e., killable and disposable) status the US government ascribes to undocumented border crossers'.

Figure 3.2 Page 43 of *La Lucha: The Story of Lucha Castro and Human Rights in Mexico* by John Sack, © 2015, used with permission from Verso.

visible in the frame. The second panel zooms out of this scene, presenting the events through a further removed perspective. While the white femicide memorial is still marked in the background, Marisela with her daughter's photograph attached to her body also enters the frame of the panel. As she gets shot from behind her back, her visual embodiment transforms into a white silhouette.

It is only when she dies that the photo/graphic spectre of her daughter also disappears from view with her. The ending of this mother/daughter activist struggle thus ends with the death of both women. Photographs of other dead or missing girls also appear in the fourth chapter of the book, which refers to the founding of the organization 'Justice for Our Daughters', by Norma Ledesma, whose daughter disappeared when she was fifteen years old to be found dead a month later (Sack 2015: 51). It is in this context that the billboard poster photograph of Viviana Rayas reappears, highlighting the organization's struggle for collective accountability, as the spectres of the dead girls trigger a form of activism that spans across Latin America.

In *The Force of Nonviolence*, Judith Butler wonders if there is an 'easy and efficient [way to] establish vulnerability as the foundation for a new politics', without editing 'our own aggression [...] out of the picture or project[ing] it onto others' (2020: 127–8). Subsequently, she asks about the implications of thinking about 'those who, in a condition of vulnerability, resist that very condition', and points out the problems of creating 'a class of persons who identify primarily with vulnerability', thus potentially erasing or unacknowledging their struggles (Butler 2020: 128). In her discussion on the Latin American femicides, Butler also mentions the 'Ni Una Menos movement', which 'has mobilized over a million women across Latin America (and Spain and Italy) to protest machista violence by taking to the streets' (2020: 128). She explains that Ni Una Menos has connected 'women across economic classes and different regional communities to oppose the killing of women and trans people, but also the persistence of discrimination, battery, and systemic inequality' (Butler 2020: 128).

Without hesitating to expose inter-national US and Mexican State and police responsibilities for the murders of Juarez, *La Lucha* presents those who lead precarious lives and are vulnerable to excessive violence, but who continuously resist this vulnerability. The photo/graphic presence of the missing girls displayed by Sack demonstrates what the dead can say about the limitations of human rights discourses. In addition, it illustrates how the spectres of the dead can trigger resistance against vulnerability and injustice. The photo/graphics of the third volume of *I Live Here, Juarez,* present a similar attempt. However, unlike

Sack's almost silent intra-diegetic presence, Kirschner's auto/biographical persona enters the narrative realm much more prominently and ambivalently, as also explained in previous chapters.

Picturing death in the journal entries of *Juarez*

The thanatic photo/graphics of *Juarez* differ from those of *The Best We Could Do* and *La Lucha* because photographs are digitally reproduced in their original form rather than being drawn. Furthermore, unlike *La Lucha*, this book refrains from presenting the activism triggered by the femicides. Instead, it includes journal entries describing Kirschner's familial past, as well as her reflections upon, and feelings about Juarez and its gendered crimes. By thus embedding her autobiographical subject in the narrative, like *Burma*, *Juarez* takes a risk and oscillates between re-silencing the dead and their families on the one hand and assigning responsibility for the femicides on the other.

Kirschner has collected photographs, autopsy and missing person reports, family letters and 'a bag of dirt from the cotton field' where the bodies of eight women were found, among which was that of Claudia Ivette Gonzalez, whose life story *Juarez* attempts to remediate (Kirschner 2008b: np). The items that become digitally reproduced are at times excessively worn by previous use. For instance, a missing person report for Claudia, a *maquiladora* worker and a femicide victim, seems damaged by excessive use. While it is easy to see the girl's returning gaze in a digitally reproduced portrait photograph, her characteristics remain difficult to decipher, underscoring the distance existing between herself and the implied reader in the Global North.

The autobiographical subject herself intra-diegetically sustains this division. 'The deaths are savage', she mentions, 'I don't know how to answer any of the questions the families have been asking for over ten years. Juárez, you won. I've choked. I decide to go home to Toronto. I miss my family' (Kirschner 2008b: np). Her self-consciousness about her inability to help the families and concerning her privilege as a white Western woman who visits the death-world of Juarez and then leaves it to return to the safety of her home and family become clearly presented, evoking the global divide that renders some femininities more prone to death than others. Such auto/biographical accounts, however, also run the risk of marginalizing the testimonies of the missing girls and their families.

This risk is present, for instance, in attempts made by Kirshner's autobiographical subject to forge identificatory bonds with the femicide victims through references to her own high-school experiences and familial past. Such attempts, similarly to those found in *Burma*, ignore the temporal, bio-, necro- and geo-political specificities of Juarez that render the lives of women and girls excessively precarious, disposable and vulnerable to death. The book's thanatic photo/graphics exist alongside such ambivalent representations of the autobiographical subject, the dead and their families.

The introduction to the third volume of *I Live Here* explains that Juarez is a border city with 'more than three hundred factories, or *maquiladoras* [attracting] economic migrants – people without land or jobs – from across Mexico and Central America' (Kirschner 2008b: np). It is also 'an international drug-trafficking center', where the scale of femicides has been increasing since 1993 (Kirschner 2008b: np). This peritext further suggests that it is possible, although not proven, that police and political authorities have been complicit in the ongoing impunity surrounding femicides. Similar information is also provided intra-diegetically, as previously explained, with narrative captions describing the low wages of the *maquiladora* workers, the percentage of migrants living in Juarez, the 'typical amount the Juárez drug cartel pays the police on its payroll [and the] estimated annual wholesale value of Mexico-U.S. cocaine trade' (Kirschner 2008b: np). The book, then, does not refrain from pointing to the involvement of the United States in the neo-colonial creation of the death-world of Juarez and to the responsibilities of State and police authorities on both sides of the border for the precarity that marks women's and girls' lives. The reader is made aware of this context prior to, and while encountering, the spectacle of gendered death through the book's thanatic photo/graphics. This is precisely why I perceive its approach to representing the dead in relation to the autobiographical self as marked by the ambivalence that characterizes Western gazes at distant suffering.

Juarez starts with the story of Erica. Polaroid photographs of different parts of her home, which have been taken by her mother, introduce her spectre as an absence from the domestic realm. Her mother's handwritten captions in Spanish explain what her daughter used to do in each of the rooms depicted in the photos, and what her favourite things were. Translations of the handwritten captions are typewritten and inserted in the visual realm of the photograph, illustrating a foreign intrusion in, and distance from, this familial space. In the final part of this photo-narrative, the narrator explains that when she went with Erica's mother to 'the highway where she first looked for her missing daughter [the] images became vague portraits of dirt' (Kirschner 2008b: np). The last pictures showing the mall where Erica went never to be found again become blurry, she explains, because her mother's 'hand must have been shaking' (Kirshner 2008b: np). Kirshner's comments about the quality of the photographs and the hands of Erica's mother charge these visual reproductions of absence with affective impact by underscoring the suffering of the person holding the camera. As Kirschner's narrator describes her meeting with Erica's mother, however, she abruptly turns to her own familial past and accounts for her grandmother's trauma of being a Holocaust survivor, at the same time as describing her feelings of guilt and shame that are caused by her distance from the people and the events of Juarez.[24]

In this narrative context, the thanatic photo/graphics of the Juarez femicides run the risk of becoming overshadowed by the very spectre of the Holocaust itself. As Rebecca Scherr writes, 'instead of continuing with writing about this mother and daughter, Kirshner suddenly veers off-topic and starts to write about her grandmother's weekly visits to the hairdresser, "chauffeured by [her] grandfather in his Cadillac"' (2021: 463). For Scherr, this attempt of forging identificatory bonds 'based on the notion of suffering comes off as [...] tone-deaf' (2021: 463). Subsequently to Kirschner's contribution in *Juarez*, a section written by her sister Lauren, 'Twenty Poems for Claudia', presents a similar attempt. In both examples, Scherr writes,

> The dead and missing women "disappear" (for a second time) into the first-world, white women's musings and recollections of their own girlhoods and experiences. The underlying message of the Kirschners' writing on Juárez goes something like, "we are so alike, it could have been me." This attempt at what might be called compassion or empathy comes across as clueless at best, and at worst complicit in the larger power structures that perpetuate global inequalities.
>
> Scherr 2021: 463–4

Scherr's harsh criticism of the narratives devoted to Erica and Claudia lies in how they seem to perform an act of aesthetic injustice in their attempt to forge cross-national gendered identifications which derive from and sustain the injurious implications and the human hierarchies produced within the context

---

[24] Attempting to create links between her own intergenerationally transmitted Holocaust trauma and that of women and girls experiencing the femicides of Juarez, Kirschner's narrator situates this gendered crime next to 'the historical calamity that has attracted by far the most attention from the Euro-American academy [and which is] still the primary, archetypal topic in memory studies' (Craps 2013: 72, 74). As Stef Craps writes, 'while it is undeniable that references to the Holocaust are increasingly being used to call attention to and demand recondition for other traumas, atrocities, and injustices', it is also crucial to remember that comparisons between the Holocaust and other crimes beyond the West are charged with risk and have at times served 'dubious and questionable purposes' (2013: 78).

of modernity/coloniality. This attempt has also been identified in Chapter 1, in Kirschner's take on sex work in Mae Sot. Nevertheless, as mentioned, the ambivalence of *Juarez* lies in that at the same time as performing this aesthetic injustice, by explaining how US and Mexican State and police authorities become involved in sustaining the femicides and the impunity that surrounds them, it refuses to edit external and internal State responsibilities out of the picture.

Consequently, Claudia's photo/graphic embodiments become embedded in the broader neocolonial context that has produced the *maquiladora* system and sustained the city's drug wars. In her photographs, Claudia is presented initially as a missing person, then in the context of a beauty pageant at her factory, and later, in a portrait photograph, which decontextualizes her presence as she smiles. Her precarious-life narrative then becomes interrupted by a visual excerpt from her autopsy report – a photograph of her decomposing face turned towards the reader similarly to her portrait-photograph depiction. This thanatic embodiment is accompanied by the caption 'femenina no identificada 189/01: Claudia Ivette Gonzalez' (Kirschner 2008b: np). The next page includes a written excerpt from the autopsy report in Spanish, on which attached are two poems that account for delays on behalf of the police to process the missing person claim and attempts to place the blame on Claudia by asking, for instance, if she was promiscuous. Later, a fabric-collage representation of the field where her body was found is shown, with a written excerpt from her autopsy report, translated in English, explaining that her skull was lying among scattered tufts of brown hair.

Subsequently, a fabric reproduction of her previously mentioned portrait photograph appears. In this repetition with a differentiation of her photo/graphic depiction, Claudia is no longer smiling. Rather, her look is sad, and the needles that are attached to the fabric seem as an attempt to artistically evoke her pain.[25] The book's thanatic photo/graphics thus temporally oscillate between Claudia's past and her precarious gendered humanity, and her posthumous, violated and dehumanized femininity. As such, they stage an unsettling juxtaposition between the grotesque spectacle of a violent femicide and the visual embodiment of a

---

[25] The fabric art of *Juarez* evokes the distinctly feminine and feminist tradition of femmage that emerged in the 1970s in the context of the Pattern and Decoration Movement, whereby artists mixed everyday materials with paint and fabric to put 'pressure on mainstream concepts of art that devalued ornamentation and handcraft as 'women's work'' (Chute 2010: 110). Embroidery was also used in Mexico City by a group of women, who collected 'reports of homicide [from] the newspapers each day' and embroidered them 'onto handkerchiefs that they then displayed publicly' in an act of public mourning for the murdered people (Boudeaux 2016: 406).

girl's precarity in the death-world of Juarez. In facing the reader, like the disappeared girls of *La Lucha*, Claudia's spectre also demands address-ability, response-ability, the acknowledgement of her precarious existence as well as that of her violent death.

Reconceptualizing death in 'La Tristeza'

The final section of *Juarez*, 'La Tristeza' whose title evokes the sadness caused by the femicides, was created, as previously mentioned, by Gloeckner. Gloeckner's work presents, according to Scherr (2021: 459), 'the extreme end-point of sexual violence: rape, murder and even an image that suggests necrophilia'. As such, 'La Tristeza' is charged with the same responsibility as the previous sections of *Juarez*. It is also likewise based on fabric art. Nevertheless, Gloeckner's feelings about her visit in Juarez are absent from the intra-diegetic realm, which constantly highlights her linguistic and cultural distance from the events and the people. As mentioned in Chapter 1, shifting her attention away from the *maquiladoras*, Gloeckner also sheds light on sex work and domestic abuse as core factors leading to femicide. At the same time as exposing the brutality of girls' and young women's murders, however, Gloeckner's thanatic photo/graphics also present an attempt to mediate a more positive take on *thanatos* through her intertextual references to Rainer Maria Rilke's 'The Death of the Beloved' and to an excerpt from Section Seven of Walt Whitman's 'Song of Myself'.

Rilke's 'The Death of the Beloved' forms part of his attempt to reconfigure death through his poetry. Death is depicted in the poem as a 'crossing over from the familiar to the unfamiliar [and] a smooth transition [. . .] to a sensuous place' (Sutherland 2003: 56). Such an understanding of *thanatos* becomes juxtaposed to its common perceptions as an 'absence [or] violent dislocation' (Sutherland 2003: 56). The speaker of the poem re-orients his perspective on death upon the loss of his beloved, expanding it beyond 'what all men may' know of how death takes people and 'thrusts [them] into dumb night' (quoted in Gloeckner 2008: np). Contrary to this view, the shadow world of the dead becomes reconfigured in Rilke's poem as the 'fortunately-placed, the ever-sweet' land (Gloeckner 2008: np).

The excerpt from Section Seven of Whitman's 'Song of Myself' which also becomes reproduced in 'La Tristeza' highlights the unity between an individual and the rest of the universe in a continuity of immortality: 'I am the mate and the companion of people', the speaker declares, 'all just as immortal and fathomless as myself,/ (They don't know how immortal, but I know)' (quoted in Gloeckner 2008: np). For Michael Sowder, this excerpt celebrates the 'intrinsic sublimity' of humans, whose unawareness of their immortality stems from their limited perception and knowledge of the world (2005: 86). Contrarily, an 'ecstatic knowledge of the world is born out of a new kind of seeing, hearing, and speaking, from a renewed relation to the world' (Sowder 2005: 114). The poems that Gloeckner chose to embed in the narrative of the gruesome femicides of Juarez invite readers to a meditation on death that can illustrate how one's dying can lift them from the precarity, injustice, suffering and pain of biological life.

The titlepage of 'La Tristeza' includes the beginning of the excerpt from Whitman's 'Song of Myself', which becomes completed in the narrative's final page. The lyrics: 'has anyone supposed it lucky to be born? I hasten to inform him or her it is as lucky to die and I know it' (quoted in Gloeckner 2008: np) accompany the narrative's title. In this first page, the photograph of a baby girl in a coffin, dressed in a white gown with a candy on her side for her journey to the underworld, visually complements the written excerpt from Whitman's poem. The girl seems as if peacefully sleeping. In Ancient Greek mythology, *Hypnos* (Sleep) and *Thanatos* (Death) are brothers and children of *Nyx* (Night) (Woodard 2007: 89), to which Rilke's speaker refers while mentioning the stereotypical view of death as associated with darkness, eternal night and the underworld.

Gloeckner's visual/verbal, photo/graphic arrangements of *thanatos* as similar to *hypnos* thus invite a meditation on death that enables a re-conceptualization of the dead's posthumous existence as other than connected to darkness. The visual conflation between *hypnos* and *thanatos* that is implied in this first page, reappears in the final one, which depicts a different perspective on the coffin shown at the beginning. A figurine of a sleeping angel and a portrait photograph of the girl with her gaze turned to the reader are also placed in the coffin. In-between the opening and the closing page of 'La Tristeza', gruesome scenes of murder become visually staged. In the middle of the narrative, a two-page-spread photo/graphic illustration includes Rilke's 'The Death of the Beloved' next to a doll that is nude from its waist downwards, with its underwear lying on the ground and its hands tied behind its back. The dead girl/doll's body is positioned in a field. In this narrative context, it is gendered life in and the place of Juarez that are marked by darkness and sadness. These harsh images become interrupted by Gloeckner's elegy and and they are enveloped in the thanatic photo/graphics of *hypnos* as/and *thanatos* and of Whitman's take on human immortality.

In order to depict the gruesome violation suffered by women and girls in the *mise-en-scène* realm of 'La Tristeza', Gloeckner sewed dolls and recreated crime scenes where she positioned them, photographed them, and then deconstructed these material scenes of violence and death, which only remain present as spectral photographic traces in *Juarez*. To these dolls, she attached photographs of actual people's heads, which she had previously collected from newspapers reporting on the crimes. As she explains in her interview with Jorge Flores-Olivier, 'in Mexico, pictures of the dead are frequently published, but the journalistic culture is different in the US, where we are much more "protected" from such images' (Gloeckner and Flores-Olivier 2011: np).

In addition to the dolls, the written captions that describe the visually staged crimes are characterized by ungrammaticality. For instance, an incident reported on the fourth of October is described as follows: 'A boy walking with dog to three meters behind school yard another minor located without life' (Gloeckner 2008: np). In the visual register, a doll is lying in a field and the camera angle zooms in on her face. Gloeckner explains that her 'first impulse was to "normalize" death by showing it' but that she also tried 'to find the beauty in death, which is, naturally, usually obscured by horror or grief' (Gloeckner and Flores-Olivier 2011: np). Commenting upon the language of 'La Tristeza', she explains that it 'is based off Google translation syntax, which was [her] first and primary way of understanding the daily news in Juárez' (Gloeckner and Flores-Olivier 2011: np). Gradually, she explains,

> I grew accustomed to the language patterns and strange verbiage of the translating engines, and began using similar patterns of word and phrase arrangement when I wrote. This way of writing seemed to reflect my experience as an artist trying to understand a situation – I was caught in-between, much like most people on the US-MX border, or really, in any active transitional space, geo-political or temporal.
>
> Gloeckner and Flores-Olivier 2011: np

The strange language of the translated newspaper entries, which was produced by earlier versions of Google Translate, presents the events through a defamiliarizing lens, as the dolls evoke the dehumanization of the people involved. That Gloeckner attaches to the dolls photographs of the actual people's heads makes this dehumanization problematic and the grotesqueness of the spectacle becomes underscored.

As Scherr points out, the dolls 'attest to the existence and ubiquity of discourses that dehumanize certain bodies, transforming them into human-like things that can be violently harmed and tossed away like garbage' (2021: 466). Laurike in 't Veld also notes that in graphic novels depicting genocide, dolls evoke the 'lack [...] of rationalised agency', they are associated with childhood, and they represent innocence, or lack thereof (2019: 27). Jocelyn Van Tuyl too, writes of their 'disquieting treatment [as] anthropomorphic playthings' in Holocaust literature for children (2015: 25), and Giorgio Agamben refers to 'the thousands of naked corpses' in Nazi camps, which the guards refused to name as such, but rather referred to them with the term '*figuren*, figures, dolls' (1999: 51, emphasis in the original). This dehumanization and objectification associated with dolls becomes mediated in unsettling ways through Gloeckner's thanatic photo/ graphics, which cast a defamiliarizing take on the femicides of Juarez, inviting the reader to reflect upon and to reconsider the meaning of death.

Gloria Anzaldúa writes that 'the U.S.-Mexican border *es una herida abierta* [an open wound] where the Third World grates against the first and bleeds' (1987: 3, emphasis in the original). For the 'Gringos' of the US Southwest, she continues, those living at the border are seen as aliens and transgressors irrespective of their Indian, Chicana or black racial background (Anzaldúa 1987: 3). Likewise, Wing notes that 'on the U.S. side of the border, Latina immigrants and their descendants are stereotyped as illegal lazy women, waiting to plop out babies in the United States in order to turn their undeserving children into citizens and collect welfare and health benefits or take jobs from "real" Americans' (1997: 346). Consequently, their lives are framed as incomprehensible, threatening, and thus, ungrievable. While Kirschner's and Gloeckner's narratives attempt to introduce the spectres of the dead of the Juarez femicides, they seem to reach an impasse when it comes to depicting their political life and their posthumous relationality in terms of how they trigger agonistic mourning and resistance against injustice, inequality and victimhood. Nevertheless, while looking at the spectacle of death, it is important that we, as readers, consider and remember who is complicit in its continuation, even if there is no or very little evidence regarding such complicities within the frame of representation. The same demand is made in Sacco's *Footnotes in Gaza* and *Palestine*, where the representation of the injustices suffered by Palestinian people is highlighted through the graphic staging of hybrid thanatic temporalities, via what I would describe as the slow tempo of dying, and through ambivalent displays of animal alongside human death.

Western reporting, thanatic temporalities and dead animals in *Footnotes in Gaza*

For Hillary Chute, Sacco's work stands as a 'mode of ethical awareness and an implicit critique of superficial news coverage' (2016: 201). His pages, she further points out, 'demand substantial cognitive engagement [and] encourage the eye to slow down [and] to tangle with the verbal and the visual' (Chute 2016: 201–2). The complexity and density of Sacco's pages, which detain the reader while critiquing the Western media coverage of the Israeli/Palestinian conflict (Kozol 2011) also affect the representation of death. *Footnotes*, for instance, structures hybrid thanatic temporalities that foreground the continuity of Palestinian suffering and death since 1948, while also critiquing Western news reporting related to them.

Sacco's second Palestinian graphic life narrative starts with his autobiographical alter ego in Jerusalem having drinks and discussing Palestinian deaths with other journalists as they 'shake their heads [and] roll their eyes' because such stories seem to have lost their shock effect (Sacco 2009c: 5). After this comment, he asks the waitress 'what's on the menu' (Sacco 2009c: 5). As she turns, three hands enter the panel eagerly reaching for the catalogue she is holding. In the following panel, the hands of Sacco or another reporter's avatar are shown holding the open menu. While the first two pages enlist food and drink options, the three that follow show a destroyed bus, a burning car and a tank. A caption in each of the pages explains that the menu also includes 'bombings [,] assassinations [and] incursions' (Sacco 2009c: 5).

In presenting suffering and subsequent death as menu items for the reporters to select and consume, *Footnotes* illustrates how human precarity to death in the context of the Israeli/Palestinian conflict becomes a commodity to be utilized by Western reporters. In a self-reflexive and ironic manner that further substantiates this critique on the ethics of Western reporting, Sacco's narrator also refers to how journalists have 'wrung every word they can out of the Second Intifada, they've photographed every wailing mother, quoted every lying spokes-person [and] detailed every humiliation' (Sacco 2009c: 5). In addition, he notes that they 'could file last month's story today – or last year's for that matter – and who'd know the difference' (Sacco 2009c: 5). This comment points to the potentially questionable validity of news reporting on Palestine at the same time as underscoring the repetitiveness and endurance of violent, lethal phenomena through time.

Underneath the three images/pages of the menu, which refer to bombings, assassinations and incursions, three panels supplement this information. The subsequent row of panels includes a question posed by the narrator regarding the meaning – or meaninglessness – of recording all the humiliation and suffering, and then three panels follow to show what comes after the above-listed menu items. This row stands out in the page because its background is washed in black. Visually, it shows Palestinian mothers, as well as other Jewish and

Palestinian people, mourning for their dead in three panels depicting scenes from three different funerals. 'Two dead! Five dead! 20 Dead!', Sacco writes, 'A week ago! A month ago! A year ago! 50 years ago' (Sacco 2009c: 5). This arrangement of still moments in time on the page effectively mediates the ambiguity and indecipherability of these killings.

The initial illustration of violence in the menu catalogue via a destroyed bus, a burning car and a tank, the representation of those burying and mourning for their dead, and subsequent depictions of corpses from different temporal points in the recent and the further removed past, may or may not be connected to each other. Hence, on the one hand, this page may sequentially and causally link the three events and their thanatic outcomes, while also situating them across different temporal points. On the other hand, it may present scenes from events that are not connected but have been selected and placed together through Sacco's montage practices. Thus, this page graphically displays what the narrator notes about the journalistic coverage of the Israeli/Palestinian conflict – that in putting together a news story, a reporter may have included past incidents, and no one would notice, showing how the comics form itself can provide fertile ground for critical approaches to mainstream reporting.

In his foreword to the book, Sacco explains that together with Chris Hedges he prepared a project on the 'barely noted historical episode [of the] large-scale killing of civilians in Khan Younis in 1956' for *Harper's* magazine, which was omitted by the editors without any justification, thus giving rise to *Footnotes* (Sacco 2009b: xi). This was, Sacco writes, 'seemingly the greatest massacre of Palestinians on Palestinian soil' but it received no attention in Anglophone journalistic and media outlets (2009b: xi). *Footnotes* illustrates how such events that have been blotted out from official history records 'often contain the seeds of the grief and anger that shape present-day events'(Sacco 2009b: xi). The ways in which past and present deaths become con/fused in Sacco's *Footnotes* produce hybrid temporalities and foreground the commonality and diachronicity of death in the Palestinian community. Both *Palestine* and *Footnotes* contextualize in/visible deaths in ways that demand a painstakingly slow engagement with their graphic displays. To a different extent, the spectres of the dead appear not because of the stillness of the framed time that was but no longer is, but because of how the reader is forced to slow down and to experience the tempo and continuity of Palestinian death through the years, alongside Sacco's critique of Western reporting as a valid source of information.

In *Footnotes*, the proliferation of Palestinian death that is embodied through violated and mutilated corpses in past and present times also becomes interrupted by and mirrored through the slaughter of bulls by Palestinian men in the context of 'Eid El-Adha, the feast which commemorates Abraham's readiness to sacrifice his son Ismael to Allah' (Sacco 2009c: 137). This religious feast that evokes commonalities between Judaism and Islam on the basis of their Abrahamic roots becomes an opportunity to introduce the animal as a figurative device that ambivalently mirrors Palestinian death, with Palestinian men themselves being placed in the position of the perpetrator. Bull slaughtering in the context of Eid El-Adha, whereby this form of killing becomes a ritualized spectacle attended primarily by Palestinian boys and men in the streets of Khan Younis, becomes depicted in equally shaped and distributed boxes that show animal suffering, mutilation and death.

In the incident Sacco witnesses, the size of the bull prevents the killing from being completed in a fast and clean way. A number of men become involved in efforts to immobilize the animal, to kill it and to then divide it in pieces to distribute it to different families. Ideally, Sacco notes, 'it should be killed with one stroke ... but the man wielding the knife can't manage; the bull takes a lot of hacking before it succumbs ... and even then, a couple of men have to add their weight to quell its spasms' (Sacco 2009c: 138). The difficulties encountered by these men in completing their task are also presented visually as the bull's blood flows in the streets, with children staining their hands with it and leaving handprints on the walls while laughing in the context of what becomes introduced as an entertaining game.

Different visual angles present the people and the slaughtered, mutilated animal, whose intestines are lying on the ground in this ritual that ends with a meal based on the fresh meat. While watching the slaughter, Sacco explains to a bystander, Abu Hamed, that he came to Gaza to conduct research on the 1956 massacre. Abu mentions that he was six years old then but still remembers the events. 'Half a century has passed', Sacco writes, 'and things seem just as bleak. We make sacrifice of the bulls', Abu tells him, 'and Sharon makes a sacrifice of us' (Sacco 2009c: 139). In 't Veld explains that in graphic novels of atrocity, the animal, like the doll, suggests 'lack of human, rationalised agency, [that its] performative quality is bound to a particular cultural and historical context [and that it can be] used as a means to comment on our human experiences' (2019: 41–2; LaCapra 1998). As such, 'the distance imposed by animals [...] opens up an affective space for readers to engage with atrocities' (In 't Veld 2019: 49). In *Footnotes*, the animal figure has the same potential. In being situated alongside graphically depicted Palestinian corpses and instances of slow death, the dead animal highlights the grotesqueness of thanatic spectacles that frequently remain invisible. At the same time, it demonstrates how Sacco's graphic life narrative ambivalently stages human, as well as human-animal hierarchies, in the context of the Israeli/Palestinian conflict.

As such, through its visual/verbal combinations, Sacco's work engages the reader in acts of 'ethical spectatorship' (Kozol 2011: 167). Through his Palestinian comics, Sacco takes up a task similar to that undertaken by Bui in her negotiations of the Saigon Execution photograph in the *Best We Could Do*, and, unlike Kirschner's intra-diegetic presence in *Juarez*, his autobiographical subject does not attempt to forge identificatory bonds between himself and his Palestinian interviewees. Rather, as discussed in the previous chapters, his distance from them is constantly underscored and the ethical issues and limitations of his journalistic project become foregrounded both through how the plot develops and via his comments about journalism.

The tempo of dying in *Palestine*

Further to *Footnotes*, *Palestine* includes a list accounting for Israeli and Palestinian deaths between March 1979 and July 1983, but a narrative caption visually disrupts this thanatic content, and Sacco's narrator suddenly addresses the reader: 'You get the picture, the list goes on … but let's skip it for now, lunch is being served' (Sacco 2001: 130). The cynicism indicated by this comment is caused by the commonality of death in the Palestinian context. At the same time, however, *Palestine* also refers to the myth of *terra nullius* – of Palestine as 'a land without people for the people without a land' (Sacco 2001: 12), which discursively erases the Arab population of the area, causing and justifying the perpetuation of death, and illustrating the lethal violence (Via) of the Israeli State (Kratos) that is driven by religion similarly to that also displayed in *Prometheus Bound*. Indeed, the narrator describes the ways in which since 1948 the Israeli State tried to change the demographics of the area now known as Israel by eliminating Palestinians, while the narrative zooms in on massacres, executions and instances of slow death caused by what Mbembe describes as '*infrastructural warfare*' (2019b: 82, emphasis in the original). In this sense, *Palestine* seems to be filling in the gaps of the religious script that has configured Palestine as an empty land to be inhabited by Israeli people, precisely by foregrounding the violence of the State.

The thanatic depictions of *Palestine* and *Footnotes* zoom in on mostly male dead bodies that also undergo different forms of necroviolence by being mutilated or deprived of the right to a proper burial. Sacco's ambivalent perspective on *thanatos* invites a readerly reflection upon the ethics of thanatic re-mediation. Simultaneously, it highlights the impasse his project reaches when it comes to actually alleviating Palestinian people's pain. Sacco's avatar is often shown unable to do anything other than listening to people's testimonies, something that is (also) done for his own professional gain, as he frequently reminds the reader. And while this impasse is also present in Kirschner's reflections on her failures upon her return home from Juarez, in *Palestine*, it is highlighted by a Palestinian mother's questions to Sacco, which bring to the fore her own critique of Western reporting on Palestine.

Through this woman's testimony, *Palestine* underscores the relational impact of death in the Palestinian community and brings to the fore the trauma that accompanies the translation process in the context of conflict. To foreground the injurious impact of his project on Sameh, his translator, Sacco's narrator explains that the former has 'heard every blow and humiliation described twice, once by the person telling [his or her story,] and again when it's come out of his mouth in translation' (Sacco 2001: 219). The translator's traumatization in the interviewing process becomes juxtaposed to the autobiographical subject's detached cynicism. Background information about the woman who is to be interviewed explains that she lost two of her sons and her husband in Rafah. During the interview, the reader shares the perspective of Sacco's autobiographical subject as he looks at her, at the same time as being aware of his cynical attitude.

The woman describes an attack with gas bombs in the area near her home, and her son's attempt to help people, during which he was shot in the head by an Israeli soldier. Her narrative of past deaths is mediated in *Palestine* through equally sized, densely packed square panels distributed across six pages, and divided by black gutter space.[26] The visual repetition of boxes that are identical in size, and the amount of information presented in each of them, demand slowing down and pausing in order to adequately process the different perspectives on, and the duration of death that becomes graphically presented. At the same time, they divide the time presented in the space of these pages equally, thus evoking the tempo of dying. From a long-distance take on the woman's son attempting to exit his home, to a perspective near the soldier who aims at and shoots him, to her reactions upon seeing the shooting, and the slowness of what happens next, the tempo of dying staged through this woman's

---

[26] A similar distribution of frozen moments of killing across equally sized and distributed panels on the page exists in *Footnotes*, p. 141, in its account of the slaughtering of bulls.

graphically remediated testimony illustrates the deliberate delays leading to the loss of Palestinian life.

The woman describes her family's attempt to save her son, Basel, who 'was taken to the health centre and then to the hospital in Khan Younis' (Sacco 2001: 236). As they follow him to the hospital, with her husband and other children, they get stopped by Israeli soldiers, who beat them up, break her other son's arm, throw stones at her, and force them to 'remove a burning tire from the street' (Sacco 2001: 236). In Khan Younis, they are ordered to take her son to a different hospital in Israel, but the soldiers refuse to let them use an ambulance. They said, she explains, that 'they would take him in an aircraft from a settlement near Khan Younis' (Sacco 2001: 236). On their way to the airport, the family gets stopped again at a checkpoint, they explain that they are accompanying a wounded person, but the soldiers only allow them to leave half an hour later (Figure 3.3).

In the visual register, they are shown standing, chatting and smoking, in a visual arrangement that illustrates the deliberate delay of the injured man's delivery to the airport. Upon their arrival there, the family sees no aircraft waiting for them, and they are directed elsewhere, only to realize that once again there is no one waiting for them. They then return to Khan Younis, where it is decided that Basel will be taken to the hospital by ambulance. His mother explains that the doctors ignored them and that 'only one came to ask about' her son (Sacco 2001: 237). In the visual register, the family is depicted together with the wounded man in the corridor, his mother breaks down and she is taken back to Gaza. 'My son', she tells Sacco's avatar and Sameh, 'died after 45 hours . . .. He had no medical care . . . no change of dressing . . . just oxygen' (Sacco 2001: 237). Sacco's manipulation of the comics form, in this instance, enables the graphic mediation of the delays leading to, and the slowness of, Basel's death. This slow tempo exaggerates the illustration of what happens when one is left to die in Foucault's terms, in the context of the Israeli/Palestinian conflict.

Delays occur posthumously as well, since forty hours intervened between this death and the time when Israeli soldiers informed the family that they should bury Basel without other attendees at eight o'clock in the evening. 'Soldiers were positioned around the graves . . .. We waited until 1 a.m. in the rain. They brought us the body and gave us 15 minutes to wash him', his mother mentions (Sacco 2001: 237–8). The rain becomes visually marked in its juxtaposition to the dark background of the graveyard where the family is standing, foregrounding its suffering, while two panels depict the actual burial, which occurred in a rush upon Israeli orders, depriving the family of the opportunity to pay its respect to

Figure 3.3 Panels from page 237 of *Palestine* by Joe Sacco, © 2001, used with permission from Fantagraphics.

Basel through required burial rituals. In this sense, these affectively charged visual images work in juxtaposition, and deconstructively, in relation to the indifference and cynicism of Sacco's narrator/the Western reporter.

Returning from the artistically recreated past to the narrative present with the completion of this part of the testimony, the reader shares Sacco's perspective as he looks at his translator, who is sitting alongside the testifying woman and her two sons. Sacco's positionality is only implied by the perspective visually mediated in this panel, which in its temporal move to the present also becomes different in size from the previous ones, rupturing the tempo that was visually presented prior to it. The faces of the people in this image charge the testimony that has been delivered with affective impact. Subsequently, the narrative zooms in on the woman's face, when she explains how her younger son died, after the death of her uncle's son. As we temporally move to the past again, the size and arrangement of panels on the following pages becomes identical to the one previously described in order to stage, yet again, the same tempo of slow death.

The second part of the woman's testimony is very similar to the first one. Her younger son got shot 'five times . . . in the forehead, the neck, the arm, the heart, and the chest', but was still alive after a clash at his school (Sacco 2001: 238). He was taken by Israeli soldiers to 'an army hospital in Israel' and because of delays on the road, his family was only able to see him very late in the afternoon (Sacco 2001: 238). On the next day, Arab doctors instructed the family to not remove him because 'he would be dead soon [and] the road was bad' and would thus cause further harm if the injured boy were to be taken to a different hospital (Sacco 2001: 240). Delays after this death also occurred, with his body arriving at home again late at night for his burial. 'We wanted to bury him next to his brother', his mother explains, 'but the soldiers refused . . . until we phoned a human rights organization in Jerusalem', which intervened, and permission was granted (Sacco 2001: 240). The body was given to the family at one o'clock after midnight, and they were only allowed five minutes to wash it. The woman explains that she had forgotten 'some of the material to cover his body' at home, but the soldiers refused to let her get it and laughed at her (Sacco 2001: 241). The reader's perspective shifts at this point, and we share her point of view, which is only implied as she is positioned outside the panel, looking at the Israeli soldiers as they laugh at her and the implied reader. The following panel depicts the graves of her two sons next to each other.

Continuing, she relates that seven months after her son's death, she lost her husband too because he had a heart condition but was not allowed to go to Egypt for treatment. Sameh then explains, crying as he translates the woman's testimony, that as a result, 'he died on the road' (Sacco 2001: 241). At this point, the narrative frame zooms in on Sameh's face, reminding the reader of how the translator articulates the voice of the Palestinian testifying subject and of how he becomes wounded through this process. As such, at the same time as displaying the spectacle of slow death and subsequent acts of necroviolence, this excerpt invites the reader to reflect upon the traumatization of the translator in the process of Sacco's preparation of a comic book on Palestinian suffering – a commodity targeting Western readers.

The ways in which the Palestinian male body becomes violated, and the ritual of the burial becomes disrupted by Israeli soldiers, constitute a form of necroviolence that reflects a social reality whereby Palestinian lives are deemed disposable and ungrievable.[27] At this instance, the ungrievability of the woman's sons becomes heightened by how they are deprived of proper burial during daytime. This prohibition seems to aim at insulting the family and the dead, and at preventing acts of resistance and protest that might become triggered in the context of a funeral, at the same time as rendering this unjust death invisible.[28] By exposing these deaths and the factors leading to them, and by forcing the reader to slow down in their engagement with them, *Palestine* introduces pre- and posthumous forms of violence as equally traumatic and painful, memorializing human loss and performing an ambivalent act of agonistic mourning that is nevertheless caught within the human hierarchies that are geographically distributed in the context of modernity/coloniality.

Indeed, in contrast to the affective impact this thanatic testimony has had on the Palestinian participants of the meeting, Sacco's avatar seems detached and is in a rush to attend his next interview. Sameh is drawn with tears in his eyes and a handkerchief in his hands and Sacco's avatar asks him to thank this woman and to tell her that 'we've got to get going' (Sacco 2001: 242). However, she forces him to stop, and repeatedly asks for substantial support. 'She's not finished', Sacco's

---

[27] Antonious C. G. M. Robben writes that 'the political practice of obstructing funerary rituals prevents people from coming to terms with their dead and from reconciling eventually with their opponents' (2004b: 145).

[28] For an analysis of Palestinian burial rituals see Hamdan Taha (2018). For the violation of the Palestinian dead and the destruction/erasure of Palestinian cemeteries by Israeli authorities see Randa May Wahbe (2020). For Honaida Ghanim, thanatopower, which supplements biopwer, denotes the 'passage from calculating life to calculating death, from managing life to managing death, and from the politicization of life to the politicization of death' (2008: 68). The excerpt analysed above from *Palestine* denotes precisely how death becomes managed by the Israeli State.

narrator mentions (Sacco 2001: 242). 'Okay, we've had a thorough run-through . . . we've shot her boys, we've chased their bodies from hospital to hospital, we've buried them in the middle of the night, their portraits have been staring down at us, and we've even fingered her son Ahmed's blood-stained school pack', the narrator mentions, 'Now what?' (Sacco 2001: 242). Sameh explains to him that 'she wants to know how talking to you is going to help her. We don't want money, she says, we want our land, our humanity. Aren't we people too?' (Sacco 2001: 242). Sacco's avatar loses his cynicism and detachment as all eyes are now turned to him demanding answers. At this point, his face shows anxiety and nervousness, even if his eyes are hidden behind his glasses.

When he responds that most people in Germany, for instance, 'support the Palestinian cause', the woman replies that they do so 'with words only [. . .,] how are words going to change things? She says she wants to see action', Sameh explains (Sacco 2001: 243). Sacco's avatar does not know how to respond. Visually, he is positioned at a distance from the Palestinians as his body faces them, while he is awkwardly looking for his shoes, refraining from sustaining eye contact with them. If seen as metonymically embodying the Western reporter visiting a precarious place to collect stories of trauma and death that will then raise his professional profile, as was the case with Adams and the Saigon Execution photograph, Sacco's graphic depiction at this instance foregrounds the ethics of his positionality, the limitations of his agency, and the impasse his activist journalism reaches. Like Alan Kurdi's photograph, there is not much *Palestine* and *Footnotes* can do in terms of influencing political decisions. However, through their contextualized depictions of the slow tempo of dying, and their hybrid thanatic temporalities, they render visible and audible those who have been deprived of channels via which to share their testimonies, thus unsettling mono-dimensional Western perspectives on the Israeli/Palestinian conflict.

Coda

Thanatic spectres in graphic life narrative, then, have important rhetorical potential. If 'death is regarded as a disturbance of the social order, a laceration of the social body, and a gap in social and family networks' (Robben 2004a: 13), in their thanatic expositions, *The Best We Could Do*, *Juarez*, *La Lucha*, *Footnotes* and *Palestine* foreground the ways in which such ruptures result from neo-colonialism, neoliberal capitalism, modernity/coloniality, and settler colonialism, all of which produce literal and metaphorical factories of death. Via their thanatic spectacles, these texts foreground people's precarity and ungrievability, and they illustrate the forms of necroviolence that become enabled within these geo-, bio- and necro-political contexts.

This chapter has illustrated how graphic life narrative can contextualize spectacles of death as shown through the thanatic photo/graphics of *The Best We Could Do*, *La Lucha* and *Juarez*. It has also shown how thanatic temporalities and tempos underscore the brutality and diachronicity of death in Sacco's *Palestine* and *Footnotes*, and it has discussed the aesthetic and affective impact of dolls and animals in thanatic graphic life narrative. The silences, erasures and injustices that sometimes mark these texts evoke the power relations within which they are produced. By inviting the reader to a critical and affectively charged meditation on death, through their nuanced thanatic representations, these texts ask that we consider what remains unsaid, and what such silences denote about the limitations of human rights discourses, and about the ethics of the Western gaze on and framing of the dead and living other.

4

Graphic topopoetics and spatial (in)justice

Further to the gendered dimensions of human suffering thus far explored, and the rhetorical implications of *thanatos*, in this chapter I examine how space, place, and the environment become connected to, reflect or sustain injustice. I demonstrate that when witnessing the human rights violations suffered by othered people in graphic life narrative, investigating depictions of space and place can nuance our understanding of how social injustices, which are always-already spatial, become distributed.[1] To substantiate this argument, I explore the contributions to meaning formation that may lie in the study of the (back)ground in graphic displays of othered people's human rights violations. I use the term graphic topopoetics to refer to the depictions of space, place, and the environment, as well as to the analytical approach that can unpack their rhetorical potential when it comes to aesthetically enriching, countering and critiquing the spatial and social injustices presented in selected print and online graphic life narratives.

The spatial turn and spatial injustice in graphic life narrative

Contrary to the 'human figure', on which comics and life narrative scholarship tends to focus, the ground, as Rebecca Scherr notes, 'is far too often overlooked as a crucial dimension of the politics of graphic representations of pain and suffering' (2020: 475). Like her, in this chapter, I am interested in 'what it means to widen the focus to include in our discussions of representational politics the ground as much as we do the figure' (Scherr 2020: 475). Achille Mbembe, for

---

[1] Robert Sack distinguishes between space and place in terms of human (un)familiarity with and experience of them. Place, he writes, 'implies space, and [a] home is a place in space. Space is a property of the natural world, but it can be experienced. From the perspective of experience, place differs from space in terms of familiarity and time. A place requires human agency, and it is something that may take time to know' (1597: 16; see also Tuan 1977; Kemal 2020).

example, writes of 'infrastructural warfare', a core component of people's necropolitical control, as being largely based on the destruction of the ground (2019b: 82). Likewise, Scherr describes the contemporary era as one of 'highly mechanized warfare and environmental disaster', arguing that it is therefore 'crucial to begin to recognize the ground as part of the whole picture of suffering, and to begin to map representational methods for including the ground within the scope of humanitarian witnessing' (2020: 476). Aligning my work alongside hers, in this chapter, I investigate how 'graphic novelists represent the built environment and the literal landscape more broadly' to unpack the ways in which this 'can add depth and fullness to how we understand the nature of political violence and loss' (Scherr 2020: 476).

Despite the predominant focus on the human as opposed to the spatial, the Latin root of the former, *humus* (earth), denotes their very connectedness to the ground (Lebech 2004), which also becomes reflected in the divine creation of man from clay in religious discourse. But the earth, or the ground, as described by Scherr, has also been systematically used as means of violence, exclusion, forced containment, and mental as well as physical torture.[2] As Henri Lefebvre writes, it serves 'as a tool of thought and of action; [but] also [as] a means of control, and hence of domination, [and] of power' (1991: 26). In *Theogony*, for example, this use of Gaea (goddess Earth) symbolizes the first divine sovereign's (impossible) attempt to stop his succession, as well as the progress and development of both the divine and the worldly realms. Here, I use the mythical narrative of Gaea as a metonymic device that embodies different manifestations of sovereign power and violence that are enacted through, reflected in, or suffered by the earth. Gaea, who came into being after Chaos (dark void), produced a multitude of offspring with Uranus (the sky, or heavens), but because the latter was afraid they would supersede him, he (ineffectively) tried to keep them imprisoned 'within [her] depths' (Woodard 2007: 86). The last sovereign deity in Ancient Greek mythology, Zeus, punished Sisyphus for having twice escaped death with tricks, by having him eternally carrying a rock up a hill in the underworld of Hades. Prometheus, as also mentioned in Chapter 2, was imprisoned underneath the earth's surface, and subsequently tied to a rock on Mount Caucasus, so that an eagle would continuously eat his liver. The earth, therefore, or the ground, constitutes, in these mythical narratives, a means

---

[2] In Chapters 1 and 2, for instance, the space of the prison, and the feeling of entrapment in small rooms, are shown to add to the detained people's suffering and mental breakdown.

through which the violence of absolute sovereignty becomes enacted and sustained.

This violence is also reflected in the Euro-American (neo-)colonial exploitation of the earth and its resources as well as in ecocides across Africa and Latin America that have transformed cities into ruins, minimizing possibilities for the sustenance of human life there (Crook et al. 2018; Mbembe 2019a). Further to ecological destruction, in the context of the so-called refugee crisis, we are increasingly witnessing Western sovereign States' use of space as a form of violence against unwanted refugee and asylum seeker populations attempting to enter their borders and jurisdictions. As Seyla Benhabib writes, 'the use of territorial exclusion to deny rights' has come to constitute 'one of the reflex mechanisms of the modern state imaginary', increasingly threatening to put an end to the 1951 Refugee Convention (2020: 77).[3] In this chapter, I examine how spatial injustices occur in the context of the industrialization of Juarez, and in that of the Sri Lankan and the Israeli/Palestinian conflicts. Such injustices as those occurring in Juarez, for instance, may take the form of environmental destruction that is caused by the disconnection between the (Western) Man and the earthly, and the perception of the former as superior both to other species and to the earth itself.[4] They also derive from the human treatment of the earth as a commodity that is available for consumption and exploitation. Further to this form of spatial injustice, in this chapter I look into how space becomes a tool that sustains, produces or suffers violence, which is directly or indirectly targeted against othered people in contexts of refugee detention and asylum-seeking sea crossings from Africa and Asia to Europe and Australia.

Ali Madanipour et al. write that 'dichotomizing space and society has its roots in the Cartesian dualism of mind and body, [but] rather than being detached, abstract and neutral, space and time are integral parts of human experience,

---

[3] 'The 1951 Refugee Convention and its 1967 Protocol are the main legal documents governing the movement of refugee and asylum seekers across international borders' (Benhabib 2020: 75). With the contemporary increase 'of displaced persons seeking refuge [. . .], states have resorted to measures to circumvent their obligations under the Convention' (Benhabib 2020: 75). The ways in which this is done are unpacked in the following sections of this chapter and in Chapter 5.

[4] In 'Decolonizing the Anthropocene: The Mytho-Politics of Human Mastery', Karsten A. Schulz explains how Ancient Greek mythology initiated the naturalization 'of human mastery' over nature 'within western cultural imaginaries' (2017: np). He also refers to 'the Judeo-Christian religious tradition [as] the second mythical tradition that played a decisive role in legitimising the human dominion over nature. Decreed by divine providence,' he writes, '"Man" was given *dominium terrae*, the cultural mandate to rule over God's creation. Occasionally this mandate was interpreted in the sense of a paternalistic stewardship, while in other cases it was taken quite literally as a divine decree to subdue the earth and all living things' (Schulz 2017: np).

finding meaning through social relations' (2022: 810). The division between the *humus* and human, a result of perspectives on the earth that conceptualize it as an exploitable means for profit, has had severe consequences on different forms of life across the globe, but these have not been evenly distributed across the Global North and the Global South (Mbembe 2019a). Hence, not looking at and into space, place, and the environment keeps aspects of the nature of this injustice unseen. Contrarily, 'a relational understanding of space means that [it] is not a passive container' (Madanipour et al. 2022: 810). Instead, it demonstrates that 'social processes are inherently spatial, and spatial processes are necessarily social' (Madanipour et al. 2022: 810).[5] In addition, and importantly, when investigated in graphic life narratives depicting human suffering, it can widen 'the empathic context in which we as readers can regard suffering – both the suffering of humans and the suffering of the larger environment' (Scherr 2020: 478).

Attention to space and place in graphic life narrative would then aim at bringing to the fore their connectedness to human experiences of suffering on the one hand, and the ways in which the earth itself suffers on the other. It would also seek to identify instances where locations such as the sea, which have been increasingly reconfigured into undocumented border crossers' lethal enemies in the context of the refugee crisis, can be represented as other than deadly. The questions I seek to explore in this chapter are therefore as follows: How is the ground, as defined by Scherr, drawn and what does the way it is drawn say in relation to spatial injustice and its uneven distribution across the Global North and the Global South? To what extent do graphic life narratives present defamiliarizing, decolonized takes on spaces that have been conventionally charged with negative connotations? How do graphic metaphors nuance depictions of spatial injustice? How can the comics form enable the writing and drawing of (neo-)colonial histories on and through space? If the spatial has been divided from the social, similarly to how reason has been divided from emotion, and word from image, how can comics politically unsettle these divisions? What would the implications of such a fusion be in relation to depictions of violence inflicted against the West's others and the spaces they navigate?

In *Disaster Drawn: Visual Witness, Comics, and Documentary Form*, Hillary Chute (2016) writes of the ways in which representations of traumatic history

---

[5] The division between the 'First', the 'Second' and the 'Third World' is also in itself quite telling in relation to how global geopolitical relations of domination have been spatially established and sustained (Dodds 2007).

can be nuanced when carried out through comics because, in being drawn, this form can account for what this history looks and feels like. For her, the sensory and the visual are of equal importance to the pressure comics place 'on traditional notions of chronology, linearity, and causality [via their] spatial syntax [when it comes to] the form's ethics and aesthetics' (Chute 2016: 4). In this chapter, I am interested in how (neo-)colonial histories, as written on, or inextricably linked to, space appear in graphic life narratives, and in decolonial reading acts, to complicate and enrich contemporary testimonies of suffering.

I examine how the landscapes of Juarez, Manus Island, Sri Lanka and Palestine become drawn in selected graphic life narratives in ways that evoke the spatial dimensions of social injustice in the following ways: firstly, by establishing causal links between space, place and human precarity and vulnerability to violence; secondly, by introducing injustice as unequally distributed across different regions; and thirdly, by illustrating how modernity/coloniality alongside global capitalism on the one hand, and settler colonialism on the other, wound the earth itself. I explore these issues by closely reading excerpts from 'La Tristeza' by Phoebe Gloeckner, *La Lucha: The Story of Lucha Castro and Human Rights in Mexico* by Jon Sack, 'Manus Island and the Death Angel' by Eaten Fish, *Vanni: A Family's Struggle through the Sri Lankan Conflict* by Benjamin Dix and Lindsay Pollock and *Palestine* by Joe Sacco. I also discuss manifestations of injustice in the context of asylum detention and border crossings in Australia and Europe, through a focus on island topographies, as well as sea and wall depictions in the aforementioned webcomic by Eaten Fish, in Safdar Ahmed's 'Villawood' and 'Affective States', Gabi Froden's 'An Empty Promise' and Francesca Sanna's *The Journey*. I argue that spatial representations in these online and print graphic life narratives can nuance our understanding of the shape that colonial violence against the West's others is presently taking, by linking it to its past versions.

As mentioned in the introduction to this chapter, I refer to depictions of space, place, and the environment in graphic life narrative and to my analytical approach to them with the term graphic topopoetics. The term 'topopoetics', which Tim Cresswell introduces in his study of Elizabeth Bishop's poetry, 'combines *topos* (place) with poetics (more or less "making") [rendering] poetry [...] a kind of place making' (2017: 114, emphasis in the original). Topopoetics is about 'the ways poems negotiate place as an idea, often through the space of the poem itself. It is about place in poems more than poems about place' (Cresswell 2017: 114). Borrowing this term for my own analysis of the *topos* that is made through the visual/verbal form of comics, I propose its displacement from the study of poetry and its emplacement in the study of online and print graphic life narrative.

My use of poetics in the sense of making refers to the *topos* that is made in the graphic life narrative itself in the artistic creation process, and to that which is (re-)created in the reading and meaning formation process. As such, it encompasses both artistic and readerly formations of space and place. In the following sections, I unpack the implications of reading space, place, and the environment in relation to human rights violations and injustices inflicted against othered people at the US/Mexico border, in the Sri Lankan and the Israeli/Palestinian conflicts, as well as in the context of border control and irregular migration in Australia and Europe.

Mapping femicide: zooming out of, and in on, the gendered crimes of Juarez

Gloeckner's 'La Tristeza' starts with a cartography of the femicides that have been ravaging Juarez.[6] A double-page spread (Figures 4.1a and 4.1b) includes a map of the border area of Juarez/El Paso. The map, as evidenced in these two pages, is linked to the 'Department of the Treasury U.S. Customs Service' and the 'United States Department of Interior Geological Survey' (Gloeckner 2008: np). It includes the names of the different '*colonias*' (neighbourhoods) and other urban areas of Juarez, Rio Grande, the river that separates Mexico from the United States, and pink pins inscribed with a red 'x' are spread across the space that is cartographically depicted. In El Paso there is one pin, and in Juarez there are forty-nine. A note explains that the pins stand for the 'approximate distribution of female corpses located from June 1990 to December 2000' (Gloeckner 2008: np). Each 'x' equals more or less 'ten bodies' per area of approximately twenty-five kilometres (Gloeckner 2008: np). This distant spatial representation of the Juarez femicides maps their uneven regional distribution without displaying the bodies of the dead, or delving into the particularities of the crimes, which become introduced in the subsequent pages.[7] Femicides are thus initially introduced in this graphic novella as inextricably linked to the geographical location of Juarez at the US/Mexico border.

---

[6] The femicides are also discussed in Chapters 1 and 3 of this monograph.
[7] As explained in Chapter 3, this is one of the reasons why Dominic Davies describes Juarez as a 'necropolis' to its Western 'metropolis', El Paso (2020: 392).

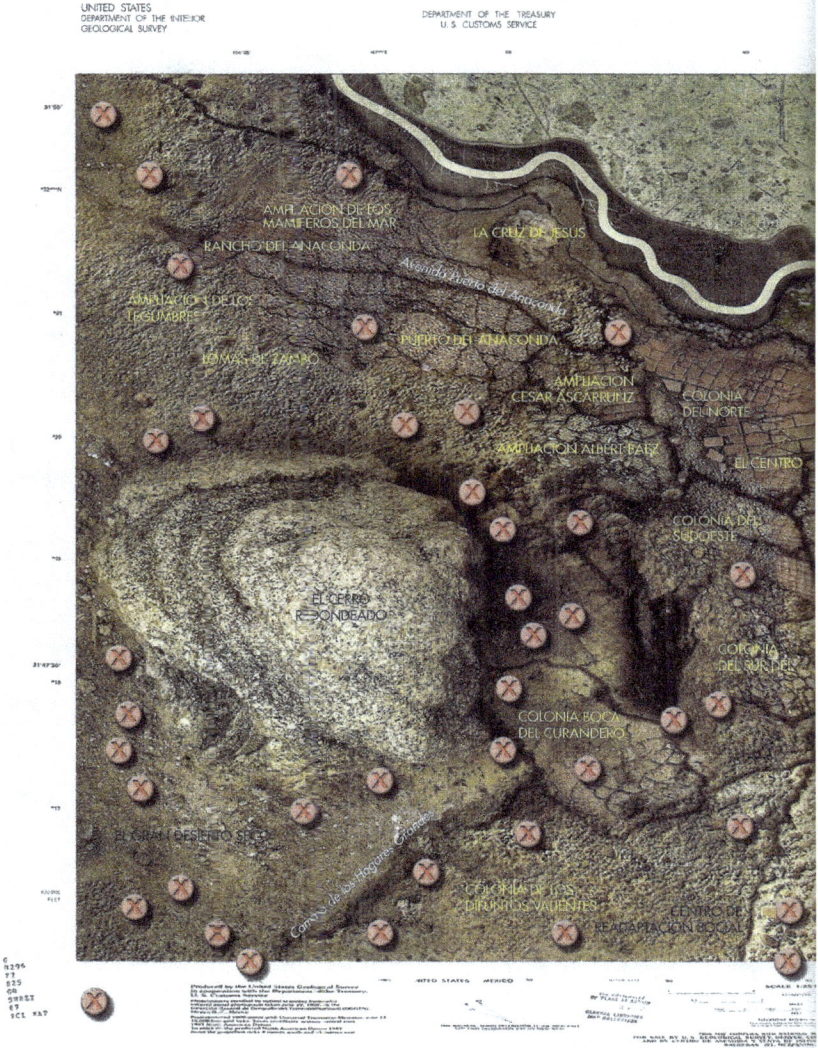

Figure 4.1a Map (part 1, left) from 'La Tristeza' by Phoebe Gloeckner, © 2008, used with permission from Phoebe Gloeckner.

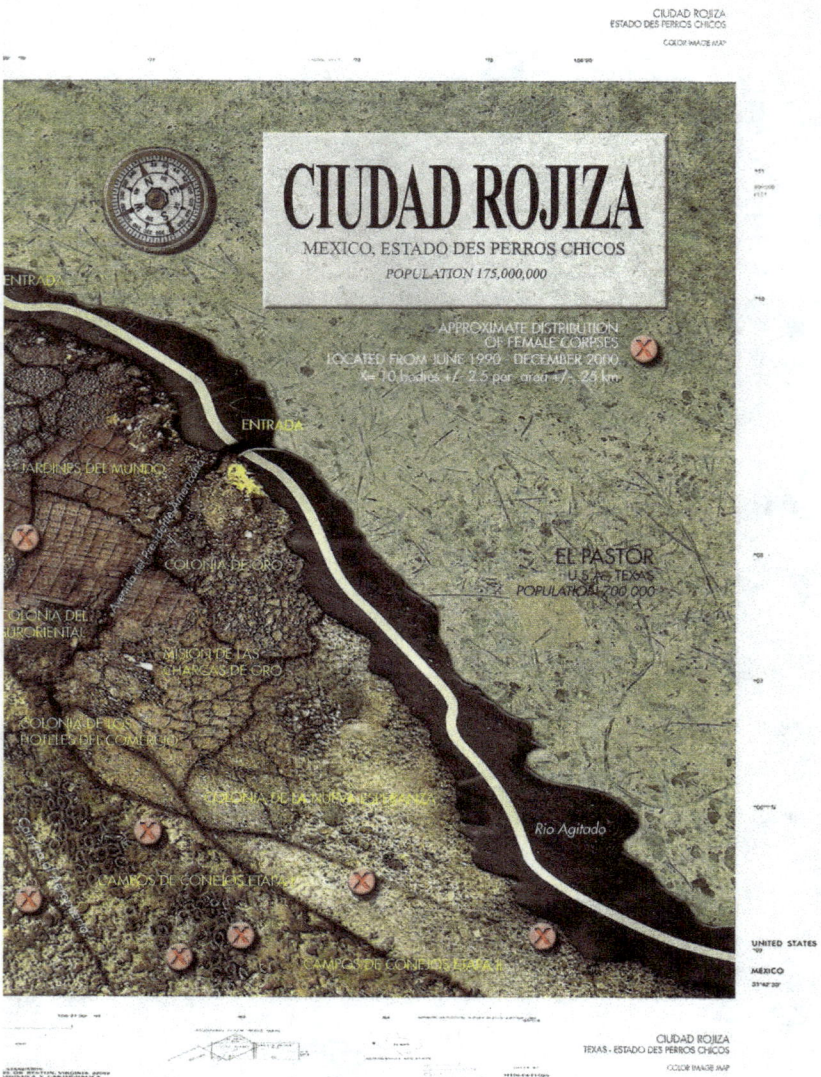

Figure 4.1b Map (part 2, right) from 'La Tristeza' by Phoebe Gloeckner, © 2008, used with permission from Phoebe Gloeckner.

Further to illustrating the uneven occurrence of gendered crimes across the two sides of the border, Gloeckner also intervenes in the map to change toponyms. Ciudad Juarez is renamed as 'Ciudad Rojiza' (the reddish city) given the dominance therein of the pink pins – and more suggestively, of blood – which stand for female deaths; Mexico is referred to as the 'Estado des Perros Chicos' (state of small dogs); El Paso is renamed 'El Pastor' (the pastor); and Rio Grande becomes 'Rio Agitado' (the agitated, or the shaken river), and it is marked with two 'entradas' (entry points) (Gloeckner 2008: np). In being distant, this first representation of the Juarez femicides hides their victims and the specificities of the crimes under symbols and numbers scattered on the map. By describing Mexico as the state of small dogs, this cartographic arrangement also mediates a dehumanizing view on the local population, while in re-configuring Rio Grande as the agitated or the shaken river, it highlights the precarity of its crossing. By introducing El Paso as 'the pastor', the map also implicitly stages a hierarchical link/division between 'the shepherd' city and the state of dogs – between El Paso and Mexico.

This divisive link also reflects the dehumanization that has been caused and sustained through centuries of Western imperial interventions in Mexico, and through modernity/coloniality as well as global capitalism, which have reconfigured the space of Juarez and the lives of Mexican workers as disposable means of exploitation. Because of its positioning at the border, after the NAFTA agreements and the creation of *maquiladoras*, Juarez has attracted poor migrant populations that temporarily or permanently live in *colonias* around factories in very bad conditions (Scherr 2021; Núñez-Mchiri 2012). The environmental pollution and health hazards caused by the factories, as well as the dire living conditions of the *colonias*, constitute an outcome of the economic and biopolitical relationship between the United States and its neighbour, which increases gendered precarity and vulnerability to violence (Wing 1997). They also constitute an example of how spatial injustice becomes manifested in the city of Juarez.[8]

Contrary to the distant depiction of femicides at the beginning of 'La Tristeza', once the page is turned, the narrative zooms in on the gruesome specificities of some of the crimes pinned on the map. Seven out of the ten vignettes that restage femicides in detail provide information about the exact location where each depicted crime was carried out, and they introduce toponyms as

[8] For further details about the impact of the NAFTA agreements on the lives of the local people see Chapters 1 and 3.

parts of the headings to corresponding narrative captions. 'Campos de Conejos Etapa I', 'Colonia del Norte', 'Rancho del Anaconda', 'Ampliación Albert Baez', 'Lomas de Zambo' and 'Colonia de los Difuntos Valientes' (Gloeckner 2008: np) are some of the places named on the map, which then become repeated in the *mise-en-scène* realm to spatially locate some of the femicides. The narrative then zooms in on domestic spaces, barren open fields and streets filled with rubbish, where the bodies of girls and women were found dead and gruesomely violated. As such, it depicts a *topos* that is deteriorating due to urbanization, lack of infrastructure, and environmental pollution, as inextricably linked to female life that is deteriorating due to (neo-)colonial violence that produces and sustains gendered precarity.[9] The toponyms that appear on the map thus become presented from a different angle as the narrative focuses on the urban areas that were further removed and marked by pink pins in their initial cartographic depiction. As such, the distant and distancing take on the crimes and the spaces where they occur, which is produced through the map, becomes undone.

For Scherr, the map that opens 'La Tristeza' underscores 'the place-specific (but not economic) dimension of these murders' (2021: 459). By renaming places, Gloeckner also charges the official script that becomes cartographically narrated with 'racial and gender irony' (Scherr 2021: 461).[10] Indeed, by transforming the map into a palimpsest in literally writing over it, the artist intervenes in the official US production of space to reinstate the racialized and gendered precarities it produces, and the (neo-)colonial links existing between the two sides of the US/Mexico border. Hence, her work foregrounds 'the suppressed, gendered dimensions of official imagery and discourse' (Scherr 2021: 461), which lead to the dehumanization of border residents and the devaluation of their lives that is both produced and sustained through space. In extra-territorializing manufacturing through the NAFTA agreements and territorializing it in Juarez, where US environmental and employment laws do not apply (Wing 1997), the United States treats both the space and the people of

---

[9] For the analysis of colonial gendered violence, see Introduction and Chapter 1 in this monograph.

[10] Mapping and cartography have been inextricably linked to past Western imperial projects. Nilanjana Mukherjee writes that 'colonial cartography involved two stages of acting upon space: first, the erasure of pre-existing indigenous space to recast it in universal terms, and second, inscribing universal space with power to outline a material place in the colonial consciousness' (2011: 429). Drawing from the work of Henry Lefebvre, Sarah Luria also refers to 'the means by which the capitalist state redefines space to achieve its own interests' (2017: 149). In its visuality, the comics form enables nuanced uses of maps. I read Gloeckner's ironic re-naming as a creative act that exposes the spatial injustices and the wounds of modernity/coloniality in Juarez at the same time as critiquing the human hierarchies emerging from the (neo-)colonial production of this border space.

Juarez as disposable, exploitable means, and it is precisely in this context that the system of the *colonias* emerges.[11]

Guillermina Gina Núñez-Mchiri describes *colonias* as 'nonincorporated communities located on the rims of larger urban centers throughout the US-Mexico border' (2012: 109). These peripheral areas are useful 'for understanding the inequities associated with life in the margins' and they illustrate 'how urban cores and peripheries are engaged in both mutually beneficial and exploitive relationships of power' (Núñez-Mchiri 2012: 109, 111). They frequently 'lack basic infrastructure and public services' and the rights as well as the humanity of their residents 'are often adversely affected by economic depression, social isolation, political alienation, and repression' (Núñez-Mchiri 2012: 11). Their development is caused and sustained by 'historical, political, and economic forces influencing human migration and immigrant population settlement' (Núñez-Mchiri 2012: 111, 112). These forces include the creation of the *maquiladoras* in Juarez, and the geographical positioning of the city at the border. In 'La Tristeza', the violation of people's human rights in the *colonias* of Juarez is linked to domestic gendered abuse.

In an interview with Whitney Joiner, Gloeckner describes one of her visits to Juarez, when she met the family of one of the murdered girls, and saw their home and the landscape wherein it was positioned. She mentions that 'twelve people [were] living in a shanty made of building pallets and tarpaper [and that] one room divided by a curtain [had] three large beds' (Gloeckner and Joiner 2015: np). She also explains that during her first visit in Juarez in 2003, 'no one had building materials, no running water, no plumbing, no sewage treatment, no garbage pickup, so there was trash everywhere' (Gloeckner and Joiner 2015: np). While these aspects of space and place are absent from the map, which zooms out of the *topos* of Juarez, they become introduced in Gloeckner's graphic crime vignettes, which zoom in on it. Small, almost claustrophobic domestic spaces, deteriorating buildings and barren landscapes become filled with female bodies alongside broken objects, rubbish and dirt.

For Núñez-Mchiri (2012: 109), 'the places and spaces in which people live and build community reveal the consequences of [...] structural violence associated

---

[11] This system is a manifestation of environmental injustice, which denotes 'the disproportionate exposure of communities of color and the poor to pollution, and its concomitant effects on health and environment, as well as the unequal environmental protection and environmental quality provided through laws, regulations, governmental programs, enforcement, and policies' (Maantay 2002: 161).

with poverty, marginalization, and underdevelopment'. Modernity/coloniality and capitalism have reconfigured the space of Juarez in such ways so as to set within and through it different forms of structural violence and injustice, which have severely impacted gender roles and relations, leading to the devaluation of female lives both within the domestic domain and outside it.[12] As Elva Fabiola Orozco aptly phrases it, the current 'spatial arrangement [of the city] reinforces the dehumanization of racialized, gendered, and sexualized peoples and "reduces [them] to being one more cog in an enormous production machine: the ultra-capitalist city"' (Orozco 2019: 142; González Rodríguez 2012; Valencia 2014).

As it stands, Juarez 'is built to sustain the assembly plant, foreign investment, and international trade instead of ordinary residents, just as [...] the former Latin American colonies' served the interests of their colonizers rather than those of their indigenous inhabitants (Orozco 2019: 142). It is precisely for this reason that 'the majority of those living in slums [around the *maquiladoras*] bear the mark of the coloniality of power and gender, which justifies their confinement in such spaces' (Orozco 2019: 141–2). The value of the graphic topopoetics of 'La Tristeza' lies in how they introduce femicides as a spatially induced and sustained injustice that is very much influenced by the border positioning of Juarez and becomes enabled by the structural violence of its *colonias*, which create the preconditions for domestic abuse.

Sack's *La Lucha* also inscribes the city's femicides spatially. In its displays of feminist activist struggles in demand for accountability for the murders, the (back)ground of the city has important rhetorical function because it is precisely through space that the memorialization of the dead occurs. The large white crosses that stand in memory of the victims across the city become presented in the narrative alongside women's struggles for justice. The writing of activist life and gendered death on space in *La Lucha* also takes the form of political graffiti inscribed on walls in demand for accountability and retribution for the murdered women and girls (Sack 2015). Lisa K. Waldner and Betty A. Dobratz explain that 'engaging in graffiti writing may be motivated by feeling excluded from the political process or that politics as usual (i.e., institutionalized politics) will not bring about change' (2013: 377). In demanding justice for the femicide victims, graffiti in *La Lucha* illustrates how space can be politicized, similarly to the white crosses, which embody the metaphorical writing of the victims' commemoration on space.

---

[12] For a more in-depth analysis of the impact of the coloniality of gender in Latin America, Mexico and Juarez, see Chapter 1.

When Marisela Escobedo Ortiz protests in demand for accountability for her daughter's murder, she gets shot in front of the capitol building of Chihuahua as explained in the previous chapter. In the page that displays the moments prior to and after her death, the presence of two crosses in the background is quite marked.[13] As she dies, these objects stand in memory of past victims, but also, as silent witnesses to yet another crime and the continuation of femicide. Like the ongoing struggles of women that become narrated in *La Lucha*, the crosses refuse to erase these unpunished gendered crimes from the public space, and to thus contribute to their invisibilization. As such, while having a similar function to the pins that become scattered on the map that opens 'La Tristeza', the crosses in Sack's graphic narrative also constitute spatial displays of agonistic mourning.[14]

Drawing from modernity/coloniality theoretical frameworks and critical Latin American geography, Orozco interprets 'the landscape of Ciudad Juárez as a counter-geography of violence assembled through the memorialization of feminicide and forced disappearance victims' (2019: 132). She argues that 'protest objects such as monuments, memorial sites, black and pink crosses, graffiti, murals, and anti-feminicide protests [...] recreate an agonizing landscape to expose the effects of an inherited colonial gender structure that normalizes extreme gender violence' (Orozco 2019: 132). In addition, she proposes that 'the memorialization of Ciudad Juárez's landscape constitutes an attempt to decolonize existing gender relations that produce zones of female death by fostering spaces of care and solidarity' (Orozco 2019: 132). In foregrounding such acts of writing on space through graffiti and crosses via the nuances of the comics form, among which are shading and colour contrast, *La Lucha* introduces the *topos* of Juarez as agonistic and, as such, participatory in women's activist struggles for justice.

Island landscapes of suffering and leisure: the heterotopias of Manus Island and Sri Lanka

Further to the femicide cartographies and the graphic depictions of the built environment of Juarez in 'La Tristeza' and *La Lucha*, 'Manus Island and the Death Angel' by Eaten Fish, and *Vanni* by Dix and Pollock introduce human suffering within, and in juxtaposition to, idyllic exotic island landscapes that often function

---

[13] For the image see Figure 3.2.
[14] For further details on agonistic mourning see Chapter 3, p.114, note 15.

as holiday destinations for affluent tourists from the Global North. In his cartoon, which exposes injustices at the Australian offshore detention centre of Manus Island, Eaten Fish draws the island landscape in bright colours and in a style that resembles children's cartoon illustrations. Palm trees and lush greenery mark the (back-)ground, and the sun has smiley facial features.[15] However, this exotic island *topos* also becomes presented as a lethal one. A refugee in a bus driven by the 'Death Angel' believes that he will be taken to his freedom, which nevertheless turns into his death (Eaten Fish: 2018: np). Thus, the idyllic landscape, to the formation of which trees, bright colours and cute cartooning style significantly contribute, comes into sharp contrast with the brutalities that occur there and have to do with how refugees are left to die in the invisibility of Australia's offshore 'black sites' (Bui 2018: 184).[16]

Despite its cuteness, the graphic depiction of Manus Island is marred by certain attributes that are figuratively suggestive of the violence that becomes enabled by its location outside the territorial borders and jurisdiction of Australia. The smiling sun has sharp teeth, there are too many flies, and the bus is driven by a skeleton wearing a black cape. As the cartoon shows the refugee expecting to reach his freedom, the caption underneath it critiques the kind of misinformation that reaches the Australian public about Manus, explaining how 'another refugee', Salim in this case, was left to die (Eaten Fish 2018: np). As such, the palm trees, the sea and the sun become presented from an angle that foregrounds the ways in which the injustice that has produced Australia's offshore detention system also causes its invisibilized violence against detained asylum seekers, turning this otherwise idyllic island space into a lethal one.

Nadine El-Enany and Sarah Keenan write of 'Australia's colonial use of the ocean as part of its ongoing mission to reign supreme as a white island in the otherwise racialised south Pacific' and of its attempt to conceal its violence 'in the distant island refugee prison camps on Manus and Nauru' (2019: 28). They describe the country's efforts 'to keep the oceans that surround it empty of migrants [. . .] as an aquatic post-script to its founding racist fiction that the land was empty (*terra nullius*) when British colonisers arrived' and they explicate how this treatment of the Pacific islands and the refugees who are detained there constitutes part of its 'racialised place-making' (El-Enany and Keenan 2019: 29,

---

[15] For the cartoon see https://eatenfish.com/2018/05/30/manus-island-and-the-death-angel/.
[16] For a detailed analysis of the term 'black sites' see Chapter 5, p. 196–97.

37). They further note that places like Manus and Nauru, 'have long been used as sites for the isolation and punishment of racialised people whose existence is perceived as a threat to white Australian sovereignty, from Aboriginal "half-castes" to Muslim refugees' (El-Enany and Keenan 2019: 29). Therefore, looking into the colonial histories of these peripheral island *topoi* allows the contextualization of Australia's contemporary treatment of refugees within a longer trajectory of colonial violence that is linked to space, place and whiteness. 'Manus Island and the Death Angel' exposes the form that Australia's otherwise invisible colonial violence is contemporarily taking, countering the 'international image as a safe and peaceful nation' that the corresponding State attempts to sustain across the globe (El-Enany and Keenan 2019: 32).

Similarly to their function in the cartoons of Eaten Fish, the sea, palms and other trees also contribute to the structuring of an idyllic island landscape in *Vanni*. However, as the narrative develops, it shows what remains invisible in distant perspectives on Sri Lanka that cast it as a paradisiac, exotic destination to be consumed by Western holiday makers. The violence of nature itself, as shown through the tsunami that left thousands of dead and mass destruction in its passing in 2004, as well as the horrific consequences of the Sri Lankan conflict, re-orient the Anglophone reader, who may be unaware of these events, in relation to their conceptualizations of the beautiful *topos* of Sri Lanka. In its focus on suffering, conflict and environmental disaster, *Vanni* illustrates how the country's recent traumatic history feels and looks like, highlighting the role of space and place in its narration.

In addition, as previously explained, peritextually, the book embeds the events that have unfolded in the recent past in longer histories. It does so by accounting for British colonial interventions there, and contemporary (neo-) colonial perspectives on Sri Lankan refugees, who try to escape death, violence and persecution, and to seek refuge in the West, where they are often treated with hostility and suspicion (Dix 2019a; 2019b). In connecting the past to the present, *Vanni* refrains from presenting today's conflict as an isolated incident that has emerged contemporarily. In contrast, it places it in a historical context that unearths its deeper causes. In doing so, it also shows that like its inhabitants, Sri Lanka's idyllic landscape also becomes wounded and suffers, similarly to, but also differently from, the industrialized border city of Juarez, due to environmental disaster and war-related violence – itself a remnant of the island's colonial past.

In order to critically and deconstructively display Western stereotypical views on Sri Lanka, *Vanni* starts with a British person's perspective on it, revealing how the same place can be experienced differently in the space of simultaneity. The first two pages of the text present a flash-forward, whereby Antoni, the protagonist, has secured asylum in the UK and works as a taxi driver in London. The heading of this section locates the events in 'Stoke Newington, London [in] February 2014' (Dix and Pollock 2019: 10). A passenger asks Antoni where he is from, and upon his response, the passenger accounts for his own memories of Sri Lanka. Having been there to attend a wedding at a beachside resort, he remembers a 'crystal clear ocean [,] palm trees [as well as] cocktails by the pool', and he asks Antoni whether he misses his country, especially in the UK weather, and if he visits often (Dix and Pollock 2019: 11). The beautiful exotic scenery he verbally recounts is significantly different from the urban London surroundings, which become visually displayed. Antoni, whose trauma and suffering during the Sri Lankan conflict become unpacked in minute detail in the subsequent pages, avoids responding to the man's question given how he had fled his country due to horrific torture, the threat of death, and ecological destruction of which his interlocutor seems unaware.

The image of the island as an idyllic paradise is also visually reproduced in the two-page prologue of the book, which moves '13 years [back in] Chempiyanpattu, 2001' (Dix and Pollock 2019: 12–13). Palm trees, a calm sea, small boats at the shore, and Antoni peacefully fishing, present a scene that is drastically different from the busy streets of London.[17] However, as the narrative progresses, this place becomes ravaged by environmental and war-induced destruction, similarly to the lives of its inhabitants. Hence, *Vanni* unsettles the image of Sri Lanka that the taxi passenger had in his mind. Given how the island becomes presented as an idyllic tourist destination, and as a locus of horrific pain, loss and destruction, it is introduced, in Dix and Pollock's graphic life narrative, as a heterotopia.

Michel Foucault describes heterotopias as 'counter-sites' that exist in all cultures and civilizations, and are charged with a mirror effect, through which other real sites become 'simultaneously represented, contested, and inverted' (1986: 24). Michel Agier describes 'precarious places' such as ghettos, refugee camps and favelas as heterotopias, noting that 'over and above [its] mirror effect, which is social, political, and moral, the heterotopia can also be seen more generally as a means of epistemological decentring' (2019: 15). He explains that these places are 'linked to one another by policies of exclusion, organisation and control [, making] visible as a global political fact the question of (in)equality'

---

[17] As such, *Vanni*'s spatial depictions may also implicitly point to the difficulties the protagonist may encounter in adopting to the completely foreign urban environment of London.

(Agier 2019: 14). In addition, they show how global and local injustices become spatially sustained and produced, similarly to the *colonias* of the border cities of Mexico. In presenting Sri Lanka through the perspectives of a British tourist and of Antoni, *Vanni* attempts to undo simplistic, distant takes on it, by zooming in on its wounds, which are peritextually linked to the British colonial project. This double framing of Sri Lanka as a locus of pleasure and suffering also illustrates its critical function as a heterotopia that renders global inequalities visible while connecting the histories of two otherwise distant countries, thus showing how local and contemporary events become shaped by global past histories.

In 'Crisis Heterotopias and Border Zones of the Dead', Joseph Pugliese also describes the simultaneous understanding of Lampedusa as a refugee detention centre and a touristic hotspot. Specifically, he writes of 'an acute sense of disorientation' he felt while reading tourist reviews of Lampedusa as 'an island of dreams' surrounded by a 'fairy tale sea', given that his own perception of it was as 'an island infamous for its overcrowded, traumatizing immigration detention centre' (Pugliese 2009: 664). For Pugliese, 'our epoch of simultaneity [opens up] the possibility of temporally juxtaposing two absolutely dichotomous figures – the wealthy tourist from the Global North and the utterly disenfranchised refugee from the Global South – within the same geographical space' (2009: 664). This juxtaposition foregrounds 'the violently disjunctive experiences of space that inscribe [the heterotopia of] a penal island/tourist resort [and enable] the conceptualization of absolute difference within the space of simultaneity' (Pugliese 2009: 664). The graphic topopoetics of *Vanni* and those of 'Manus Island and the Death Angel' have similar consequences in evoking two radically opposing views on the same spaces, critically unsettling distant takes on them, and illustrating the uneven distribution of and (un)awareness about injustice across the Global North and the Global South.

The olive trees of Palestine

While the palm trees in the island landscapes of Manus and Sri Lanka stage exotic destinations for people from the Global North that simultaneously function as locations of suffering for persecuted people from the Global South, olive trees and the ground in Sacco's *Palestine* illustrate how the people and the earth of Palestine become wounded in the context of Israeli occupation. Their suffering, in other words, is presented as relationally experienced. In her analysis of Sacco's Palestinian comics, Scherr notes that the cartoonist 'understands the contiguous relationship between figure and ground deeply, and uses his comics artistry to reveal the ties that make the suffering of the people and the suffering of the built environment into one piece' (2020: 477). Via his 'detailed line drawings and the use of sequentiality', she further notes, 'Gaza City appears less of a "thing" or object and more like a "subject," capable of telling a story, of giving testimony' (Scherr 2020: 477).

Davies also discusses Sacco's two-page spread depiction of the Jabalia refugee camp in *Palestine* as 'a space of infrastructural deterioration [but also as one of] vibrant urban life, enduring economic activity and social resilience' (2019: 1). In this sense, like Scherr, he too unpacks the rhetorical potential that foregrounds human and spatial Palestinian resistance under Israeli occupation. Attention to space and place as drawn in *Palestine* has also been paid by Edward Said in his 'Homage to Sacco' at the beginning of the book. As he points out, the inhospitality and the unfamiliarity of the place that is graphically mediated through the cartoonist's detailed drawings of the ground relates to 'harrowing experiences of houses demolished and land appropriated, torture, [roadblocks,] waiting [. . .,] the sense of confinement, [as well as the] permanent muddiness and ugliness conveyed by the refugee camp which is so iconic to the Palestinian experience' (Said 2001: iii–v).

In Sacco's second book on Palestine, *Footnotes in Gaza*, the deterioration of the built environment is also quite important for the narrative structuring of Palestinian suffering. A man, for example, shows Sacco's autobiographical avatar the 'bullet scars in his home' while the narrator explains that these exist in 'one room, and another, and another' (Sacco 2009c: 253). This repetition highlights the intense precarity that marks the family and its dwelling place in the context of Israeli infrastructural warfare. As Sacco's avatar walks through the rubble left behind by Israeli demolition practices, the narrator explicates how 'bulldozers have scooped out the earth as if it were ice cream [to] push and bury the homes they destroy' inside the holes they formed (Sacco 2009c: 256). Further to the built environment, however, and the mud that is characteristic in Sacco's visual depictions of life in Palestine's refugee camps, the olive trees in the (back)ground also have important rhetorical function.

Similarly to *Vanni*'s mediation of an outsider's perspective on Sri Lanka, Sacco's work of graphic journalism, as previously mentioned, repeatedly highlights his own positionality as a visitor in an alien, unfamiliar *topos*. The narrator's captions also frequently remind readers of how the testimonies of suffering he witnesses become commodified for his professional gain, ironically acknowledging the power dynamics and the distance between his Palestinian testifying subjects and himself. This is also true for the graphic account of the destruction of olive trees. As they drive to a village to interview people, the narrator sarcastically describes this place as 'a veritable goldmine of Palestinian misery' and expresses his wish that it will be worth the '89 sheks' he had paid his driver, whom he later asks whether they can 'talk to the people who've had their trees destroyed' (Sacco 2001: 59). A panel zooms in on the bare trunks of the trees, whose branches have been cut. 'See?' the narrator mentions addressing the reader, 'trees destroyed' (Sacco 2001: 59). This kind of narrative distancing and the continuous objectification and 'commodification of suffering' (Smith 2011: 71) that Sacco sustains through his intra-diegetic persona's cynical perspective concerns both the *topos* and the people of Palestine, and it affirms hierarchies that are geographically distributed and sustained, which the autobiographical subject himself does not pretend to overcome in his witnessing role.

In the subsequent page, a woman's testimony, and that of her father, unsettle Sacco's initial cynical staging of environmental injustice that is reflected through the destruction of olive trees. The woman explains that a Palestinian man was wounded while preparing a bomb 'beyond [her] neighbor's house' (Sacco 2001: 60). Because of this, a curfew was immediately imposed in the area, and in the next two days Israeli soldiers returned to cut down the trees across the street and those belonging to the people living there. The narrative moves spatially outside the domestic space, where the woman is being interviewed by Sacco's intra-diegetic persona, and temporally to the past, to recreate the scenes, whereby Israeli soldiers cut the trees and she cries while witnessing their suffering that she experiences relationally. Overall, she relates, 'they cut down 70 olive trees, the trees of 13 families' (Sacco 2001: 60). Through her statement, the trees become linked to familial belonging, a bond that is further explicated through her father's testimonial account.

His testimony supplements her affectively charged response to the cutting down of the trees, at the same time as detailing the impact this form of wounding has had for himself. 'The olive tree is our source of living', he explains, 'we use oil for food and we buy our clothes with the oil we sell [...]. Here we have nothing but the trees [because] the Israelis don't give people from our village permits to work in Israel' (Sacco 2001: 61). Spatial segregation, in this sense, becomes a means for the imposition of sovereign State power and people's deprivation of their human rights. Mbembe writes that the destruction of olive trees constitutes a core component of Israel's *infrastructural warfare* against the Palestinian people (2019b: 82, emphasis in the original). In combination with becoming deprived of the opportunity to work in Israel given their positionality in the particular *topos*, these people's means for sustaining a life thus become severely affected. Further to the exposition of this injustice, comics enable a complex graphic mediation of the affective impact of the trees' destruction on the Palestinian people.

A panel zooms in on the face of the old man, which is marked by wrinkles that look similar to tree roots as he explains that 'the Israelis know that an olive tree is the same as our sons' and that two years before they 'cut down 17 of [his] trees' (Sacco 2001: 62; Figure 4.2). The trees were planted by his father, and some were close to one hundred years old. As such, they constitute an inter-generationally preserved means of sustenance and familial bonding.[18] The old man was asked to cut his trees because 'a Molotov or stones were thrown from [his] field' and he did not have money to build a fence as he was ordered to do by Israeli soldiers (Sacco 2001: 62). A second panel zooms further in on his face as Sacco's intra-diegetic persona predatorily asks how he felt in being forced to do so. The man's eyes are filled with tears as he explains how he was given a chainsaw to cut down the trees. 'I was crying', he explains, 'I felt I was killing my son when I cut them down' (Sacco 2001: 62).[19] In this sense, the pain that is visually inscribed on this man's face, and becomes articulated via his speech bubbles, is caused by how he was forced to put an end to the life of the trees that he understands as his offspring. The resemblance of his wrinkles to roots visually mirrors a connectedness to the ground, which becomes wounded and ruptured through the destruction of the olive trees.[20] In this sense, the *humus* (the earth) and the human seem to conflate in this graphic articulation of spatial injustice that occurs in the Israeli/Palestinian conflict.

The thickness of the trees' trunks, which becomes visually presented in Sacco's restaging of how they looked prior to being cut down, denotes their age and the years during which they had been rooted in Palestinian soil. Their destruction

[18] Nasser Abufarha writes of the olive tree that 'it is a medium for Palestinians to experience the relationship to the land across time through the chain of exchange. The cross-generational reciprocity is uniting people with their land and history. It fuses history, the present life, the land, and the future. Furthermore, as a gift from past generations, the olive tree carries meanings and sacred, mystical qualities' (2008: 358).

[19] In her discussion of the significance of the olive tree in the Palestinian collective memory, Carol B. Bardenstein also writes that 'in the wake of more than 3,300 olive trees being uprooted, black banners were raised at the entrance to the village [of Midya] and on individual homes, as done in mourning the death of a human being' (1999: 156).

[20] In Naji al-Ali's political cartoons the human and the ground also become conflated to illustrate Palestinian connectedness to the land and the human body becomes hybridized in being fused with a tree to denote perseverance through persecution and rootedness to the ground (Sacco 2009a).

Figure 4.2　Panels from page 62 of *Palestine* by Joe Sacco, © 2001, used with permission from Fantagraphics.

therefore seems to mirror the enforced uprooting of the Palestinians from their land, which causes the pain that becomes manifested through Sacco's aesthetic choices for his depiction of the old man's face. As Sacco's autobiographical avatar leaves the family with his driver and the photographer, the narrative perspective zooms out of the domestic space yet again. The family is standing among cut down olive trees which had been planted in order. Its positioning in-between them configures its own suffering as equal to, and continuous with, that of the trees. At the same time as mutually suffering from Israeli injustice, the trees and the people also bear witness to it.

By foregrounding the relational impact of the trees' wounding on their Palestinian owners under Israeli occupation, Sacco's graphic life narrative presents a human relationship to the earth and the environment that does not posit the former as superior, but rather as equal to the latter. As such, it advances knowledge about the environment, space and place from an other body-political and geo-political location. In Latin American decolonial feminist geography, 'Cuerpo-Territorio (Body-Territory) [refers to] a decolonized embodied ontology [that] places the community and territory as a single subject of political agency that resists and identifies violations against women's bodies and territories as part of the same process' (Naylor et al. 2018: 204) as also shown through the analysis of the Juarez-femicide comics. While Sacco's depiction of the destruction of the olive trees does not have feminist implications, it is important to note how it also presents the suffering of the people and that of the environment as mutual. As such, it demonstrates a thinking '"otherwise" about space and power from and with marginalized knowledges' (Radcliffe and Radhuber 2020: 2).[21]

Indeed, as Carol B. Bardenstein writes, in Palestinian collective memory, 'nature is not inert; the olive tree is not "just" a tree. It is presumed to have a longevity sufficiently extensive for it to survive both the tragedy and its protagonists and has thus been designated as a proxy Palestinian witness, aligned with and testifying to Palestinian collective memory' (1999: 156). In this sense, the 'broken' trees and people that become visually embodied in Sacco's work resist occupation precisely by bearing witness to its violence. Closing the narrative account of the olive trees' destruction, Sacco's narrator explains that 'the Israelis uprooted 120,000 plus [trees] in the Intifada's first four years ... for "security reasons" [as in the aforementioned cases] or in constructing the network of roads that link Jewish settlements to Israel' (Sacco 2001: 62). The official justification for

---

[21] This kind of thinking constitutes one of the objectives of decolonial political geography (Radcliffe and Radhuber 2020).

this spatial injustice thus becomes undone through the narrator's critical commentary that illustrates how the Israeli transformation of the landscape inscribes shifting socio-, necro- and bio-political realities on space.

This spatial transformation can be understood through the lens of a decolonial, post-colonized interpretation of space and place. Mbembe, for instance, notes that:

> *Colonial occupation* consisted of seizing, delimiting, and asserting control over a geographical area – of writing a new set of social and spatial relations on the ground. The writing of new spatial relations (territorialization) ultimately amounted to the production of boundaries and hierarchies, zones and enclaves; the subversion of existing property arrangements; the differential classification of people; resource extraction; and, finally, the manufacturing of a large reservoir of cultural imaginaries.
>
> Mbembe 2019b: 79, emphasis in the original

Sacco's *Palestine* illustrates, in minute detail, the writing of new social relations on space through the transformation of land, which evokes a colonial production of space. Further to damaging the environment and depriving Palestinian people of their means to a life, the destruction of olive trees has further political and affective impact, given that they symbolize Palestinian rootedness to the land and resistance to occupation.[22] As such, in addition to presenting how violence shapes urban infrastructure, Sacco's attention to the suffering of olive trees as relational to that of the Palestinian people also politically transforms them into witnesses to violence, potentially re-orienting the reader's understanding of the human connection to the earth and the environment.

Spatial violence and irregular migration

The sea

While conflict causes specific types of environmental destruction, as seen through the example of *Palestine*, different forms of spatial injustice also occur in the context of forced and irregular migration. As mentioned earlier in this

---

[22] Ahmed Abofoul writes that 'in light of the gravity and intensity of Israel's violations of the Palestinian people's basic human rights, such environmental aspects [as the uprooting of olive trees] often do not get enough attention' (2021: np).

chapter, Western States are increasingly using space to deter unwanted populations from trying to make their way into their borders. This is illustrated, for instance, in the Australian State's (neo-)colonial management of the sea and the function of the Pacific islands of Manus and Nauru as offshore detention prisons, where othered asylum seekers are exposed to increased precarity and vulnerability to death. In this section, I focus on online and print graphic life narratives of detention and irregular migration to examine representations of the sea, and its rhetorical contributions in relation to the suffering of others in the context of the so-called refugee crisis and its management in Australia and Europe.

Ahmed's 'Affective States', for instance, starts with a collage of images used by the Australian State in online graphic narratives that have been published to deter migrants from attempting to enter the country without documents (Figure 4.3). Released by the Department of Home Affairs, 'No Way' is one of these publications, and it explicates, in rather threatening and hostile language, the impossibility of undocumented entry into the country, while warning the intended reader that boats arriving on the shores of Australia and New Zealand will be sent back to their countries of origin.[23] The sea, in this narrative, is presented as threatening and destructive. Such visual oceanic depictions are positioned alongside a map of Australia underneath a red stop sign.

Figure 4.3 Excerpt from Ahmed, S. (2023), 'Affective States', *Image [&] Narrative* 24(3): 1-4, © Safdar Ahmed, image courtesy of the artist.

---

[23] For the 'No Way' graphic narrative, see: https://www.homeaffairs.gov.au/foi/files/2019/fa-190801764-document-released-p4.PDF.

'Affective States', which accounts for Safdar's bonding over music-making with an Iranian refugee who had been detained in Manus Island, starts by repeating this threatening spatial imagery, as well as a statement that accompanies it and becomes repeated throughout 'No Way', reminding readers that 'Australia's borders remain strong' (Ahmed 2024: np). The force of the sea is shown in photo-realistic images of boats being shipwrecked in waves, in what seems as an attempt to visually highlight the increased possibility of such an occurrence. Contrarily, as also explained in the following chapter, the depictions of refugees in 'No Way' are more abstracted, thus distancing them from the reader and rendering them unknowable.

Refugee comics often display the ways in which the sea is increasingly becoming excessively dangerous in the context of Western nations' border control policies, transforming into a *topos* that threatens refugees with death.[24] Massive waves, for instance, as those included in 'No Way' and reproduced by Ahmed, also exist in Froden's 'An Empty Promise', which accounts for the dangers a Nigerian woman faced during her own irregular crossing from her home-country through Libya and the Mediterranean to Sicily. Small dinghies are often depicted hopelessly struggling to overcome huge waves in an imagery that underscores the lethal impact of the force of nature/the sea in juxtaposition with human powerlessness.

Ahmed's and Froden's webcomics illustrate how the sea is becoming reconfigured into a aquatic wall in Western States' attempts to prevent people from entering their territories and jurisdictions. El-Enany and Keenan note that Australia's control of the waters that surround it in the context of its deterrence policies has remained 'consistent with [its] long history of white supremacist violence and racialised assertions of territorial and maritime sovereignty' (2019: 32). For this reason, in addition to interpreting the country 'through the critical lens of *terra nullius* and the ongoing racist theft of land [from its indigenous inhabitants,] there is [also] much to be gained from analysing [its] relationship with the sea', they argue (El-Enany and Keenan 2019: 32). To illustrate the State's hostility to refugee sea arrivals, El-Enany and Keenan discuss the semiotics of the 'menacing sea' that 'No Way' features, introducing Australia's current deterrence policies as a contemporary version of the colonial foundations, upon which a white Australian nation has been built in the 'otherwise racialised South Pacific' (2019: 33, 28).

---

[24] Such texts as *Illegal*, by Eoin Colfer et al. (2017) and *Zenobia* by Morten Dürr and Lars Horneman (2018) also show how the sea conceals deaths occurring in the context of irregular migration rendering them invisible.

While refugee comics tend to present the sea as a menacing, deterring threat, the visual/verbal hybridity of the form offers cartoonists opportunities to foreground the ways in which this transformation in the context of migration governmentality is caused by Western (neo-)colonial violence against underprivileged people from the Global South. Indeed, those who are forced to flee their homelands are those who become more severely impacted by the Western (neo-)colonial exploitation of the earth and of people elsewhere.[25] The biopolitical and necropolitical control of the waters around Western States sustains the modern/colonial hierarchies that produce the disposability of certain lives from the Global South, which become charged with further precarity in people's enforced irregular crossings through liquid and territorial borders. While graphic depictions of seascapes as those found in 'No Way' and in 'An Empty Promise' cast nature – the sea, in particular – as dangerous, Ahmed's 'Affective States' foregrounds its violence as man-made.

In an act of meta-commentary, Ahmed's narrator explains how the language of comics works, quoting Erin La Cour and Anna Poletti, who note that it 'incites "an affective experience in readers by drawing them into the story while at the same time prompting them to consider how feeling influences their interpretation of experience"' (Ahmed 2024: np). In the visual register, a boat full of people is at sea, and a massive human hand that is emerging from underwater, as opposed to waves, is blocking their way forward. Through this visual metaphor, Ahmed illustrates that the agent behind the ocean's deterring and at times lethal function is human. As such, the sea's violence is attributed to the Western Man and not to the force of nature.

The narrative's visual/verbal combinations and meta-commentary thus invite readers to affectively witness the consequences of Australia's violent control of the waters that surround it, and the spatial injustices that produce and become produced through the country's deterrence policies. As such, the conflation of the human and the thalassic in this visual image foregrounds the ways in which the sea becomes instrumentalized in white Western sovereign aggression against Australia's others. In this way, preconceptions regarding the violence of nature/the sea as disconnected from human agency become reconfigured as 'Affective States' presents the violence of Man as being implemented through this aquatic *topos*.

---

[25] As El-Enany and Keenan (2019: 34) remind us, 'those who travel irregularly by sea today are for the most part racialised people from poor southern countries with histories of colonisation, neoliberal exploitation in the form of debt, land-grabbing, and calamity-inducing International Monetary Fund (IMF) and World Bank-imposed structural adjustment programmes and of military intervention by northern countries, and are disproportionately suffering the effects of climate change'.

European States' policing of the sea in the context of their own deterrence policies is equally violent to that of Australia and similarly linked to the continent's colonial national histories. European border control authorities are funding non-EU nations across the Mediterranean to prevent undocumented migrants from entering Europe. Regarding the Libyan route, which Mary pursues in 'An Empty Promise', Pat Rubio Bertran notes that there has not been 'an active [EU] search and rescue mission for migrants at sea attempting to flee from Libya [...]. Instead, the current policy consists of pushing migrants and refugees back to the North African country by training and funding the Libyan Coast Guard (LCG) to intercept migrants [who] end up in detention' there (2021: 302–3). Such pushback operations have currently 'become standard procedure, without regard to their illegality in the eyes of customary international human rights law' (Bertran 2021: 319). In other words, with the passing of time, as Europe's borders, like those of Australia, are becoming stronger, their thalassic violence is also increasing, with a complete disregard for the severe human rights violations that accompany it. Such practices illustrate how Europe's extra-territorialization of its refugee management increases spatial violence and injustice against people on the move, while the States that are responsible for it remain unaccountable given the occurrence of the crimes caused by such spatial injustices outside European borders and national jurisdictions.

In 'An Empty Promise', the orange dinghy in which Mary and the rest of the asylum seekers were put by the people smugglers in Libya looks tiny in relation to the waves wherein it was abandoned, and which take up almost all the space of a full-page panel. This image presents human powerlessness, that of the asylum seekers, in the face of the overwhelming force of nature/the sea. Contrarily, in the panel showing the Italian rescue boat that saved Mary together with other people, the waves have subsided, and it is the ship that dominates in the narrative space, in a visual arrangement that seems to imply the taming of the sea upon its arrival (Froden 2017). *Mare Nostrum* (our sea), 'the military-humanitarian operation' that was in place 'in the channel of Sicily' until 2014, later became replaced by Triton, which was coordinated by Frontex (Tazzioli 2016: 1).[26] Rather than rescuing people, however, Triton aimed mostly at blocking their entry into Italy (Bertran 2021). While 'An Empty Promise' does not provide information regarding the name of the rescue operation through which Mary was saved, it is useful to look into how *Mare Nostrum* evokes links between Italy's

---

[26] Tazzioli unpacks the implications of this transition in her analysis of the 'ongoing spatial and political recrafting of the Mediterranean Sea as a space of migration governmentality' (2016: 1).

contemporary management of irregular migration in the Mediterranean with its imperial and Fascist pasts.

The Mediterranean is a *topos* that has been central in Italian Fascisms and expansionist visions (Agbamu 2019). *Mare Nostrum* is a term that was taken from the lexicon of the Roman Empire and was used to 'anchor modern Italian imperialism within the authority of the classical past' during Benito Mussolini's rule, when Italian aggression in the country's African colonies also increased (Agbamu 2019: 250).[27] With the end of the Second World War and decolonization, *Mare Nostrum* 'receded from popular discourse, [and] previous claims to the Mediterranean' were abandoned (Agbamu 2019: 250). Contemporarily, however, 'in the context of the so-called refugee crisis, Italy resurrected [this term], in the naming of its military-humanitarian operation, a move rejected by the contemporary Italian far right' (Agbamu 2019: 250).

At the same time as foregrounding the colonial histories that have shaped the *topos* of the Mediterranean in relation to Italy, the re-surfacing of *Mare Nostrum* in the context of the refugee crisis speaks to the ways in which the country's management of undocumented migration becomes embedded in a trajectory that includes its imperial, colonial and Fascist pasts. For this reason, it is important to read the human precarity and vulnerability in the rough seas between Libya and Sicily, which becomes visually evoked through the waves in 'An Empty Promise' alongside, and through the lens of, Italy's colonial histories. Such a reading of the sea in this online graphic life narrative can expose the traces of modernity/coloniality in Italy's control of the Mediterranean and its spatial management of irregular migration.

Gillian Whitlock refers to the temporal coincidence of Australia's 'Operation Sovereign Borders' and Italy's *Mare Nostrum* 'in the global politics of forced migration' (2015b: 248). She also discusses massive loss of life in the context of Triton, which 'renewed debates about [...] the ethics of hospitality' (Whitlock 2015b: 248).[28] Unlike Triton, she writes, *Mare Nostrum* 'arose in mourning for loss of life at sea, and reconfigured the maritime border in a temporary opening to the foreigner, welcoming the stranger into the homelands' (Whitlock 2015b: 263). But even if the use of *Mare Nostrum* in this context is seen as an attempt to decolonize this term and to reconfigure its meanings, reactions to it from the

---

[27] In a speech he delivered in Tripoli, Libya, in 1926, Mussolini talked about the need for an Italian expansion in the Mediterranean and towards the East (Srivastava 2018).
[28] On the hostility that is implied in acts of European hospitality in the context of the contemporary refugee crisis, see Michael and Mastilovic 2022.

Italian far right and its replacement by Triton illustrate that this effort has not been brought to fruition as Europe's neo-colonial management of the Mediterranean is increasingly becoming more violent, causing more deaths at 'our' sea.

In Sanna's *The Journey*, which addresses younger readers, as mentioned in the Introduction, depictions of the sea are particularly nuanced. Because it addresses younger readers, Sanna's drawing style is characterized by cuteness, brightness, but also strong contrasts between bright and dark colours. While the spaces and places that become visually depicted in this narrative are not named, Sanna writes that the story told in this picture book is based on that of two girls she met at a refugee centre in Italy and on additional testimonies she collected from other refugees. Initially, the book's child narrator explains that together with their family, they lived 'in a city close to the sea' (Sanna 2016: np). While in the past they used to spend their weekends at the beach, this is no longer possible.

The architectural style and design of the buildings in the first two pages of the narrative, as well as the visual embodiments of the family, imply that the city may be located somewhere in the Middle East. Mosques, buildings with domes and cactus plants compose an oriental landscape in the initial two-page spread representation of the family's homeland. At the right side of the page, the sea, which washes the town's shores, is painted in dark blue and black colours, coming to stark juxtaposition to the brightly coloured landscape of the city. In the following two-page spread, the sea transforms into a monstrous entity, it takes up almost all of the space of the second page, it is washed in black, and the monstrous hands with sharp ends, which represent its edges in a visual metaphor with ominous implications, are destroying the city.[29] The chaos brought about by the war that the child narrator describes becomes visually represented through the destruction of the city's landscape and infrastructure, which the family is trying to escape.

The beginning of the war, in this sense, becomes represented through a monstrous, lethal sea, which destructively enters the town. This depiction may suggest that the factors leading to the war are external. It may also visually capture the environmental damage that comes along with the infrastructural

---

[29] In her analysis of children's responses to this 'ambiguity [of the monstrous hands] (over who or what is responsible for the traumatic event)', Kate Douglas writes that 'the child reader might interpret the scene as real and human inflicted (if they are ready to) or as a fairy-tale monster (if they are not)' (2023: 110).

destruction caused by war. When the children's father dies, their mother decides
to flee with them to another country. The sea is one among other spaces they
have to cross in this process. The narrator mentions that it 'stretches far and wide
ahead of us and we must cross it', further wondering how they will manage to do
so (Sanna 2016: np). A two-page spread presents a distant take on a landscape
that is significantly different from that of the family's homeland. Mountains with
grass and tall trees end in a calm bright blue sea. The family is almost unnoticeable
in this vast landscape as they stand at the top of a mountain looking across the
sea they will have to navigate. At the mountain's foothills there is also a tiny
orange boat, similar to the dinghy in Froden's webcomic, and people about to
board on it. The vastness of the landscape and the seascape in contradistinction
to the minuteness of the visual embodiments of the people and the boat unsettles
the narrative of human dominion over nature at the same time as underscoring
the family's refugee precarity.

The following page presents the dinghy as it navigates sea waves, which
similarly to those of 'An Empty Promise', take up almost all the space of the page.
In this case, however, the sea is not presented as a lethal border nor as a dangerous
threat. Cute fish and cephalopods accompany the boat and the sea itself becomes
personified, breathing towards the direction of the boat as if to keep it afloat
(Figure 4.4). As such, contrary to the configuration of border violence as
attributed to the harsh environment of the open seas, *The Journey* reconfigures
this aquatic space as a witness to, and facilitator of, the family's precarious border
crossing. When the narrator explains that the waves 'grow bigger and bigger
[and] it feels like the sea will never end', in the visual register the colours of the
waves shift from brightness to darkness (Sanna 2016: np). However, the facial
features drawn on yellow droplets emanating from the position of the boat at sea
indicate worry over the refugee precarity caused by the turbulence of the waves.
As such, *The Journey* presents the environment, that is, both the earth and the
sea, as other than threatening and lethal. Through her visual depictions of
seascapes and landscapes, Sanna recasts nature as a *topos* of refuge and assistance
for people on the move.

In making the aesthetic decision to personify the sea in its transformation
into a protective force for the refugees, Sanna draws from the realm of the
fantastic to tell this family's border-crossing story. The real and the imaginary, or
rather, the mythical, become conflated to articulate the ways in which the earth
is neither enemy to, nor dominated by, the humankind. The female figure whose
face is shown in Sanna's visual sea depiction can be read as evocative of the
Nereids of Greco-Roman mythology. These 'sea nymphs [...] watched over the

Figure 4.4 Page from *The Journey* © 2016 Flying Eye Books © 2016 Francesca Sanna.

Mediterranean Sea and attended the sea divinities Poseidon and Amphitrite'
(San Martín Bacaicoa and Perea Horno 2003: 14). They lived underwater and
only appeared on the sea surface to dance in the waves. Like other forest,
mountain, and sea nymphs, they 'were friendly and kind to mortals' (San Martín
Bacaicoa and Perea Horno 2003: 14). Sanna's representation of the sea as a spirit
of nature that assists asylum seekers in *The Journey* illustrates the ways in which
art is connected to and can articulate 'the geopower of the earth' (Yusoff 2012:
972) in nuanced ways.

For Elizabeth Grosz, 'art is geographical (rather than psychological) [because]
it involves the earth and the movement of its qualities so that they may intensify
the sensations of living beings with otherwise imperceptible forces' (2012: 975).
Kathryn Yusoff writes that it constitutes 'the opening up of material and
immaterial forces of the universe to elaboration and experimentation. In this
way [it] taps into the substrata of the earth, its geography and its time, to unearth
and repurpose its forces' (2012: 972). Contrary to conventional geopolitics that
treat the surface of the earth as a stage on which human political dramas are
performed, 'Grosz's notion of geopower permits the dynamics of the earth to

leave their mark on human and other bodies' (Clark 2012: 976). The value of the graphic topopoetics of *The Journey*, then, lies in how they introduce a defamiliarizing perspective on the earth and on geopower; specifically, on the forces of the sea in the context of the refugee crisis that is other than weaponized by Western States to deter undocumented migrants and to threaten them with death. In incorporating the fantastic and the mythical in the articulation of this family's life narrative, Sanna's picture book presents a different way of conceptualizing the sea, reconfiguring its meaning, and illustrating how irregular migrant precarity therein is a result of biopower and necropower (Foucault 2003b; Mbembe 2019b), thus delinking it from the forces of the earth and geopower.

Unfamiliar places, forests and walls

Further to its thalassic representations, *The Journey* also depicts walls in nuanced ways, as does Ahmed's 'Villawood'. After crossing through dark forests populated by tall, green trees and animals that witness its journey, the family arrives at a border that becomes spatially embodied via a wall. Sanna's graphic life narrative presents elements from the genre of the fairy tale in its articulation of a contemporary refugee life story. This is shown, *inter alia*, through its depictions of the sea as a nymph, and its references to 'big green forests [...] filled with kind fairies that dance and give us magic spells to end the war' (Sanna 2016: np). The earth, in other words, and the mythical spirits inhabiting (or constituting) it, seem to assist this family to overcome its precarity.

Donald Haase writes that settings, in fairy tales, 'are polarized and valorized according to whether they offer characters familiarity and security, or threaten them with exile and danger. Place', he further points out, 'signals the alienation and endangerment that characters experience, as it does their return to safety and security' (2000: 363). While the forest constitutes one of the 'typical locations that threaten characters with isolation, danger, and violence, including imprisonment and death', other familiar places like one's home may 'become defamiliarized and threatening' (Haase 2000: 364). The familiar *topos* of the family home can therefore be 'an ambiguous location, embodying both the danger of violence and ultimate security' (Haase 2000: 364).

In *The Journey*, the children's hometown becomes destroyed by the arrival of the war and Sanna's visual images illustrate how this familiar and familial environment becomes reconfigured into an alien, dangerous *topos*, which they are forced to flee with their mother. During their border crossing, they navigate dark forests. Their visual embodiments, as previously discussed, render them an almost unnoticeable part of the pages that depict vast landscapes. During their territorial crossing, the family is standing at the edge of a forest drawn in dark green colours and with trees that are too tall to fit into the space of the page. Behind them lies 'the border', the child narrator explains – 'an enormous wall [...] we must climb over' (Sanna 2016: np). The enormousness of the wall however becomes unsettled in the visual register which shows a spatial image dominated by the forest rather than the man-made border. As they get closer to the wall, it is still not this built structure that becomes foregrounded, but rather a monstrous guard that protects it and orders the family to 'go back' because they 'are not allowed to cross' (Sanna 2016: np).

Upon running away from the wall, whose human guard – rather than its spatial force – threatens them with violence, they find refuge in the forest, a place that otherwise signals danger for fairy tale characters. As such, similarly to its representation of the sea, by embedding the wall within the forest, and configuring its surveillance and control as enacted by a human/monstrous guard, to whom I return in the following chapter, *The Journey* once again delinks the forces of nature from the factors leading to spatial injustice and undocumented border crossers' precarity. Even though the border is verbally described as an enormous wall, physically, its presence is overshadowed by that of nature – the forest – and that of the border guard. When the mother pays a people smuggler to help them cross over it, once again, this built formation is drawn as significantly smaller than the agent assisting the family's irregular crossing, who, like the border guard, is also visually embodied with monstrous rather than human attributes.

In Ahmed's 'Villawood', the structure of the wall becomes used figuratively to account for how those in detention become deprived of online access to the world. In the carceral *topos* of Villawood, which exposes detained asylum seekers to a number of human rights violations and to increased vulnerability to mental illness and death, people's access to the external world is blocked via limitations imposed on to their internet access.[30] In chapter 3 of 'Villawood', which is entitled 'The Human Rights Firewall and Other Deprivations', Khadija, an adolescent girl, accounts for her inability to study properly because of the centre's poor internet connection and the blockage of access to useful websites. The term 'firewall' in the title of this chapter denotes a wall that is

[30] See Chapter 5 for an analysis of trauma and vulnerability in 'Villawood'.

built in order to prevent fire from spreading. Further to its literal meaning, in Information Technology it refers to 'a security device [...] that can help protect [a] network by filtering traffic and blocking outsiders from gaining unauthorized access to the private data on [a personal] computer' (Johansen 2021: np). Firewalls also prevent 'malicious software from infecting [a] computer' (Johansen 2021: np).

While the term has moved from the physical built environment to the virtual, in both realms it constitutes a defensive structure against unwanted threat. Its positioning in the title of chapter 3 is rather paradoxical because it becomes situated in a semantic environment that denotes its use to prevent the entry of human rights, which it reconfigures into a threat, in the detention centre of Villawood. Khadija explains that 'the internet is so slow it's impossible for [her] to study', and that 'Mathletics [,] an educational website that all the schools use [is] blocked' leaving her with Wikipedia as her only option for studying and researching, which students are discouraged from using at school (Ahmed 2015: np). The centre's management of the Internet to deprive people of their human rights, such as access to education, is confirmed by a human rights lawyer who realized while working with detained asylum seekers 'that a number of human rights websites were [also] blocked' (Ahmed 2015: np). This, the lawyer explains, 'impedes the legal process [...] by barring the information that would help refugees prove their case' (Ahmed 2015: np). In the visual register, a spatial illustration shows the globe situated in front of a thick brick wall, and a person behind this structure, trying to see over it. This person's vision becomes restricted by the limitations imposed by the wall that blocks their (online) access to, and view of, the globe (Figure 4.5).

Like the detention centre itself, this wall can be read through the metaphor of the firewall that is used in the title of the chapter. If read through this lens, the space of detention functions as a blockage for those who are perceived as a potential threat to the white Australian nation – racially and religiously othered refugees, whose human rights become violated in this carceral structure, which, similarly to the virtual firewall, is supposed to filter access to Australia and to block unwanted human traffic therein.[31] Indeed, the centre's initial depictions upon Safdar's entry into it present it first and foremost as a preventive, carceral *topos*. As the narrator explains, this is 'an environment of chain link fences ...

---

[31] Liam Apter unpacks the racialized and colonial violence of this site that is similar to Australia's management of the waters surrounding it. He writes that Villawood was inhabited by the indigenous Gandangara tribe, which was eliminated with colonialism (Apter 2016). During the Second World

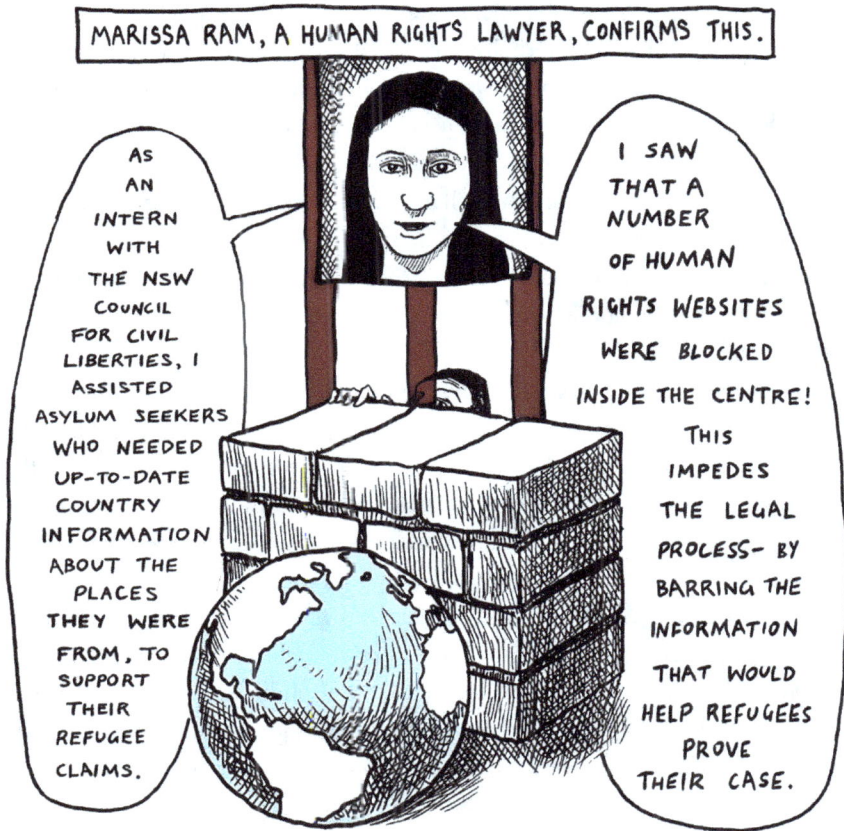

Figure 4.5 Excerpt from Ahmed, S. (2015), 'Villawood: Notes from an Immigration Detention Centre', *The Shipping News*. © Safdar Ahmed, image courtesy of the artist.

and tall, sharp palisade rods topped with electric wire [,] where even the trees are bound in corrugated iron and steel spikes [. . .] to prevent [people] from climbing them and jumping off' (Ahmed 2015: np). The brick wall that is drawn in chapter 3 of 'Villawood', which blocks the refugee's access to the globe, constitutes another

War, the area was used for the construction of a factory that created explosives, while in the post-war period, the factory transformed into the 'Villawood Migrant Hostel' in the context of the 'immigration policy [. . .] "Populate or Perish" [which aimed to] to increase Australia's population following World War Two' (Apter 2016: 6). The Australian State's 'racial fear of Asia' as well as fears stemming from its supposed 'isolation in the Pacific' led to the Australian prime minister's belief that it was essential for the country's white, Western population to increase, and so 'assisted migration from the UK' in particular was initiated (Apter 2016: 6). In the 1970s, the site started holding people that were to be deported from the country, and currently it constitutes a carceral site for Australia's unwanted others (Apter 2016). It is precisely for these reasons that colonial and racial violence is inextricably linked to this space.

variation of the firewall. As a spatial metaphor that is visually presented, this wall embodies the information verbally accounted for by the lawyer, which regards the blocking of human rights websites and other means that would help those detained to strengthen their asylum cases and to thus gain access to Australia, and to the world. As shown through this example, comics enable the structuring of the wall in 'Villawood' as both a physical and virtual construct that represents the multiplicity of the ways through which the Australian State tries to block people from securing asylum in the country, enacting its (neo-)colonial violence against them through both physical and virtual wall-building.

In *Walled States, Waning Sovereignty*, Wendy Brown discusses the preoccupation of nation-States with walls, noting the marked difference between their 'stark physicalism' and the currently available 'capacities for destruction [that are] historically unparalleled in their combined potency, miniaturization, and mobility' (2010: 20). The frenzied building of walls across Western nations, she writes, constitutes a spectacle that is supposed to spatially embody the power of State sovereignty. However, this project is a failed one given that walls are instead 'iconographic' of the erosion of sovereign State power (Brown 2010: 24). 'Notwithstanding their strikingly physicalist and obdurate dimensions', Brown points out, walls 'often function theatrically, projecting power and efficaciousness that they do not and cannot actually exercise and that they also performatively contradict' (2010: 25).

Contrary to capital and goods that freely circulate in the context of globalized neoliberal economy, the movement of people is supposed to be blocked by liquid and territorial walls. Human movement, however, does not stop. Rather, it diverges from previous routes, finding new ones, which may nevertheless be more dangerous. It is for this reason that walls spatially embody 'the effects of waning state sovereignty on the psychic-political desires, anxieties, and needs of late modern subjects', who were promised to be protected from their others (Brown 2010: 107). Consequently, they function as fetishes falsely promising 'restored potency' (Brown 2010: 119). In their visual depictions of literal, metaphorical, virtual, liquid and built walls, and the perseverance of refugees and asylum seekers as they endure their violence, *The Journey* and 'Villawood' also highlight their inadequacy.

According to Michel Agier, walls crush 'borders, making them disappear, until the "walled" (who include, of course, those walled out) overthrow [them] or transform [them] and make [them] disappear by cutting holes in [them], putting up ladders or equipping [them] with gates' (2016: 17). Walls 'provoke indignation. They reassure. They prevent seeing what happens on the other side. They are the mark and means of a "war". They are visible, [they] lead to deaths [...]. They are permeable and spur people to study informal ("clandestine") ways of crossing them' (Agier 2016: 55). They are excessive, anachronistic spectacles that render the lives of those trying to overcome them unliveable, and 'they produce new political subjectivities' (Agier 2016: 56). In the graphic life narratives examined in this chapter, walls also become spatial figurative devices that critically underscore the political, colonial violence that becomes manifested through their erection reconfiguring and underscoring the violence of Western borders. At the same time, they also foreground asylum seekers' resilience against Western States' spatial injustices.

Coda

Through the preceding analysis, I have unpacked the role of space and place in graphic life narratives that account for different forms of injustice and human rights violations inflicted against othered people. From the cartographies of the Juarez femicides, to the heterotopias of Manus Island and Sri Lanka, and from the destroyed olive trees of Palestine to the weaponization of the sea and the erection of walls in Australia and Europe, the online and print graphic life narratives examined in this chapter demonstrate how looking at and into the (back)ground matters in graphic testimonies of suffering.

Sarah A. Radcliffe and Isabella M. Radhuber write that 'political geography has much to contribute to interdisciplinary decolonial scholarship through contextualized, grounded, multiscalar and granular analysis of socio-spatial relations' (2020: 1). The graphic life narratives examined in this chapter present localized knowledge about the earth from body-political and geo-political locations of alterity, showing how modernity/coloniality wounds both othered people and the earth itself. They politically re-connect space and society, the *humus* and the human, myth and reality, reason and emotion, as well as word and image, in displaying the shapes that sovereign violence is contemporarily taking in Western States' governmentality of irregular migration, in the Israeli/Palestinian and the Sri Lankan conflict, and in the transformation of Juarez into an 'ultra-capitalist city' (González Rodríguez 2012: 37). Radcliffe and Radhuber also explain that to decolonize analysis and knowledge production means to draw 'from postcolonial, critical, feminist and racism critiques, and [to problematize] accounts of knowledge, subjectivity and power [in ways that address] global inequalities' (2020: 1). This chapter has unpacked the contribution of graphic topopoetics and graphic life narrative in human and political geography's explorations of the workings of space and place in the global distribution of inequality and injustice.

5

Western borders, violence and *ponos*

In this chapter, I examine one print and four online graphic life narratives accounting for human rights violations that occur in the context of forced, undocumented migration at the borders of Australia and Europe. Focusing on Safdar Ahmed's 'Villawood' and 'Affective States', two cartoons by Eaten Fish, Gabi Froden's 'An Empty Promise' and Francesca Sanna's *The Journey*, I investigate the extent to which they adequately foreground Western (neo-) colonial complicities in human rights violations inflicted against undocumented migrants in origin, transit and destination countries and their corresponding borderzones. I argue that the selected texts' depictions of monsters, icons of (in) justice and witnessing animals alongside the othered people who become configured into the living dead of European and Australian borders, enrich the spectacle of border violence, and expose the *ponos* of (neo-)colonial border policing regimes in Australia, Europe and beyond.

Border *ponos*

I use the term 'border' as described by Achille Mbembe, who introduces it as 'the name we should use to describe the organised violence that underpins both contemporary capitalism and our world order in general' (2019a: 9). The border is not merely a static territorial point because the 'new global partitioning between [bodies that are] potentially risky [and those] that are not' has transformed it into the name to be given to 'the moving body of the undesired masses of populations' (Mbembe 2019a: 9). The border hence refers to the collective (im-)mobile othered border-crossing body, as well as to the violent sovereign State powers that injuriously interpellate a given subject as belonging to it. Borders also constitute (neo-)colonial death-worlds that configure those they constrain within their limits as living dead populations (Mbembe 2019b; Zocchi 2021). And while in Chapter 3 I examine literal deaths, my investigation of graphic life narratives displaying the living dead of Western borders concerns metaphorical, social ones. It also relates to whether undocumented border-crossers' (neo-)colonial subject formations demonstrate how 'bodies are shaped by histories of colonialism [and how they] remember [these] histories, even when we forget them' (Ahmed 2007: 153–4).

Benedetta Zocchi, for instance, describes the Bosnian-Croatian border as a colonial one because it does not 'participate in the collective amnesia of war, conflict, and darkness that Europe brought on itself' (2021: 31). In that impenetrable for some zone, Europe's 'dark side [. . .] was not hidden', she writes, 'to the contrary, signs of a dark past were more visible than ever [and its violence was] visible and legitimatized' (Zocchi 2021: 31). In their production of othered living dead populations, white Western borders within and beyond the West, in places such as Australia, Nauru and Manus Islands in the Pacific Ocean as well as Italy and Libya, share the same characteristics.[1] The graphic narrativization of their violence is therefore charged with the potential to expose the colonial wounds and the *ponos* (pain) they cause, opening up spaces towards decolonial healing precisely by breaking into the darkness and invisibility that are cast over them.

For Walter D. Mignolo, the border is a space from which decolonial thinking can emerge. Borders, he notes, 'matter [decolonially] when the enunciation is enacted in [them], by enunciators dwelling' therein (Mignolo and Gaztambide-Fernández 2014: 199). Border epistemology, he further explains, 'emerges from the senses, from the body sensing the power differential of the border (any border, geo-political and body-political)' (Mignolo and Gaztambide-Fernández 2014: 199). Comics produced collaboratively by artists, and asylum seekers crossing or remaining stranded within Western borderzones may constitute a fertile ground for articulating such decolonial knowledge emerging from liminal, non-Eurocentric loci of enunciation. It is precisely this aspect of the border that has fruitful potential regarding the creative work it can enable, which can expose border-crossers' human rights violations, showing how the border itself is much more than a territorial entity.

With the term border *ponos*, I refer to this double dimension of both the suffering caused by border violence, and the creative strife that exposes it. In Hesiod's *Theogony*, Ponos (pain) was the son of Eris (strife, conflict) and

---

[1]   Western borders extend outside the West through 'border externalization processes, including "assisting, funding, or training agencies in other countries to arrest, detail, process, rescue, or disembark and return refugees or migrants" [, processes that have] raised serious concerns where [by] the recipient states are alleged to be responsible for serious crimes' (Bertran 2021: 304).

grandson of Nyx (night). It was one of the dark forces given as punishment to humans for accepting the fire Prometheus had stolen from the gods for them. Jonathan P. Zarecki writes of how Prometheus undid the injustice committed by Zeus, who had robbed humans of their 'means of life, the βίος', by gifting them with fire (2007: 16).[2] In this chapter, I use this mythical narrative as a metaphorical exposition of the violence suffered by undocumented border-crossers, which is caused by centuries of Western (neo-)colonial (at times religiously justified) sovereign State interventions elsewhere, and through contemporary border policing practices that deprive them of a biographical, political life.

Zeus with Via and Kratos, who in their union embody the violence of absolute sovereignty in *Prometheus Bound*, punished both Prometheus and the humankind for having proverbially crossed the line in their effort to restore the possibility of human *bios*. And while people did gain the means to a life by accepting Prometheus's gift, this would be marked by *ponos* (pain and strife). In *Theogony*, Ponos is connected to 'physical or mental conflict' and suffering, while Homer uses this term to refer to 'the toil of war, or as a synonym for war itself' (Zarecki 2007: 16).[3] As used in this chapter, *ponos* is associated with physical and psychic strain and trauma, and with the strife for survival, for the right to a human, that is, to a biographical as well as a biological life, to a *zoe* and a *bios*, of which undocumented border-crossers become deprived in being reconfigured as the living dead of Western borders.

When it comes to these populations, *ponos* and the other evils brought about by Eris stem from the death-worlds existing in their countries of origin, those they are forced to navigate en route to, and those they encounter upon arriving in, destination countries. These evils are the offspring of Western (neo-)colonial sovereign interventions elsewhere, and of the violent biopolitical and necropolitical governmentality of migration. As Mbembe reminds us in 'Bodies as Borders', 'millions of people [have been lost] during the centuries of the Atlantic and Arab slave trades. Colonialism, its endless wars, its political economy and its epidemiological and ecological consequences [also] killed many' (2019a: 15). Further to these past crimes, contemporarily, Western countries continue 'destroying other people's living environments, extracting

---

[2] Giorgio Agamben (1995) distinguishes between *zoe* (biological life) and *bios* (political life) of which one is deprived when existing outside the law of the State.
[3] The 'harmful creatures' born by Eris alongside Ponos, such as 'Fights, Battles, Murders, Slaughters, Feuds', Lethe (forgetting/amnesia) and Limos (famine) have connotations related to the evils brought about by war (Zarecki 2007: 16).

their oil, gas, timber, diamonds and gold, shipping it all home, leaving nothing behind, turning their cities into rubble, bringing to an end the possibilities of life in faraway places, and expect those affected by such upheavals to survive in the midst of the ruins' (Mbembe 2019a: 16).[4] This diachronic (neo-)colonial violence produces othered border-crossing populations as mere bodies, it deprives them of a *bios*, and often of a *zoe*, and it reconfigures them as living dead othered spectres. For this reason, it is necessary to examine embodied human rights violations at Western borders while being 'mindful of [the] empire' and its transformations through the centuries (Sidaway 2019: 271).

Precisely because Western borders and their biopolitical control deprive people of life, the irregularly crossed border is similar to that other liminal border, the Acheron River, which connected the world with the underworld, the Earth with Hades, the state of the living with that of the dead. In Ancient Greece, it was believed that in order to enter the underworld, people had to pay Charon, the ferryman, to carry them with his boat across the river, so that they could continue living as dead. The name Acheron denotes a 'stream of pain' (St. Fleur 2020: 6). This liminal borderzone between the world of the living and that of the dead is, in this sense, characterized by its flowing *ponos*. Those crossing it were perceived as neither fully dead nor alive, but rather as ambivalent spectres existing in-between, but not quite in either of the two states. As such, Acheron embodied 'the conditions of the Hadean afterlife: an endless limbo of grievous pain, wailing, [...], hatred, and mindless oblivion' (St. Fleur 2020: 6). These attributes also characterize the lives of people contemporarily trying to irregularly cross Western borders both within and beyond the West in search for a life that is both biological and biographical.

In Greek mythology, falling into oblivion or *lethe*, being erased from memory, denotes (a kind of) death.[5] Western State-initiated narratives about border violence are characterized by a tendency to justify it, to erase it from public discourse and from collective memory, and to cast a veil of amnesia (*lethe*) and silence over it (Humphrey 2017). While prior to 2020 social and mainstream

---

[4] Kalypso Nicolaïdis describes Europe's 'virgin (re-)birth' noting that the 'European Community was born not only of a desire for a radical break with the past, war and nationalism; it was also born out of desire for continuity and collective management of a colonial world – above all the African continent – that was slipping out of the grasp of its member states individually' (2015: 285–6).

[5] Lethe was also born by Eris and is one of Ponos's siblings. Eris is also a sister to Thanatos that was discussed in Chapter 3.

media were flooded by images showing dead people at the shores of European countries in the Mediterranean, the separation of families and the caging of children at the US/Mexico border, as well as the brutality of Australian deterrence policies (MacFarlane 2014; Davies 2020; Pécoud 2020), the outbreak of the Covid-19 pandemic has silenced stories of border suffering.[6] The analysis that follows aims to show how graphic life narratives depicting such pain counter this tendency towards forgetting or *lethe*.[7]

This is where the second set of implications of *ponos* as used in this chapter are located. The verb 'πονέω'/*poneo*, its root, means 'to labor, endure hardships, suffer, [but also] travail' (Montanari 2016: 1720). It further denotes accomplishing something, while a second derivative of the same root denotes work, which may be literary and is completed after intellectual, creative and/or physical strife (Montanari 2016). Hence, *ponos* can also be associated with creative labour. In this chapter, I perceive the texts under investigation as illustrative of and embodying such (creative) strife and pain. My analysis points to their potential for countering colonial textualities, such as those previously described.[8] In doing so, it demonstrates how icons of monstrosity and (in)justice, as well as witnessing animals, appear at Western borders in the selected texts to enrich the graphic depiction of their violence for adult and child readers. It also introduces the ways in which detained asylum seekers in Australia, as well as those precariously crossing European borderzones, resist their status as living dead and their configurations as undesired, mute, bodies.

---

[6] Jennifer Boum Make and John Patrick Walsh write that three years after its outbreak, COVID seems 'to have eclipsed stories about migrants and refugees' (2021: 294). The pandemic also caused further human rights violations and immobility for irregular border-crossers, who in many cases were exposed to higher risk of contamination due to detention, lockdowns and prohibition of movement, and were deprived of the right to health care. As such, it has foregrounded the stark juxtaposition between lives that matter and those that do not. In *Migrants and the COVID-19 Pandemic: An Initial Analysis*, Lorenzo Guadagno explains how 'the pandemic has [also] been weaponized to spread anti-migrant narratives and call[s] for increased immigration control and reduction of migrants' rights' (2020: 12).

[7] Memory was personified through the figure of Mnemosyne in *Theogony*, the binary opposite of, Lethe, which I discuss in Chapter 3. On time, death, forgetting and remembering in relation to Lethe and Mnemosyne in literary and graphic narratives depicting irregular border crossings from Africa and Asia to Europe, see also Michael 2024.

[8] Binita Mehta and Pia Mukherji define colonial textualities as 'persistent and strategic practice[s] of epistemic violence: self-identifying as legitimate systems of knowledge, engaged in naming the self/other binary, and encoding names in hierarchies of significance in (post)imperial contexts' (2015: 2). Contra to those, online and print graphic life narratives exposing human rights violations at borders may constitute samples of decolonized 'postcolonial textualities [that] enter colonial discourse deconstructively, inhabiting its ambiguities and fissures, and thus initiate a "persistent questioning of the frame, which at one level, is the space of representation, and at another level, the frame of western modernity itself"' (Mehta and Mukherji 2015: 2).

Border monstrosities

Asylum detention in Australia

In their graphic narrativization of border violence, 'Villawood' and 'Affective States' by Ahmed, like 'An Empty Promise' by Froden and *The Journey* by Sanna, are populated by monsters; creatures that are marked by their visible difference, and the pain they can cause, as well as by their liminal existence in-between the human and the inhuman. Maaheen Ahmed writes that monsters embody 'figurations of social identity constructions and mechanisms of othering' (2019: 4; Diamond and Poharec 2017). In this book, I have thus far unpacked the ways in which racially and religiously othered men have been discursively formed and hence become perceived as monstrous terrorists, and I have pointed to the ways in which graphic life narrative can undo their injurious formations as such. Elsewhere, I have also argued that such formations can stand in opposition to news reporting on post-9/11 terrorism as a largely decontextualized product of the current moment (Michael 2022a). In this chapter, I focus on the graphic depictions of monstrosities appearing at Western borders that do not embody the religiously and racially othered refugee and asylum seeker.

In 'Villawood', border monstrosity can be seen as metaphorically reflected in how detained people are left to suffer health and other issues, and to eventually die. Because most of Ahmed's interlocutors are male detainees, by presenting their stories and perspectives, the narrative re-orients readerly preconceptions regarding male migrant monstrosity, as those previously described. One of the detainees Safdar meets, Ahmad Ali Jafari, is a Hazara refugee from Afghanistan, whose illustrations and poems form a core part of 'Villawood'. The narrator describes him as 'a generous, warm-natured man' and relates how he prepared 'drinks for everyone' during the art workshops at the centre, performing acts of hospitality in an extremely inhospitable context (Ahmed 2015: np). He also notes that 'his artwork displays the frustration of being indefinitely detained with no certainty of release' (Ahmed 2015: np).

In the visual register (Figure 5.1), a panel shows an abstract drawing of a boat, the scale of (in-)justice weighting on one side, a leg chained to a wall, an eye crying, and a hammer directed towards a human brain, which is bound to be wounded due to the approaching violence. In one of his couplets, which are written in Urdu, but become translated into English by Ahmed, Ahmad writes that 'in this night of solitude, there are thousands of dreams, but there are more

Figure 5.1 Excerpt from Ahmed, S. (2015), 'Villawood: Notes from an Immigration Detention Centre', *The Shipping News*. © Safdar Ahmed, image courtesy of the artist.

pains in my heart – thousands of sorrows' (Ahmed 2015: np). His poetic references to pain, sorrow and an endless night of solitude, alongside his visual depictions of suffering in Villawood, artistically embody the attributes of the non-life of Acheron – the liminal border between the world of the living and that of the dead.

In the account of Ahmad's death in 'Villawood', the figure of the monster becomes embodied by the female guards of the detention centre. Safdar relates how this man was left to die, explaining that his chest pains had been systematically ignored by the guards, like his psychologist's instructions to place him in a room separately from other detainees due to his severe mental health issues. At this instance, border monstrosity also becomes manifested via how a guard decides to stop people from participating in mourning rituals organized by the detainees in the visitors' area of the centre. Upon a detainee's request to allow people to enter, the guard gets infuriated. Her rage is visually depicted initially through the shape of her irises, and subsequently, via the veins on the side of her head, and the bright red colour in which her figure is washed (Figure 5.2).

Border monstrosity thus concerns how a man was left to die and how those left behind become deprived of the right to appropriately mourn him. A detainee explains to Safdar, and the implied reader, that through their behaviour the guards 'were trying to say: "Who gives a shit that someone died"' (Ahmed 2015: np).

Figure 5.2 Excerpt from Ahmed, S. (2015), 'Villawood: Notes from an Immigration Detention Centre', *The Shipping News*. © Safdar Ahmed, image courtesy of the artist.

The dehumanization of refugees therefore continues posthumously and becomes relationally experienced by the living dead of the Australian border. Ahmad's family were also denied visas to attend his funeral due to their status as Afghan refugees living in Pakistan (Ahmed 2015). In the visual register, Ahmad's parents, and his younger brother, those the Australian State strives to keep outside its borders, are shown crying over the loss of their loved one. As such, 'Villawood' displays how the *ponos* of the border becomes experienced well beyond the spatial boundaries of Australia as it also exposes the State's colonial violence.

Border monstrosity, which also becomes metonymically embodied through the female guards of Villawood, deprives refugees of adequate health care, at the same time as preventing their communities from showing respect for their dead. Similarly to the walls of the detention centre, the white scroll of Ahmed's online graphic life narrative is marked by the presence of Ahmad's photograph, which enters the diegetic realm to present the violence of the Australian border more realistically. A caption accompanying the photograph explains that this man was 'killed by immigration' (Ahmed 2015: np), pointing to State responsibilities for this death. However, the guards, the State's monstrous extensions, quickly remove these photographs from the walls to erase Ahmad's death from public discourse and from collective memory. The political impact of 'Villawood' lies precisely in how, by exposing the lethal impact of border monstrosity, it also counters attempts to force it into oblivion/*lethe* embodying an act of creative, agonistic mourning and strife in its demand for justice.

Another liminal creature, the zombie, which is caught in-between the living and the dead, also appears in Ahmed's 'Affective States'. Penny Crofts and Anthea Vogl discuss this figure in their analysis of 'inhuman/human constructions that feature in state responses to refugees' in the Australian context (2019: 29). They write that the refugees' representations as zombies constitute one of the ways through which they become dehumanized and demonized. In addition, they propose that 'reading the demonised refugee as the contemporary zombie monster and inversely, reading the resurgence of the zombie monster through the prism of the so-called refugee and migrant crisis, reveals the precise anxieties brought about by refugees and asylum seekers' (Crofts and Vogl 2019: 29). The zombie, like other monsters, signals 'a category crisis' as Jeffrey Jerome Cohen writes (1996: 6).

According to Crofts and Vogl, both the refugee and the zombie 'represent the transgression of borders, as well as the failure of containment, borders and border walls as a response to crisis' (2019: 29). The contemporary reconceptualization of the zombie 'as a race-less catchall monster figure mirrors the erasure of colonial histories, race and race relations in the casting of refugees as dehistoricized, invading and disorderly bodies' (Crofts and Vogl 2019: 29). Like the (neo-) colonial histories that remain outside the frame of representation in State-initiated narratives regarding refugees and the refugee crisis, the structuring of border-crossers as unified zombie masses strategically introduces them as a threat that is other than and external to the Australian people and sovereign State.

Rather than metaphorically or metonymically depicting border violence or the living dead of the border, however, the figure of the zombie in 'Affective States' is a creature that enables, at the same time as embodying, bonds of solidarity and creativity between Safdar and Kazem Kazemi, an Iranian asylum seeker, who was detained in Manus Island for six years. These bonds emerged via their collaborative metal music-making. Ahmed's short graphic life narrative starts with his autobiographical avatar looking at the implied reader and explicating how the State's 'language of exclusion generates affective arrangements that instil hostility, xenophobia and indifference' (2024: np). In the first row of three panels, the artist reproduces the narrative of the Australian State's take on 'the boat people [who] threaten the border' by evoking 'the spectre of invasion' (Ahmed 2024: np). Images used in hostile deterrence narratives become reproduced in the visual register. Darkness, a black silhouette and abstracted human icons over a boat become displayed. While in *Understanding Comics* Scott McCloud (1994) argues that abstraction in comics' iconicity enables readerly identification, at this instance, the abstracted figures of the boat people visually trigger distance and estrangement. Through their abstracted embodiments, in this initial row of panels, undocumented border-crossing populations become presented as elusive, indecipherable and threatening.[9]

In the second row of panels, the narrative frame turns away from this distancing view on asylum seekers and zooms in on xenophobic and Islamophobic comments. The first panel shows a man wearing a 'refugees not welcome' T-shirt as he explains that 'we need to protect our culture' (Ahmed 2024: np). The second shows another person holding a poster with a visual prohibition symbol over a mosque and saying that 'no more mosques' should exist in Australia (Ahmed 2024: np). The narrator intervenes in this narrative fragment to explain that the

---

[9]   For the image, see Figure 4.3 in Chapter 4.

State's abstracted, hostile take on the people seeking refuge in Australia, as presented in the previous row, becomes 'amplified in the public mind [, especially] when [it] attack[s] Muslims and other racialized minorities' (Ahmed 2024: np). This, he continues, 'shouldn't surprise anyone [because] the colonial state was built on' such processes (Ahmed 2024: np).

The third panel zooms in on the face of Pauline Hanson, an MP who stated, in 2017, that 'Islam is a disease and we need to vaccinate ourselves against that' (Ahmed 2024: np). Hanson's visual depiction is similar to those of the monstrous guards of 'Villawood'. In the post-Covid-19 pandemic context, her comment is charged with heightened injurious implications. The visual depiction of her face mediates the anger and hatred entailed in her words, which produce two categories of Australian citizens, those who are, and those who are not infected by what she presents through an injurious metaphor as a contaminating disease.[10] Those who are not contaminated in this metaphorical schema become represented through her use of the first-person collective pronoun 'we', casting those who do not belong in this category as her diseased others, sustaining, in the contemporary Australian context, affectively charged (neo-)colonial perspectives on Muslim people.

Contrary to the abstracted images of unknown refugees, the embodied articulations of religious hate are presented as being too close, and thus too familiar for the autobiographical subject. Indeed, the narrator explains that as a Muslim Australian national, he experiences this form of violence as a 'pre-verbal experience . . . [a] kick in the guts [that] also describes affect' (Ahmed 2024: np).[11] Safdar's autobiographical avatar is shown crouching because of the *ponos* caused by such statements. Presenting affectively charged knowledge deriving from his geo-political and body-political locus of enunciation, Safdar

---

[10] In 'Metaphors We Discriminate By', Elisabeth el Refaie accounts for verbal metaphors found in Austrian newspapers, which introduce 'the arrival of Kurdish asylum seekers in Italy in January 1998 [. . .] as water, as criminals, or as invading army' and warns 'that the "naturalization" of particular metaphors can contribute to a blurring of the boundaries between the literal and the non-literal' (2001: 532). Elsewhere, she discusses visual metaphors found in political cartoons in Austrian newspapers, which portray 'immigration as a criminal activity, an invasion and a flood' alongside 'the highly conventional verbal metaphor of "fortress Europe"' (El Refaie 2003: 83). Highlighting the affective impact of visual images in relation to verbal ones, el Refaie explains how these enhance the naturalization of negative discursive formations and understandings of the asylum seeker. In this monograph, I also illustrate the opposite effect lying in graphic metaphors found in online and print graphic life narratives accounting for the human rights violations suffered by othered people.

[11] Sara Ahmed also writes that 'the body recognized as "could be Muslim", which translates into "could be terrorist"' gets stopped and becomes 'singled out' more frequently thus being deprived of the opportunity to inhabit and navigate certain spaces 'habitually' (2007: 162–3).

exposes colonial wounds at the same time as embedding contemporary refugee and asylum detention in Australia in a broader, painful trajectory. He thus introduces border violence as colonial and as spreading beyond territorial and temporal boundaries. The transition from the abstracted visual depictions of the boat people to individual people's hate expressions, and to the display of Safdar's embodied affective experiences of Islamophobia, illustrates the potential of comics for critiquing preconceptions about threat coming from othered populations and from beyond Australia's borders. By accounting for Safdar's experiences of religious hate as an Australian citizen, the narrative also implies that racism and Islamophobia are more severely injurious for noncitizens, for asylum seekers and undocumented migrants, who become further wounded and marginalized within this (neo-) colonial setting.

It is in this narrative context that the figure of the zombie appears to embody affective bonds of solidarity created through collaborative music-making (Figure 5.3). After accounting for the injurious impact of Islamophobia, Safdar relates how in 2018 he met Kazem, who had been imprisoned for six years in Manus Island. He explains that Kazem 'would practice guitar in the laundry room [. . .] and send [him] riffs recorded on his phone' (Ahmed 2024: np). A poem he wrote, entitled 'Manus Hell', provided the lyrics of a song the two men wrote together (Ahmed 2024: np). Similarly to Acheron, the liminal border that is characterized by pain and suffering, and like Ahmad's description of detention as a long, dark, night of pain and solitude in 'Villawood', Kazem describes Manus Island as hell – the kind of afterlife that is supposed to function as eternal punishment and torture (Ahmed 2024). The indefiniteness of suffering in hell corresponds to that of his detention in Manus Island.

Figure 5.3 Excerpt from Ahmed, S. (2024), 'Affective States', *Image [&] Narrative* 24(3): 1–4. © Safdar Ahmed, image courtesy of the artist.

In the final page of the narrative, Safdar explains that the two met in person in 2021 and bonded through 'Brethren in the Dark', a song by the Norwegian black metal band Satyricon. In the visual register, an elongated panel shows a zombie quoting/singing lyrics from this song: 'Forever torn, forever gone through the mirror of despair . . . . Pass a torch to your brethren in the dark' (Ahmed 2024: np). The despair suffered by the living dead who navigate darkness becomes embodied visually, through the figure of the zombie and the colour of the panel, and verbally, through the lyrics of this song. The zombie visually embodies border *ponos* – the suffering and the collaborative creative strife emerging from Australia's border. In rejecting categories and collapsing borders between inside/outside, and between the living and the dead, the zombie in 'Affective States' embodies solidarity and resistance at the border that is also reflected via the torch of light it holds and through Safdar and Kazem's music-making in a genre that is deeply subversive and political. This creature's contextualization and reconceptualization in 'Affective States' stands as a counter-narrative to its discursive use for the demonization and dehumanization of refugees.

Subsequently to the presence of the zombie in the intra-diegetic register, Kazem explains to Safdar that he 'cannot remember riffs because [his] brain is wrecked from detention' (Ahmed 2024: np).[12] This statement presents literally what Ahmad's abstract drawings illustrate figuratively in 'Villawood' in relation to the psychic injuries caused by detention.[13] In 'Affective States', step by step, and piece by piece, the two men compose their song. The narrator explains that 'in this context, our collaboration was not just about telling a story, or relaying how racist Australia's border policies are, but an attempt to evoke feelings through music' (Ahmed 2024: np). Kazem's face is cut in half by the panel's border, but as he plays his guitar and sings, his facial expressions also illustrate the pain that becomes expressed acoustically and verbally through his song.

In 'Affective Economies', Sara Ahmed writes that 'emotions *do things*, and they align individuals with communities – or bodily space with social space – through

---

[12] Australia's detention centres have been described by the psychiatrist Patrick McGorry as 'factories for producing mental illness' (quoted in Fiske 2016: 199).

[13] A study conducted in Sidney, Australia, connects pre- and post-migration trauma. According to it, 'a diagnosis of PTSD was associated with greater exposure to pre-migration trauma, delays in processing refugee applications, difficulties in dealing with immigration officials, obstacles to employment, racial discrimination, loneliness and boredom' (Silove et al. 1997: 351). Aamer Sultan, a medical practitioner from Iraq, who was detained in Villawood, co-authored a paper for the *Medical Journal of Australia* with Kevin O Sullivan, where they explain that because 'the process of applying for refugee status in Australia is complex, lengthy and often poorly understood by asylum seekers' it often leads to mental strain (2001: 593). They further note that 'the prolonged detention of asylum seekers appears to cause serious psychological harm' (Sultan and O'Sullivan 2001: 593).

the very intensity of their attachments' (2004: 119, emphasis in the original). They 'work by sticking figures together (adherence), a sticking that creates the very effect of a collective (coherence), with reference to the figures of the asylum seeker and the international terrorist' (Ahmed 2004: 119). The feelings of the Australian public and politicians accounted for by Ahmed at the beginning of 'Affective States' exist in juxtaposition with those produced at its end. While fear brings about hate, and according to Ahmed, the intersectional-feminist scholar, the creation and control of the border itself, the ways in which Kazem and Safdar stuck together shows how affective bonds can also open up spaces towards decolonial healing and solidarity precisely by exposing the impact of the Australian border's colonial wounds. 'Affective States' thus shows, on the one hand, the injurious impact of violent border monstrosities, the mental strain, and the trauma that they cause, and on the other, it illustrates, through the figure of the zombie, how creative resistance and affective bonds of solidarity can emerge from the domain of the living dead.

In *Human Rights, Refugee Protest, and Immigration Detention*, Lucy Fiske writes that 'as recently as the 1990s, immigration detention was used by only a few states and almost entirely as a last resort, whereas in 2015, almost all states practice immigration detention, creating a global carceral web' (2016: 6; Nethery and Silverman 2015). Further to those within their borders, Australia, Europe and the United States fund detention centres elsewhere, in Nauru and Manus Islands and in Indonesia in the first case, in Libya in the second, and in Mexico in the third (Fiske 2016). In the post-Brexit context and its attempt to 'tackle [...] "illegal" migration', the UK also signed agreements to send 'people who arrive by small boats [and those] hidden in lorries to have their asylum claims processed in Rwanda' (Limb 2022: np). In so doing, Western States purposefully keep asylum seekers 'outside the potentially protective embrace of western liberal democratic states' legal systems' (Fiske 2016: 6). Western border monstrosities thus move beyond the West while reconfiguring undocumented border-crossers as living dead populations deprived of the right to a *zoe* and a *bios*.

Commenting upon Australia's offshore detention sites in the Pacific, Michelle Bui writes that they operate 'under a veil of secrecy, outside of an effective state jurisdiction and with little independent oversight', something that 'has led to their characterisation as black sites' (2018: 183–4). This term, which reflects processes of invisibilization occurring at borderzones, but also their function as the domains of the living dead, was introduced by Researchers Against Pacific Black Sites (RAPBS). In defining it, they explain that it has been widely used in the war on terror to describe locations where the US and its allies maintain secret prisons or conduct other illicit activities away from public or legal scrutiny. These sites are characterized by secrecy and lack of accountability. They are most often located in racialized and/or formerly colonized territories, and they continue practices of abuse and torture perpetrated there against colonized peoples.

RAPBS quoted in Bui 2018: 184

Even though NGOs and the media have been routinely denied access to such carceral spaces in Australia, with this prohibition leading to the increased invisibility of human rights violations occurring there, 'as long as there has been violence enacted upon the bodies of asylum seekers and refugees there has, too, been resistance' (Bui 2018: 184). This resistance is displayed in Ahmed's online comics through their exposure of border *ponos* and their monster figurations. Bui highlights the value of 'social media platforms and online communication channels [,which] have strengthened the ability of Australia's political prisoners to reach through the wire, to defy fences, seas and borders, and connect with people who the government does not want their voices to reach' (2018: 185). The political value of Ahmed's webcomics lies in that they break into the seal of darkness that hides the violence inflicted on the bodies of detained asylum seekers.

European deterrence and border control policies

Further to suffering that occurs in the Australian detention system, Froden's online comic, 'An Empty Promise', illustrates anthropomorphized monsters of border violence in the female protagonist's crossing from Nigeria through Libya in her attempt to reach Italy.[14] The violence encountered by asylum seekers crossing through Libya derives from European efforts to keep them outside the borders of its otherwise democratic, protective, liberal States. Mary relates that when she arrived with other people in Quatrun, Libya, after having crossed through Nigeria and Niger, their trafficker abandoned them, and they 'were held prisoners by the Bogas and the Madames for three months' (Froden 2017: 11).[15]

---

[14] Mbembe describes Libya as one of the 'lawless places [...], where Europe is funding militias and encouraging them to capture would-be African migrants to detain them in makeshift camps or to sell them into slavery' (2019a: 16).
[15] The madames are women who control the trafficked people through their journey and get discounts for their own, and the bogas are men who accompany trafficked girls (Pascoal 2020).

She also mentions that 'girls were chosen at random for sex work and boys worked all day without food' (Froden 2017: 11). Her avatar is located at the centre of the panel. The rest of the people around her are depicted minimally through white outlines that foreground their dehumanization and their status as the semi/visible, indecipherable living dead spectres navigating Western borders outside Europe.

Mary, the testifying subject, is drawn in colour in this graphic life narrative that relates her horrific border-crossing experiences in a drawing style that evokes children's illustration. As she relates how she and other border-crossers were forced into slavery, six black hands that are larger than the visually depicted border-crossers approach them from the sides of the panel. A man's hand grabs that of a boy, and a woman's (as indicated by its embellishments) grabs that of a girl. These monstrous perpetrators of violence, who force boys and girls into labour and sex work, are thus gendered and racially marked, but remain elusive, outside the frame of representation. The same applies for the ways in which European deterrence policies cause human trafficking and torture in Libya. In this sense, at this instance, 'An Empty Promise' depicts the monster of violence as othered, and as disconnected and far-removed from Europe.

Prior to describing the violence she suffered in Libya, Mary accounts for why she left her village in Nigeria. Paternal abandonment and poverty led her to seek a better life in Europe, after having tried to survive by cleaning, selling fruit and begging. The impact of the British colonization of Nigeria, as well as British and European (neo-)colonial interests there, which have deprived the local population of their means to a *bios*, are not mentioned in this narrative. Toyin Falola, however, writes of how the country's natural resources were seized through British colonization, which also left its mark on political life after decolonization through its 'legacies [of] postcolonial disorder', also describing Nigeria as 'torn from within' (2009: 180), similarly to the other British post-colonies discussed in this monograph. In the Nigerian (post-)colonial context, Mary's survival chances are limited due to poverty and lack of access to education and employment. Her account of how a friend introduced her to a man named John, who promised a short trip to Italy, where she 'would make plenty of money', and she would have the opportunity to study (Froden 2017: 7), is quite representative of the stories told to young women to deceive them into being trafficked (Pascoal 2020).

Rafaela Pascoal (2020) writes of the restrictions imposed by the European Union on Nigerian migration, which has increased trafficking and trafficked women's vulnerabilities to exploitation in transit and destination countries. She further relates how the 'European dream' is deeply rooted in the Nigerian community, explaining that 'a cultural framework has been created around [. . .] migration flows to Italy and Spain due to a "quick money syndrome"' (Pascoal 2020: 35). Because of it, 'women often have high expectations when departing for Europe' and due to their poor educational and socio-economic background, they frequently become victims of trafficking (Pascoal 2020: 35). While the Libyan smuggling route had been previously well-controlled because of agreements signed between Italy and Libya, which prevented undocumented African migrants from entering Europe, the Libyan civil war and Gaddafi's death caused 'military forces [to lose] control of the smugglers [who] started to use Libya as a transit country' (Pascoal 2020: 40). In the context of modernity/coloniality and global capitalism, the smuggling of migrants through this route has become 'a high-profit activity, which has led to an increase of individual *passeurs* operating' across the country (Pascoal 2020: 41). It is precisely in this context that Mary, in 'An Empty Promise', becomes victimized and the monster of border violence appears as that which forces her into sex work and male border-crossers into forced labour.

The grotesque, large, racially marked hands of the bogas and the madames that accompany the trafficked people are those that visually embody the kind of border violence that is inflicted against Mary and those around her (Froden 2017). In her description of trafficked Nigerian women's suffering in transit places like Libya, Pascoal writes that when 'migrants are not able to pay the border agents, the smugglers offer the sexual services of the women to [them], in exchange for passage' (2020: 41). As Mary crosses from Quatrun to Sabha in Libya, male perpetrators of rape and murder are drawn minimally, through black outlines and dark holes at the position of their heart. They are, in this sense, liminal, indecipherable, monstrous (in-)human, heartless spectres. The causes leading to this kind of border monstrosity, which are inextricably linked to European deterrence policies and become implemented in the context of modernity/coloniality, remain unaddressed in this fictionalized testimony.[16]

After having been saved by the Italian rescue boat, further to the pain she suffered and witnessed in Libya, Mary also endures a different kind of border *ponos* while awaiting a State decision on her asylum claim. 'I am still waiting for my papers so that I can work', she explains (Froden 2017: 22). 'I wish I could keep myself busy to take my mind away from that awful journey' (Froden 2017: 22).

---

[16] Bertran writes that Europe can be considered responsible for 'crimes against humanity' enacted upon migrants in Libya through 'aiding and abetting' (2021: 302).

In the visual register she navigates a city, while textual representations of xenophobic and racist insults float around her avatar. She is being called a 'whore', and 'a prostitute' by people who demand that she goes 'home' because she is unwanted, but who are not visually present in this panel (Froden 2017: 22). In this sense, her injurious journey is presented as in-progress even after her arrival to her destination, where she is still waiting for the opportunity to work – to have a dignified life that is not characterized by the immanent *stasis* of inactively waiting for a State decision. Like Ahmed's avatar in 'Affective States', in this instance Mary is also depicted in a crouched bodily posture that illustrates the affective impact of hate and inactive waiting on her psyche. As such, her graphic depiction foregrounds the ways in which her racialized and gendered body has been shaped by, and remembers, even if we forget, as Ahmed writes, painful histories of colonialism.

Like Froden's online comics, Sanna's picture book, *The Journey*, also concerns a woman's border crossing and her encounter with monsters in the process.[17] In this case, however, as explained in the previous chapter, this woman is a mother who is also accompanied by her two children. Monstrosity in this picture book is embodied through the figure of the border guard, whom they encounter once they reach Europe or the West. Vassiliki Vassiloudi criticizes *The Journey* for presenting a beautified version of the refugee experience, and notes that 'true awareness and empathy by Western child readers cannot be raised by portraying the displacement suffered by underprivileged children in the East as a sugar-coated, risk-free journey' (2019: 42). She argues that in *The Journey* this beautification is reflected in how the family's 'long, harrowing trip toward safety is designated as a "great adventure"' (Vassiloudi 2019: 42). While this is indeed how the mother describes the journey to her children, I read her lexical choice as her intra-diegetic attempt to protect them, rather than as indicative of (unconscious) authorial intent that results in minimizing the perils of refugee border crossings. In fact, the book introduces the refugee mother, who is often depicted as a vulnerable victim in need of a Western (male) saviour, as a resilient heroine. She encounters obstacles and monsters, but overcomes them, constantly protecting her children in the process (Figure 5.4).

The monstrosity of the border guard in *The Journey* is indicated by his hands, his size and his teeth, and by how the mother with her two children are almost invisible in comparison to him, as he angrily shouts at them that they 'are not

[17] The publisher's website explains that the book is appropriate for ages between three and fourteen years old. See https://flyingeyebooks.com/shop/the-journey/.

Figure 5.4 Full-page image from *The Journey* © 2016 Flying Eye Books © 2016 Francesca Sanna.

allowed to cross the border' and that they must 'go back' (Sanna 2016: np).[18] This monster is also marked by his visible, racial difference from the family, which is implied by the colour of his beard and hair. The people smuggler whom the mother pays to help them overcome a wall is also visually embodied as a monstrous creature. Unlike the border guard, he is not anthropomorphized, but rather he is visually embodied as a black creature, which is also significantly larger than the mother and her children, but less easy to decipher due to his appearance.

In the textual register, the child narrator relates that as they cross the sea in an overloaded ferry together with other people, they tell each other 'tales of terrible and dangerous monsters that hide beneath [their] boat ready to gobble [them] up if the boat capsizes' (Sanna 2016: np). The cartoony images of underwater creatures, cephalopods, fish and, as explained in the previous chapter, the sea nymph, do not correspond to the textual account of monsters that are about to

---

[18] The monstrous representations in *The Journey* share attributes of the monstrous guards in 'Villawood'.

devour them. Rather, like the visual embodiment of the guard and the people smuggler, this narrative fragment foregrounds Western/European deterrence policies as the monsters that deprive the family of the right to mobility, safe travel and asylum.

As such, despite addressing younger readers and softening harsh images of border suffering, *The Journey* does not refrain from underscoring the monstrous violence of European/Western border policing. Even if it does not embed this family's border-crossing journey within longer colonial histories, it explicitly illustrates how the spectre of (neo-)colonialism is contemporarily embodied in border control practices and the governmentality of undocumented migration. As such, like Froden's webcomic, it shows how bodily vulnerabilities and precarities become shaped by colonial histories and how bodies remember these histories, thus exposing the colonial wounds and the pain they cause.

In *Monster Theory: Reading Culture*, Cohen writes that 'the monster's body [...] incorporates fear, desire, anxiety, and fantasy [, and it] signifies something other than itself' (1996: 4). In 'its ontological liminality, [it] appears at times of crisis as a kind of third term that problematizes the clash of extremes' (Cohen 1996: 6). In being a 'third' entity, it 'questions binary thinking and introduces a crisis' similarly to the 'third sex', as described by Marjorie Garber (1997: 11), and the comics form itself, as presented by David Carrier (2000).[19] The monster 'dwells at the gates of difference', it embodies our 'dialectical Other [, and] polices the borders of the possible' (Cohen 1996: 7, 12). It 'prevents mobility (intellectual, geographic, or sexual) [and delimits] the social spaces through which private bodies may move' (Cohen 1996: 12). The monsters examined in this chapter illustrate the attributes described by Cohen. In being the products of border crisis, they also necessarily evoke its violence, but also, and importantly, the transgressions and the acts of resistance it produces.

Their connotations expand when they enter the narrative frame to embody creative work, solidarity and strife at the border. If 'the monster's body is a

---

[19] Garber borrows this term form Sandra Gilbert's analysis of the figure of the transvestite in early-twentieth-century modernist literary texts and theoretical writing about gender. In this analysis, the 'third sex' constitutes 'a way of securing *power* for (and coping with the anxieties of) modernist *women*' (Garber 1997: 10, emphasis in the original). The 'third' also appears in Bhabha's postcolonial theoretical writings on the 'third space', which offers opportunities 'for elaborating strategies of selfhood – singular or communal – that initiate new signs of identity, and innovative sites of collaboration, and contestation, in the act of defining the idea of society itself' (1994: 1–2). This hybrid, liminal and marginal space 'displaces the histories that constitute it, and sets up [...] new political initiatives, which are inadequately understood through received wisdom' (Bhabha 1990: 211). Understood as a 'third' creature, the figure of the monster in the selected graphic life narratives also shares this political impact of re-signification regarding both the notion of monstrosity itself, and the violence of Western borders.

cultural body', and if this creature embodies 'a certain cultural moment – of a time, a feeling, and a place' (Cohen 1996: 4), then border monsters reflect the fear, anxiety and violence of the cultural and biopolitical moment and of the geopolitical location wherein they are produced. In figuratively embodying solidarity, creative work and resistance at the border, the zombie in Ahmed's 'Affective States' resists its mono-dimensional perception as a harbinger of evil. In being contextualized in sequential graphic life narratives of border *ponos*, these creatures can also foreground the monstrosity of (neo-)coloniality. Their presence in the selected texts becomes political in its exposure of border injustice, against which asylum seekers fight from their positionalities of the living dead, which, in so doing, they also resist.

Icons of (in)justice

In 'Villawood', asylum seekers' experiences of injustice are also foregrounded through iconic symbols related to justice, which emerged from mythology and have been adopted in juridical and court contexts. The injustice of Australia's detention system becomes embodied, as previously mentioned, in Ahmad's abstract drawings. The scale, which is found therein, is an object that, in ancient mythology, was held by anthropomorphized female deities embodying justice, namely Maat in Egypt, Themis and Δίκη/*Dike* in Greece, and Justitia in Rome. In their contemporary fossilized versions, these deities have become embodied by Lady Justice, who is also blindfolded while holding the scale, suggesting equal and impartial distribution of justice (Dandurand and Jahn 2021). Yvon Dandurand and Jessica Jahn note how gradually this anthropomorphized deity 'is being replaced by the instrument alone, suggesting that human intervention in justice [is] no longer required, [and] that the system – the scale – has acquired a life of its own' (2021: 568). Such symbolic representations of justice as disconnected from the human agent behind its delivery, suggest that 'the instrument itself [...] should be sufficient to weigh any matter, as long as it is artificially maintained in a perpetually simulated state of equilibrium' (Dandurand and Jahn 2021: 568).

In 'Villawood', the scale, as drawn by Ahmad, is located within a state of disequilibrium that causes and is caused by Australia's refugee crisis. In weighing on the one side and being embedded in a sequence of abstracted images that illustrate the *ponos* of this border, it becomes connected to embodied experiences of suffering in detention. It also stands for the juridically approved injustice of the Australian State's attempt to restore order and equilibrium, by sealing its borders and through its detention system. While the agent behind the distribution of injustice is, in this case, also abstracted in their absence from this iconic depiction, the placement of this symbol in the sequential narrative of border *ponos* foregrounds the State as its elusive perpetrator (see Figure 5.1).[20]

And while being blindfolded enables the impartiality of justice, in Australia's detention system it is precisely the invisibilization of border violence that enables its perpetual continuation. In showing this, 'Villawood' illustrates how 'the tool itself [– the scale –] is imperfect and can be tempered with or corrupted' (Dandurand and Jahn 2021: 568). Dandurand and Jahn write that in being represented through the object only, justice becomes reconfigured as a device which we can only access through the system and not directly, 'if we [can] have any access at all. Access to the scales is rigidly controlled and unevenly distributed', they further point out (Dandurand and Jahn 2021: 568). 'Villawood' displays the impossibility of a detained asylum seeker's access to justice at Australia's borders, and those who guard them as the monstrous agents behind the delivery of injustice.

Another object that has symbolic connotations related to juridical authority and order is the gavel, which also appears in 'Villawood'. In the first chapter of the narrative, Safdar meets a group of asylum seekers from Iran. Some of them are stateless Kurds, born and raised in that country. Due to their statelessness, that is, their configurations as non-beings, they were deprived of 'access to education, health care and employment. Denied the rights of citizenship', the narrator explains, 'they've been deemed illegal their whole lives' (Ahmed 2015: np). Prior to this narrative fragment, whereby the three men also turn their gaze to Safdar and the implied reader in demand for address-ability and response-ability as they share their testimonies, we come across stereotypical injurious characterizations of asylum seekers and refugees, as related by old white male politicians. As such, 'Villawood' has a similar structure to 'Affective States' in how it initially presents distant, racist and xenophobic othering perspectives on asylum seekers that cause fear and hate in the local population. This injurious political discourse becomes subsequently undone through its sequential juxtaposition to the three detainees' testimonies.

---

[20] Dandurand and Jahn (2021: 568) write that by being removed from contemporary iconic depictions of justice through the scale, 'the subjective aspect of weighing or taking a measurement of any kind is dissimulated or denied, as if fairness was an attribute of the human-made contraption and not of those who invent, build, and use such devices'.

Scrolling down into the narrative, the reader encounters Hassan, for instance, who explains that they 'are caught in a legal maze', and that their 'stories are doubted at every step by case managers, immigration officials and judges who make it their job to reject' them (Ahmed 2015: np). Their citizenship status, alongside their gender, race and religion, render these men's testimonies doubted and unreliable, tainting them, as Leigh Gilmore (2017) writes in her analysis of the reception of testimonies by women and girls of colour.[21] Hassan's verbal metaphor, which mediates the Kafkaesque nature of the asylum clearance process in Australia, becomes accompanied by a visual one drawn by Ahmed (Figure 5.5).

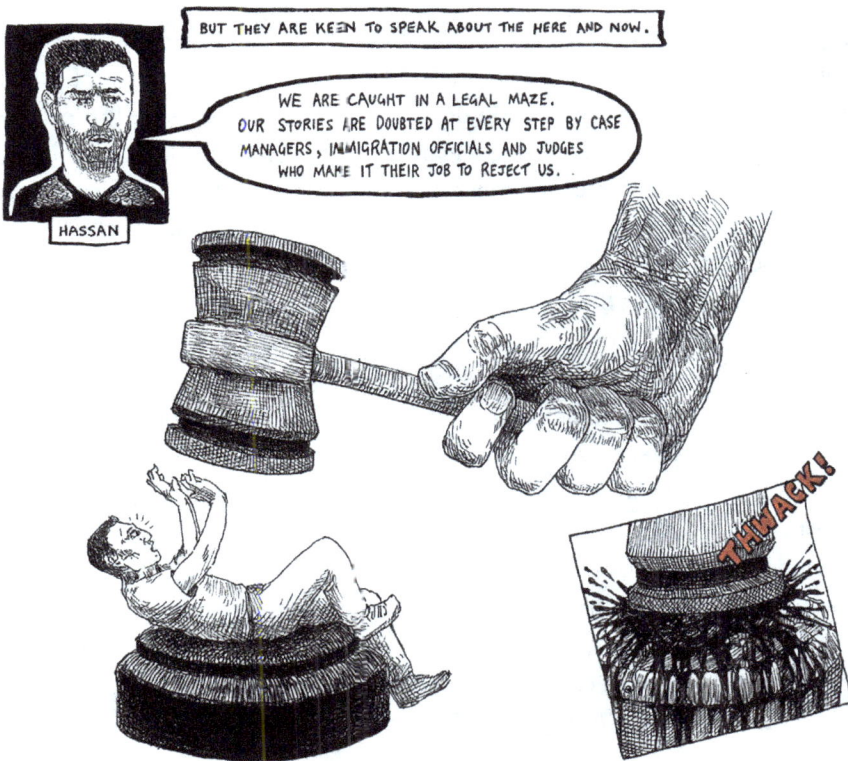

Figure 5.5 Excerpt from Ahmed, S. (2015), 'Villawood: Notes from an Immigration Detention Centre', *The Shipping News*. © Safdar Ahmed, image courtesy of the artist.

[21] Gilmore explains that 'to taint' a testimony means 'to contaminate [it] by doubt, stigmatize [it] through association with gender and race, and dishonor [it] through shame, such that not only the testimony but the person herself is smeared' (2017: 2). While Gilmore's analysis refers to women and girls, I also perceive the lack of citizenship as well as race as intersecting with masculinity in cases of asylum detention as factors leading to the tainting of men's and boys' testimonies as lucidly displayed in 'Villawood'.

A hand, like those appearing in 'An Empty Promise', is larger than the asylum seeker. It holds a gavel and is about to hit and crush him. In this visual metaphor, he is drawn in a position of complete powerlessness against the violence of the State – of Via and Kratos – and the Law, which he is nevertheless trying to resist from this precarious bio-political positionality. Next to this image, an inset zooms in on what happens after the moment previously presented. The gavel has now crushed this man's body, which becomes replaced by dark, splashing liquid, presumably blood, visually displaying the inevitability of the male asylum seeker's juridically approved obliteration, alongside an onomatopoeic 'thwack' that evokes the violence of the asylum system auditorily, visually and textually.

James Parker writes, in *International Law's Objects*, that the gavel is used in court contexts 'to "call proceedings to order"' (2018: 217). He further explains that 'what this amounts to in institutional terms is a call for silence' (Parker 2018: 217). In his analysis of its acoustic semantics, he notes that its 'knock stand[s] out or cut[s] through a soundscape consisting predominantly of voices' in its demand for order and silence (Parker 2018: 217). Like the imbalanced scales, the gavel in 'Villawood' also points to the disorder of the border that is further reflected through the monsters that inhabit it. In its onomatopoeic knock, its loud demand for and production of silence and order, it obliterates the male asylum seeker, whose testimony becomes tainted in the process of asylum clearance, but adequately witnessed in the alternative jurisdiction of 'Villawood'.

The asylum system, the narrator explains elsewhere, causes innumerable 'daily deprivations and abuses that result in mass depression and mental illness. As most refugees see it … it does not work and nor is it designed to. They are in detention to be punished … not processed' (Ahmed 2015: np). The violence of detention is visually embodied through a circle that envelopes another, three-dimensional spherical shape, within which trapped faces in despair and suffering can be deciphered. The circle, a symbol of 'eternal recommencement' as Thierry Groensteen writes in *The System of Comics* (2007: 155), metaphorically captures the indefiniteness of juridically approved border violence and *ponos*, which are also embodied through the gavel that exterminates the male asylum seeker.

Further to demanding and producing order and silence in court contexts, this object also signals that a verdict has been reached. In symbolically embodying the violent demand and production of silence and order on the one hand and signalling that 'a judgement was rendered' (Parker 2018: 218) on the other, the gavel in 'Villawood' crashes the male asylum seeker under its authority. As such, it stands as a reminder 'of the necessary imbrication of law and violence' (Parker

2018: 222) and the implications this has for those stranded in Australia's detention system. In its connection to the hammer, it is both a tool and a weapon. In its function as the latter, it constitutes 'a technique of violence: a reminder of the intimacy between apparently anodyne juridical speech and sheer brute force' (Parker 2018: 224). In 'Villawood' a hammer also appears, as mentioned, in Ahmad's abstract drawing (Figure 5.1). Like the gavel, which is directed towards and subsequently crushes the asylum seeker under its brute force, metaphorically staging his experiences of the legitimized violence of the asylum process, the hammer in Ahmed's abstract drawing is also directed towards the brain of an abstracted detainee figure, highlighting the mental strain and damage caused by detention.

In 'Comics and the Iconography of Illness', Ian Williams notes that 'the medium of comics uses and extends the language of classical art in signalling mood states using an expressionist mix of posture, expression, and visual metaphor, while also having the advantage of narrative text with which to fortify the effect' (2015: 127). In its contextualization in 'Villawood', where the narrator explains that 'there's evidence of anxiety, depression, and self-harm' everywhere, while in the visual register an arm is marked by cuts and scars, the hammer presents one of the many takes on the psychic pain prevailing at Australia's borders (Ahmed 2015: np). By displacing the scales, the gavel and the hammer from their regular contexts and embedding them in the space of detention, the narrative expands their connotations that come to encompass the country's juridically approved border violence, which nevertheless, the living dead of the border resist by bearing witness to it, as also illustrated by the comics of Eaten Fish.

The animal as witness at Western borders

The animal in these webcomics, similarly to those found in *The Journey*, often bears witness to border injustices. David L. Clark asks what it means 'to fall under the gaze of a non-human animal [;] to be glimpsed by a creature whose eyes are not so much unmet as met without the consolation of recognition or comprehension' (2015: 143). In the comics of Eaten Fish, the animal has anthropomorphic attributes and exists in-between the human and the non-human, both recognizing and bearing witness to border *ponos* in Australia's offshore detention centres. The artist himself, as explained in the introduction, uses Eaten Fish as his pen name, in a decision that evokes, according to Suvendrini

Perera and Joseph Pugliese, 'the lives that are being relentlessly consumed, expended, chewed up and spat out in the service of Australia's calculatedly cruel policy of "deterrence"' (2016: np). Dorani's pen name appears in his comics textually, visually or in a combination of both. The figure of the eaten fish, as reflected through its iconic representation as a skeleton, a living dead animal, is used as a signature in his graphic testimonies. To further illustrate the political impact of this animal's presence in Dorani's cartoons, it is useful to look into its history.

The connotations of the fish as a visual symbol go back to early Christianity. Todd Edmondson writes that in its symbolic representation of Jesus Christ, through the word 'ΙΧΘΥΣ' (fish) and its corresponding visual image, it 'was an important sign in the apostolic age, when Christians were a minority sect in [. . .] the Roman Empire' (2010: 57). 'ΥΧΘΥΣ', which means fish in Ancient Greek, is also an acronym for 'Jesus Christ, Son of God' in the same language (Edmondson 2010: 58). Prior to the fourth century CE, in order to avoid persecution, early Christians carved the word, the icon or both onto the walls of their homes to articulate their religious identity for those who shared the same system of communication, and to avoid the persecution caused by its open expression given their marginal positionality as subjects to the Roman Empire.

Its visual depiction was based on a simple drawing 'of a fish formed by joining two arcs' (Edmondson 2010: 57). Edmondson explains how 'in the two millennia since the image first appeared, this crude likeness of an ancient Mediterranean dietary staple has undergone a cultural evolution, provoking myriad responses along the way' (Edmondson 2010: 57). Its appearance as a witnessing animal in the comics of Eaten Fish constitutes a literal and metaphorical deterritorialization of the religious symbol, which becomes political in bearing witness to and exposing suffering in Australia's offshore detention prison in Manus Island, at the same time as having protected Dorani by hiding his identity, thus repeating the earliest concealing/revealing function of the fish as a graphic symbol.[22]

Commenting upon the cartoons of Eaten Fish, Aaron Scott Humphrey writes that they 'defy the narrative component of "graphic narratives" because they depict the dehumanized conditions of detention where asylum-seekers were kept indefinitely' (2020: 437). Given their production in the temporal *stasis* of

---

[22] As used here, 'deterritorialization' is influenced by the conceptualization of the term by Gilles Deleuze and Félix Guattari (2016) in *Kafka: Toward a Minor Literature*, where they explain how Franz Kafka's literary work demonstrates the deterritorialization of German language, the language of the oppressive Nazi majority that became used by a Jewish author of minority descent writing in Prague, Czech Republic.

detention, they articulate, he aptly notes, a 'life denied' – rather than a life – narrative (Humphrey 2020: 437). While Humphrey introduces the generic defiance of these comics as what allows them to present the state of the living dead and the *ponos* of the border, he also explains that drawing, Dorani's creative strife, became a mechanism that helped him cope with obsessive compulsive disorder in detention.

Eaten Fish shared his comics with other detainees in 'the bubble of the black site', and after having gained 'permission to use the Internet once a week [. . .], for forty minutes', he photographed and shared them with the Australian public using a borrowed mobile phone (Humphrey 2020: 438). This process shows how the political impact of testimony lies in the existence of an audience, who 'is party to the creation of knowledge *de novo*' (Laub 1992: 57). It is indeed through their online circulation that they exposed the violations occurring at Manus Island, the harassment Dorani suffered, as well as his protest, and it is largely because of them that he was granted asylum in Norway.[23] By introducing his authorial avatar and signature as an animal that is both human and non-human, Dorani's cartoons connect his own human precarity at the border with animal precarity in patriarchal modernity/coloniality that wounds other species as well.

Further to the artist's pen name, a second witnessing animal in his comics is the figure of the crab. Like Handala, the child witness in Naji al Ali's cartoons, the crab in the comics of Eaten Fish does not in any way influence the development of events captured in the diegetic realm. It is, however, embedded in these texts to bear witness to the cruelties occurring in Australia's detention prisons from its own marginalized positionality. Unlike Handala, who has his back turned to readers as he silently witnesses Palestinian suffering, the crab in Dorani's comics faces readers and addresses them while commenting upon the injustices it witnesses.

In one of his cartoons, which takes the form of a 'spot the difference' game, Eaten Fish draws parallels between the extermination of Jews in Auschwitz during the Holocaust and what he describes as 'Manus Regional Processing Centre – Australia's refugees Concentration Camp from 2013 onwards' (2019: np).[24] The structuring of this graphic life narrative as a game, its bright colours and drawing style alongside its personified animals evoke children's illustration,

---

[23] See https://eatenfish.com/.
[24] Unlike the re-surfacing of the Holocaust in Kirschner's diary entries in *Juarez*, which I discuss in Chapter 3, in this case it does not risk overshadowing or minimizing the refugee experience at Australia's borderzones. Rather, it foregrounds the brutality of the biopolitical and necropolitical governmentality of Australia's borders.

like the comics of PositiveNegatives. In placing the violence suffered by Jewish people detained in Auschwitz and that experienced by asylum seekers on Manus Island next to each other, this cartoon shows how the killing of undesired populations has contemporarily transformed into letting them die in detention. This presentation of the biopolitical and necropolitical governmentality of undocumented migration at the Australian border in a bright, colourful graphic text comes off as eerily unsettling.

In the first image, two guards are dressed in Nazi uniforms with the corresponding insignia, as one of them instructs the other to 'kill them all' and to 'leave no Jewish behind', while the other points his gun towards a person tied to a wooden pole, awaiting their execution (Eaten Fish 2019: np). The Jewish detainees are depicted in white abstracted, spectral shapes. Instead of their attributes, their faces are marked with the Star of David. Their visual embodiment as such strips them of their individuality and reduces them to their racial and religious otherness as perceived by Nazi German soldiers in the dehumanizing context of the Holocaust.

In the repetition and differentiation of this image, the Nazi insignia on the guards' uniforms are replaced by the flags of Australia and Papua New Guinea. The guards do not hold guns and, as opposed to ordering the extermination of refugees, one of them explains to the other that they 'do not need to kill refugees to keep them from entering Australia. It's not right' (Eaten Fish 2019: np). To this, the second guard responds that they should instead keep them detained and let them 'die slowly by illness and suicide' (Eaten Fish 2019: np). As such, the responsibility for the perpetration of crimes at the border becomes elusive. Like the Jewish people imprisoned in Auschwitz, the refugees are also depicted as spectral white shapes, but the Star of David is replaced by a question mark, reducing them to complete indecipherability and otherness that goes beyond a particular race and/or religion. The only refugees who are named are those who died in detention and their names are inscribed on their tomb stones. On Hamed's grave there is also a rope, suggesting suicide.

In these two distinct contexts, the crab appears facing the reader to explain, in the first case, that 'most people usually read about terrible stories that happened in the past and feel so sorry about them'(Eaten Fish 2019: np). The crab's arms are raised upwards at this instance, contrary to its second appearance, where they are lowered, like its eyebrows, visually reflecting sadness and disappointment when explaining how 'most people usually read terrible stories about Australia's refugee camps on the news and they do not feel sad and sorry' (Eaten Fish 2019: np). As it exposes the cruelty of detention at Manus Island, the anthropomorphized animal thus also critiques public inaction in the face of human rights violations suffered by those detained there.

In a different cartoon, the crab bears witness to children's rights violations. A girl is drawn in ragged clothes, thinking of all that she is deprived of while being detained, namely her family, education, '[sic] happyness, kindness, [and] freedom', *inter alia* (Eaten Fish 2016: np). She sits on the ground playing with a rope that signifies the suffocating and potentially lethal implications of her detention and her separation from her family. The crab addresses the reader explaining that 'children [need] some more kindness' and asking that they 'help them to get it' (Eaten Fish 2016: np). The language errors in the cartoons of Eaten Fish do not prevent his message from coming across. At the same time, they show how English, this otherwise oppressive language, is used from within the border and Dorani's marginalized locus of enunciation to counter official State narratives that render the violence inflicted against asylum seekers invisible. It is precisely for this reason that his comics constitute an instance of what Mignolo and Rolando Vazquez (2013: np) have introduced as 'decolonial aestheSis'.[25] As such, they can potentially trigger affective responses in their demand for justice, without relegating the violence of the State outside the frame of representation. The visual signature of Eaten Fish, a small fish skeleton, is attached to the girl's dress, accompanying the crab in this human/non-human animal testimonial project.

For Ursula Le Guin, animals, like women and children, 'are the obscure matter upon which Civilization erects itself, phallologically' (1988: 10). Their otherness is produced from within the same patriarchal system of modernity/coloniality that also reconfigures (post-)colonized people from the Global South, who attempt to cross into the Global North in search for a better life as threatening and disposable others. Marian Scholtmeijer (1995) writes of how the otherness of animals has been used to justify human cruelty against them, as well as their exploitation. The same is also true for a number of people, among whom undocumented migrants, refugees, asylum seekers, those detained in, or precariously crossing Western borders across the globe.

Noting the value of feminist work that has 'politicized animal oppression', Susanne Kappeler embeds animal rights within masculinist structures that also deprive women and racially othered people of their rights, and she foregrounds intersections between 'speciesism, racism and nationalism' (1995: 320). Likewise,

---

[25] For Mignolo and Vazquez, 'decoloniality is at once the unveiling of the [colonial] wound and the possibility of healing. It makes the wound visible, tangible; it voices the scream' (2013: np).

A. Breeze Harper urges 'social justice activists to [acknowledge] the interconnections' between different kinds of abuse and violence because 'human-nonhuman animal relationships help shape our relationships with one another, and they help to shape our consciousness of race and ethnicity (as well as class, national identity, gender, and sexual orientation)' (2011: 75).[26] The human and non-human animals bearing witness to border violence in the comics of Eaten Fish, and, likewise, in *The Journey*, politically embed this injustice in a masculinist, modern/colonial structure that causes additional forms of suffering, discrimination and devaluation across species, genders, sexualities, classes, abilities and nationalities.

In Sanna's picture book, when the family is about to abandon their home, the girl protagonist is shown hugging her cat in tears prior to her departure. On the following page, the child narrator explains that they put all their belongings in suitcases and said 'goodbye to everyone' they knew (Sanna 2016: np). The cat watches the family leaving it behind, and the boy waves his hand at it in a final valediction. In this sense, the cat witnesses this family's forced uprooting at the same time as showing how human/non-human animal bonds become ruptured through forced migration. As they cross Western borders and navigate a dark forest, a fox, a fairy tale animal known for its cunning, worryingly watches the family's encounter with the monstrous border guard.

Unlike the witnessing animal in the cartoons of Eaten Fish, in Sanna's book animals do not speak. However, they do illustrate anthropomorphic awareness of border *ponos* and affective responses to the family's precarity. Clark asks whether 'in the wake of atrocities, [we] can [. . .] think of animals acting as testamentary remnants, attesting to unregarded deaths and useless suffering. How does animal witnessing – if there is such a thing – make irrefutable demands on the present and on the future?' he wonders (2015: 144). While in Dorani's cartoons the witnessing animal foregrounds the violence of detention, in Sanna's picture book it highlights the precarity that comes with enforced irregular border crossing journeys. In their co-existence with, and while also constituting a different category of marginalized others at Western borders, animals become political by bearing witness to violence emerging from the black sites of Australia and the dark borderzones of Europe.

In *The Wretched of the Earth*, Franz Fanon writes that 'the first thing the colonial learns is to remain in his place and not overstep his limits' (2004: 15). Like those who crossed the line to acquire the means for a *bios*, hence being

---

[26] Mbembe (2018: 88) also discusses the 'ecocide' caused by 'borderization'.

punished with *ponos* by Zeus, Via and Kratos, the (post-)colonized people who refuse to stay in their place and cross borders to enter the West resist their (neo-) colonial positionings. In crossing the line and persevering through dangerous journeys and detention, they defy the violence of Western borders, at the same time as bearing witness to it through their testimonies.

Refugee resistance in Villawood and beyond

Fiske writes that a lot of scholarship on asylum detention, 'focuses on the practices of the state and considers "the refugee" in abstract form, as a passive, inter-changeable object caught in an extraordinary exercise of state power. The refugee is [...] a concern as the victim of human rights violations, yet [they are] not present in any distinct or recognisable form' (2016: 1). Very little scholarship, she continues, engages 'with detained refugees as agents in the exercises of power or the challenges to human rights that immigration detention entails' (Fiske 2016: 1). Those subjects whose acts of resistance remain absent from such work become centralized in the graphic life narratives examined in this chapter. These texts' value as alternative sources of information regarding human rights violations at Western borders lies in how they recast refugees beyond utter victimhood.

Further to bearing witness to human rights violations, 'Villawood' accounts for other forms of resistance emerging from the zone of the living dead. Detained men support each other, they play games, they preserve familial, religious and cultural traditions, they learn English to 'ensure their release' and to make sense of the official language of the reports and forms they are asked to sign (Ahmed 2015: np). Scrolling down into the narrative reveals other forms of resistance. The men's faces become more desperate and angrier, with their reactions to their oppression becoming more painful and more severely punished. These reactions include refusal to sign 'petty documents such as behaviour contracts [...] foot-dragging, defiance, resisting deportation, speaking to the media, hunger strikes and refusing to take medication' (Ahmed 2015: np). These verbally mediated acts are placed in an image of a red fire that charges the narrative with affective impact through its symbolism.

As means of showing resistance become even more painful, a visual embodiment of a man's silhouette is coloured in red, and his head is turned down. 'Self-harm', Ahmed writes, 'is an expression of abject despair, but in detention it's sometimes more than that' (2015: np). A panel underneath this caption zooms in on the sewn mouth of an asylum seeker. 'Because refugees are objectified and dehumanized', the narrator notes, 'because they are reduced to the status of incarcerated bodies . . . to harm themselves is to defy the system that locks them away' (Ahmed 2015: np). Protest and riots often lead to repression, punishment and further State-initiated violence. Nevertheless, by shedding light on acts of resistance and solidarity, 'Villawood' lifts the detained other from the position of the in/visible monstrous terrorist on the one hand, and of the silent, passive victim on the other.

Fiske writes that 'when detainees go on hunger strike or riot or occupy the roofs of detention centres, their actions are usually narrated by governments keen to discredit them and their actions as criminal, manipulative and evidence of "their" barbarity and difference' (2016: 16). Contra to such narratives, 'Villawood' zooms in on detention suffering, functioning as 'a counter [narrative that explains such] actions as evidence of detainees' distress and deteriorating mental health' (Fiske 2016: 16). The same is true for the cartoons of Eaten Fish. Alongside these detention comics, Froden's 'Empty Promise' and Sanna's *The Journey* foreground refugee perseverance through hardships and expose the violence of Australian and European borders.

Antoine Pécoud and Paul de Guchteneire write that 'the right to leave a country is a human right and the line between discouraging and forbidding people to leave is thin. The responsibilities for the human rights violations surrounding migration control are therefore difficult to establish' (2006: 74). The texts examined in this chapter illustrate this difficulty. The State as a perpetrator of border violence remains elusive. From the transformation of killing people to letting them slowly die while suffering a number of daily deprivations and humiliations that cause psychic pain, to the metaphorical and metonymic depiction of border violence through monsters, the selected texts foreground the difficulty of establishing single agents as those responsible for border injustice. At the same time, however, in bearing witness to it, they foreground border violence as inextricably connected to the (elusive) sovereign State.

Coda

In 2000, Teresa Hayter noted that 'the morality of frontiers, where human rights are at their lowest, is threatening the interiors of the countries' (2000: 150). Two and a half decades onwards, this statement seems truer than ever across the Western world. Pécoud and de Guchteneire (2006: 74) note that 'the way in which a society handles the fate of foreigners ultimately reflects the values upon which it is based, and the evolution of migration controls toward greater harshness may eventually backfire and threaten the principles and freedoms that lie at the core of democratic societies'. Europe, Australia and their freedoms and democracies, however, have been diachronically based on (neo-)colonial values, which are contemporarily reflected in their border and migration control policies. Contra to the collective amnesia regarding their (neo-)colonial pasts and presents, through their monsters, (in)justice icons, animal witnesses and accounts of embodied border *ponos*, the selected graphic life narratives, and their decolonized postcolonial readings, foreground the violence of Western borders as (neo-)colonial and those trying to navigate it as constantly resisting their configurations as mere living dead bodies.

6

Final remarks on the implications of reading graphic life narratives and bearing witness to other people's distant suffering

The preceding chapters have demonstrated that graphic life narratives bearing witness to other people's distant suffering, and decolonized postcolonial approaches to them, can prove useful for better understanding the ambivalences and limitations of human rights discourses, and the risk entailed in artistic and journalistic attempts to speak for othered people. The texts I have discussed illustrate how different forms of suffering and injustice become unevenly distributed and experienced across different parts of the globe. Further to those, the texts' interpretation from intersectional, interdisciplinary, decolonized postcolonial standpoints can expose the ways in which injustice can become aesthetically reproduced or critiqued within the graphic life narratives themselves. From the border cities of Juarez and Mae Sot to the conflict zones of Palestine and Sri Lanka, and from Vietnam to Australian and European borderzones, the selected texts account for a plurality of injustices suffered by people who become injuriously othered in the context of modernity/coloniality, which has a similarly wounding/othering impact on non-Western (post-)colonized places.

In Chapter 1, I have discussed the limitations of human rights discourses in relation to women and girls from the Global South, and I have looked into how graphic life narratives display female precarities in the contexts of Juarez, Mae Sot and Palestine, reading the primary texts alongside the mythical narrative of Philomela's visual testimony of sexual violence. After having noted the marginalization of adolescent boys and adult men in legal, humanitarian and migration policy discourses, as well as their injurious othering through stereotypical Western media representations, in Chapter 2, I have examined how selected graphic life narratives expose vulnerable masculinities, as well as hierarchies of masculinity, both global and local, in the contexts of the Tamil/Sinhala, the Israeli/Palestinian and the Burmese/Karen conflicts. Reading the selected texts alongside the story of Prometheus's suffering, I argue for their potential for connecting spectacle, testimony, male suffering and acts of witness and remembering through the notion of *graphic martyria*.

Turning my attention away from the living, in Chapter 3, I have looked at the dead, and I have unpacked their posthumous political existence, their relational bonds with those left behind, and what their presence in graphic life narratives says about the limitations of human rights in the contexts of the Juarez femicides, the Israeli/Palestinian conflict and the Vietnam war. I have read representations of death in the framework of a Foucaultian *melete thanatou* and I have argued for the political potential of graphic thanatopoetics. In Chapter 4, I have examined depictions of space, place, and the environment through the lens of spatial justice. Having read the selected texts alongside the story of Gaea and its use as a means of containment and torture, I have demonstrated how the earth exposes, sustains and is affected by (neo-)colonial violence, and how spatial and human suffering are relationally linked. From the cartographies of the Juarez femicides to the heterotopias of Manus Island and Sri Lanka, to the destroyed olive trees of Palestine, as well as the walls and the seas at European and Australian borders, through the lens of graphic topopoetics, spatial, like other forms of injustice, become introduced as deeply rooted in (neo-)colonial approaches both to the human and the *humus* (the earth).

Lastly, in Chapter 5, I have looked at people, monsters, animals and objects circulating in European and Australian borders. I have read narratives of suffering in the contexts of Australian asylum detention and precarious sea and terrestrial crossings into Europe alongside the story of Acheron and its production of ambivalent living-dead (non-)humans, and I have explained how refugees and asylum seekers become reconfigured into living dead people by and at Western borders. I have argued that in their displays of border *ponos*, the selected graphic life narratives and decolonized postcolonial approaches to them expose the violence of Western borders as neocolonial and introduce people whose media representations configure them as sensationalized spectacles of threat and/or vulnerability as other than muted, passive victims or monstrous violence perpetrators.

Through the preceding analyses, I have demonstrated what contemporary graphic life narrative has morphed into, and what its contribution can be, in social justice, in decolonial, postcolonial and intersectional-feminist literary studies, and in critical race, refugee and migration studies. In the spirit of Gillian Whitlock's work, I have pointed to the hospitality of graphic life narrative, of the fictionalization of testimony, and of decolonized postcolonial reading acts of secondary witness for exposing colonial wounds, and for foregrounding the ambivalence that characterizes Western gazes at other people's distant suffering (Whitlock 2015a, 2015b). This study is of course limited, and further theoretical work on the reception of such texts as well as the forums in which they circulate would shed light on their social impact that spans beyond that implied by my own reading.

In *Human Rights and Narrated Lives: The Ethics of Recognition*, Kay Schaffer and Sidonie Smith note 'that those who publish their stories of oppression, abuse, trauma, degradation, and loss can neither know nor control how that story will be received and interpreted' (2004: 31). In a society saturated with spectacles of violence, how are graphic life narratives accounting for other people's distant suffering received in virtual and physical contexts? A lot has been written about the potential of human rights literature and visual arts to trigger empathy and activism, for instance, but I remain skeptical about the extent to which such texts can cause substantial change. As shown through the preceding analysis, graphic life narratives accounting for the suffering of others are many times vested in ambivalence, and often reproduce the power dynamics and hierarchies of modernity/coloniality they seek to counter thus bringing to the fore the limitations they are marked by.

James Dawes also writes that representations of atrocity can fail for a number of reasons; they can 'be rejected in the global North because accepting their reality can require first acknowledging our complicity, guilt, or the ways we benefit from systemic violations; and they can be rejected in the global South because they are experienced as hypocritical imperialist incursions on state sovereignty' (2007: 64–5). They can fail because of compassion fatigue, or indifference, because we have seen or heard them too many times, or because they are 'too unfamiliar' (Dawes 2007: 64). Their failures are inextricably linked to their ambivalence, and to the fact that they circulate in the global power hierarchies they seek to expose and unsettle.

This is also true for the artworks that are increasingly taking up Europe's refugee crisis as their subject matter. Jerome Phelps, for instance, wonders why 'so much art about the "refugee crisis" is so bad' (2017: np). In his essay, he focuses on Ai Wei Wei's artistic negotiations of this so-called crisis and on his approach to art and humanitarianism. He discusses, *inter alia*, his re-enactment of the photograph showing the dead body of Alan Kurdi, the Syrian toddler who was washed ashore in Bodrum in 2015. Ai Wei Wei went to Lesvos, Greece, and posed for a photographic depiction that was meant to show suffering caused by what he described as a human rather than a refugee crisis. '"There is no refugee crisis,"

Ai has said, "but only a human crisis". His artistic project is "to relate to humanity's struggles", his Lesvos image a straightforward attempt to embody this suffering humanity', writes Phelps (2017: np).

In decontextualizing Kurdi's death from longer trajectories that include the historical and contemporary factors leading to forced migration, his photograph, which became excessively used and misused in the media, social or otherwise, captures the spectacle of utter, innocent victimhood (Michael 2022b). Ai Wei Wei's re-enactment of this thanatic scene is supposed to critically foreground the child's suffering as potentially that of every person – of the Universal Human. As Phelps notes, however, the artist's 'focus on that great abstraction "humanity" lifts his gaze far above the humdrum political decision-making that actually cost Alan Kurdi his life. The crisis becomes the existential one of death, the great sea that awaits us all' (Phelps 2017: np).[1] The sea, however, does not await us all. As shown through the methodological approach to the study of graphic life narratives pursued in this book, the violence of colonialism and of modernity/coloniality, as well as the suffering and the injustices that they have caused through the centuries and contemporarily, have not been equally distributed and experienced across the globe. Some lives have been configured as disposable and more precarious and vulnerable to death than others. The Universal Human is an impossibly abstracted version of humans in their diverse body- geo- and biopolitical positionalities. Thus, to speak about universal suffering constitutes another form of injustice, silencing and marginalization of othered people.

I am writing this monograph from Cyprus, my country of origin. As I am writing, pushbacks in the Aegean Sea have been on the increase.[2] The Aegean Boat Report accounts, through its Facebook page, for such pushbacks through photographs and messages sent by people on dinghies, who have been abandoned at sea, often subsequently to having been beaten.[3] These online visual/verbal narratives bear witness to suffering caused by the violence of the Greek State's approach to irregular migration at the very moment or shortly after such events occur, while the mainstream media have remained conspicuously silent about it. In May 2022, the European Union's Anti-Fraud watchdog exposed evidence of misconduct, harassment and pushbacks involving Frontex, the European Border

---

[1]   Phelps further points out that 'in its very failures, Ai's work points obliquely to the key political content of the "crisis": the collapsing of distinctions between the "here" of comfortable Western lives and the "there" of humanitarian catastrophe and war' (2017: np).

[2]   For more details about the pushbacks see the report published by Forensic Architecture, a Goldsmiths research unit, which investigates human rights violations through architectural evidence: https://aegean.forensic-architecture.org/.

[3]   For more information, see https://www.facebook.com/AegeanBoatReport.

Control Authority, in Greece and Hungary, which continue despite being 'incompatible with EU law' (Krvade 2022: np).[4] As I am writing, people are left, or rather pushed back, to die in the sea that surrounds Cyprus and Greece. The fact that I have secured a postdoctoral grant to write this book in Cyprus, a partitioned British (post-)colony, an EU member that is located at the continent's south-eastern margins, is in itself quite telling in regard to the unequal global distribution of violence and precarity on the one hand, and safety as well as opportunities on the other. Our positionalities on this earth, in other words, matter, and we are not all equally exposed to violence and injustice, as I have shown in the previous chapters.

Pramod Nayar writes that the human rights graphic novel 'is a pre-eminent form to thematize [human rights] concerns, with its ability to merge text and image, force a critical literacy upon the reader, enable a visibilization of the act – and politics – of witnessing, capture trauma, embody violence, generate empathetic and affective connections' among other potentialities (2021: 4). In his discussion on the representations of other people's distant suffering, he argues that 'the proximity generated through our encounter with stranger faces inside the panel-as-place leads to an acknowledgement of the completely alien Other's common ground with all humans: the potential for suffering' (Nayar 2021: 185). It is important, however, to always remember that this potential is not equally distributed across all humanity, and the biocularity of comics constantly reminds the reader of this precisely by en-fleshing, en-gendering and geographically positioning the abstracted Universal Human of Human Rights.

Returning to the pushbacks of the Aegean, in July 2022, I came across a one-page graphic narrative drawn by Yorgos Konstantinou, which was published in *Πενάκια Εναντίον Γκλομπ// Pens Vs Batons*, a Facebook group that includes political cartoons and comic strips uploaded by its members and speaking against police brutality and State corruption in Greece (Figure 6.1).[5] This single-page text captures the potentialities of the comics form for articulating a complex, historically informed take on Greece's contemporary crisis and the pushbacks occurring in its context. The comic starts with a temporal transition to the past, to explain that during the Second World War, with the help of lieutenant Elias Kazakos from Lesvos, the navy lieutenant Georgios Kotoulas 'organized an illegal network for helping people to escape Nazi-occupied Greece into different'

---

[4] Fabrice Leggeri, the president of Frontex, resigned in April amidst allegations (Rankin 2022).
[5] See https://www.facebook.com/groups/pens.vs.batons.

Figure 6.1 'Not in My Name', one-page webcomic by Yorgos Konstantinou, © 2022, used with permission from y0rgos/IMAGISTAN.

countries in the Middle East (Konstantinou 2022: np). In the visual register, a hand helps people cross the aquatic corridor between Greece and Turkey in the opposite direction from that contemporarily taken.

While they did not take advantage of those they helped cross, in today's terms, the two men could be considered as having operated similarly to people smugglers in helping individuals escape the famine and violence caused by German occupation. Countries such as Palestine and Syria, Congo and others offered refuge to Greek people in times of need (Mrad Abu 2016). The short webcomic explains that the two men who helped many survive by 'illegally' crossing were betrayed and subsequently executed by the German forces, and that after the liberation, a navy school was named after Kotoulas, and a statue was erected in Mytilene, Lesvos, in memory of Kazakos (Konstantinou 2022). Visually, the narrative zooms in on the places that become inscribed with and thus enable the public commemoration of the two men. In the verbal register, the narrator turns to the present to explain that in 2022, the Greek coastguard was equipped with vessels funded by the European Union, one of which was named after Kotoulas. In July, he continues, the boat took 'a leading role in a pushback-mission, just some miles [away] from Lesvos', abandoning thirty-five people at sea (Konstantinou 2022: np). In the visual register, what was previously drawn as a helping hand transforms into one that removes people from Greece, and the map through which the country was previously cartographically presented morphs into a monster ordering for the refugees to be thrown in the sea. In the background, a newspaper reportage on 'illegal trafficking networks' represents one of the causes leading to the justification of pushbacks and the human rights violations they cause (Konstantinou 2022: np). In the visual register, the statue of Kazakos is drawn in tears.

Konstantinou has used comics to embody the suffering of othered people spatially, through the map, and via two graphic metaphors: that of a monstrous Greece, which metonymically represents the State, and that of the crying statue, which stands as a silent witness to people's plights at sea and to the State's criminal actions. Through its conflations between different temporalities and traumatic histories, it shows how the thalassic corridor between Greece and Turkey has been used by people desperately reaching for opportunities to escape death at different historical points. But rather than suggesting that people's contemporary suffering is potentially universal, and that it can be ethically approached if we all recognize that we are prone to it in our humanity, this short webcomic instead demonstrates that when history is erased, distorted or forgotten, further violence, xenophobia and suffering occur, and that certain people and places are more prone to them than others. In addition, it refrains from neatly placing Greece in the position of the victim by showing how it violates the human rights of those attempting to cross the surrounding waters. In further referring to mainstream reporting on the crimes of the Aegean, this webcomic constitutes a counter-discourse to it, much like Sacco and Ahmed's graphic journalism do. Its political value also lies in that it has been published online, through the social media, reflecting the additional democratization of a genre that is deeply rooted in popular (counter-)culture.

In *Writing Human Rights: The Political Imaginaries of Writers of Color*, Krystal Parikh refers to 'conventional approaches to literature, humanitarianism, and human rights [that] have long been yoked to [a] type of "sentimental education" [...], wherein shared emotions provide the basis for progressive change' (2017: 87). Contrary to those, she proposes an 'ethical critique [that] emphasizes the alienating or disarming effects that the literary can induce, such that our responsibility to the other resides neither "in the head" nor "the heart," but with a certain discomfort in our own skin, the difficulty of "living (at home) with ourselves" when brushed by the Other who is the impossible subject of rights' (Parikh 2017: 87). In this book, I have shown how graphic life narratives that account for other people's distant suffering, and intersectional, decolonized postcolonial approaches to them, can have a similar outcome. I have further demonstrated that the responsibility to the other needs to stem both from the senses and from the mind.

References

Abdelrazaq, L. (2015), *Baddawi*, Charlottesville: Just World Books.

Abofoul, A. (2021), 'Israel's Ecological Apartheid in the Occupied Palestinian Territory', *OpinioJuris*, 22 October, available online: https://opiniojuris.org/2021/10/22/israels-ecological-apartheid-in-the-occupied-palestinian-territory/ (accessed 22 July 2022).

Abufarha, N. (2008), 'Land of Symbols: Cactus, Poppies, Orange and Olive Trees in Palestine', *Identities: Global Studies in Culture and Power* 15(3): 343–68.

Abu-Lughod, L. (2002), 'Do Muslim Women Really Need Saving? Anthropological Reflections on Cultural Relativism and Its Others', *American Anthropologist* 104(3): 783–90.

Agamben, G. (1999), *Remnants of Auschwitz: The Witness and the Archive*, New York: Zone Books.

Agamben, G. (2008), 'Beyond Human Rights', *Social Engineering* 1(15): 90–5.

Agbamu, S. (2019), '*Mare Nostrum*: Italy and the Mediterranean of Ancient Rome in the Twentieth and Twenty-First Centuries', *Fascism* 8: 250–74.

Agier, M. (2016), *Borderlands: Towards an Anthropology of the Cosmopolitan Condition*, trans. D. Fernbach, Cambridge: Polity Press.

Agier, M. (2019), 'Camps, Encampments, and Occupations: From the Heterotopia to the Urban Subject', *Ethnos* 8(1): 14–26.

Ahmed, A. (1992), *Postmodernism and Islam: Predicament and Promise*, London: Routledge.

Ahmed, L. (1992), *Women & Gender in Islam: Historical Roots of a Modern Debate*, New Haven: Yale University Press.

Ahmed, M. (2019), *Monstrous Imaginaries: The Legacy of Romanticism in Comics*, Jackson: University Press of Mississippi.

Ahmed, S. (2013), *Reform and Modernity in Islam: The Philosophical, Cultural and Political Discourses Among Muslim Reformers*, London: I. B. Tauris.

Ahmed, S. (2014), 'The Refugee Art Project', *Overland* (217): 81–3, 1 December, available online: https://search.informit.org/doi/epdf/10.3316/informit.878871171475723 (accessed 11 May 2021).

Ahmed, S. (2015), 'Villawood: Notes from an Immigration Detention Centre', *The Shipping News*, 5 March, available online: https://medium.com/shipping-news/villawood-9698183e114c (accessed 11 May 2021).

Ahmed, S. (2021), *Still Alive: Notes from Australia's Immigration Detention System*, Melbourne: Twelve Panels Press.

Ahmed, S. (2024), 'Affective States', *Image [&] Narrative* 24(3): np.

Ahmed, Sara (2004), 'Affective Economies', *Social Text* 22(2): 117–39.

Ahmed, Sara (2007), 'A Phenomenology of Whiteness', *Feminist Theory* 8(2): 149–68.

Ahmed, Sara (2014), *The Cultural Politics of Emotion*, London: Routledge.

Akesson, B. (2014), 'Contradictions in Place: Everyday Geographies of Palestinian Children and Families Living Under Occupation', PhD Diss., McGill University, Montreal.

Albanese, P. F. and L. Takkenberg (2020), *Palestinian Refugees in International Law*, Oxford: Oxford University Press.

Anzaldúa, G. (1987), *Borderlands/La Frontera: The New Mestiza*, San Francisco: Aunt Lute Books.

Apperley, H. (2015), 'Hidden Victims: A Call to Action on Sexual Violence against Men in Conflict', *Medicine, Conflict and Survival* 31(2): 92–9.

Apter, L. (2016), 'Villawood & Violence – A History of the Site of One of Australia's Most Well-Known Detention Centres', *Human Rights Defender* 25(2): 5–7.

Arendt, H. (1958), *The Human Condition*, Chicago: University of Chicago Press.

Arendt, H. (1976), *The Origins of Totalitarianism*, San Diego: Harcourt Brace & Company.

Arriola, E. (2000), 'Voices from the Barbed Wires of Despair: Women in the Maquiladoras, Latina Critical Legal Theory, and Gender at the U.S.-Mexico Border', *DePaul Law Review* 49(3): 729–816.

Astor, M. (2018), 'A Photo that Changed the Couse of the Vietnam War', *The New York Times*, 1 February, available online: https://www.nytimes.com/2018/02/01/world/asia/vietnam-execution-photo.html (accessed 12 August 2022).

Athanasiou, A. (2017), *Agonistic Mourning: Political Dissidence and the Women in Black*, Edinburgh: Edinburgh University Press.

Bal, M. (1999), 'Introduction', in M. Bal and B. Gonzales (eds), *The Practice of Cultural Analysis: Exposing Interdisciplinary Interpretation*, 1–14, Stanford: Stanford University Press.

Bal, M. (2002), 'Autotopography – Louis Bourgeois as Builder', in J. Watson and S. Smith (eds), *Interfaces – Women/Autobiography/Image/Performance*, 163–85, Ann Arbor: University of Michigan Press.

Bal, M. (2004), 'Dispersing the Image: Vermeer Story' in N. Brison (ed.), *Looking in: The Art of Viewing*, 68–71, London: Routledge.

Bales, K. (2003), 'Because She Looks Like a Child', in B. Ehrenreich and A. R. Hochschild (eds), *Global Woman: Nannies, Maids, and Sex Workers in the New Economy*, 229–56, New York: Henry Holt and Company.

Bardenstein, C. B. (1999), 'Trees, Forests, and the Shaping of Palestinian and Israeli Collective Memory', in M. Bal, J. V. Crew and L. Spitzer (eds), *Acts of Memory: Cultural Recall in the Present*, 148–70, Hanover, NH: University Press of New England.

Barreto, J. M. (2012), 'Decolonial Strategies and Dialogue in the Human Rights Field: A Manifesto', *Transnational Legal Theory* 3(1): 1–29.

Barthes, R. (1982), *Camera Lucida. Reflections on Photography*, trans. R. Howard, New York: Hill and Wang.

Bartra, R. (1992), *The Cage of Melancholy: Identity and Metamorphosis in the Mexican Character*, New Brunswick, NJ: Rutgers University Press.

Baudelaire, C. (1980), 'The Modern Public and Photography', in A. Trachtenberg (ed.), *Classic Essays on Photography*, 83–91, New Haven: Leete's Island Books.

Baxi, U. (2008), *The Future of Human Rights*, Oxford: Oxford University Press.

Benhabib, S. (2020), 'The End of the 1951 Refugee Convention? Dilemmas of Sovereignty, Territoriality, and Human Rights', *Jus Cogens* 2: 75–100.

Berger, J. (1972), *Ways of Seeing*, London: British Broadcasting Corporation.

Bertran, P. R. (2021), 'Aiding and Abetting: Assessing the Responsibility of European Union Officials for Crimes against Humanity Committed against Migrants in Libya', in J. L. Diab (ed.), *Dignity in Movement: Borders, Bodies and Rights*, 302–15, Bristol: E-International Relations.

Bhabha, H. K. (1990), 'Introduction: Narrating the Nation', in H. K. Bhabha (ed.), *Nation and Narration*, 1–7, London: Routledge.

Bhabha, H. K. (1994), *The Location of Culture*, London: Routledge.

Bhambra, K. G. (2014), 'Postcolonial and Decolonial Dialogues', *Postcolonial Studies* 17(2): 115–21.

Boltanski, L. (1999), *Distant Suffering. Morality, Media and Politics*, Cambridge: Cambridge University Press.

Borren, M. (2008), 'Towards an Arendtian Politics of In/Visibility: On Stateless Refugees and Undocumented Aliens', *Ethical Perspectives: Journal of the European Ethics Network* 15(2): 213–37.

Borren, M. (2010), 'Amor Mundi. Hannah Arendt's Political Phenomenology of World', PhD Diss., Amsterdam: University of Amsterdam.

Boum Make, J. and J. P. Walsh (2021), 'Literature and Art in the Time of Migration', *Crossings: Journal of Migration & Culture* 12(1): 293–9.

Bourdeaux, C. (2016), 'Public Memorialization and the Grievability of Victims in Ciudad Juárez', *Social Research: An International Quarterly* 83(2): 391–417.

Brambilla, C. and H. Pötzsch (2017), 'In/visibility', in J. Schimanski and S. F. Wolfe (eds), *Border Aesthetics: Concepts and Intersections*, 68–89, Oxford: Berghahn.

Brown, W. (2010), *Walled States, Waning Sovereignty*, New York: Zone Books.

Brown, W. (2012), 'Civilizational Delusions: Secularism, Tolerance, Equality', *Theory & Event* 15(2): np.

Buchanan, S., B. Grillo and T. Threadgold (2003), *What's the Story? Results from Research into Media Coverage of Refugees and Asylum Seekers in the UK*, London: Article 19.

Bui, M. (2018), 'Resistance and Visibility: How Technology Has Prompted Activism from Australia's Black Sites', *Coolabah* 24–25: 183–97.

Bui, T. (2018a), 'Preface', in T. Bui, *The Best We Could Do*, np, New York: Abrams Comicarts.

Bui, T. (2018b), *The Best We Could Do*, New York: Abrams Comicarts.

Burkert, W. (1995), *Near Eastern Influence on Greek Culture in the Early Archaic Age*, trans. M. E. Pinder, Cambridge, MA: Harvard University Press.

Butler, J. (1997), *Excitable Speech: A Politics of the Performative*, London: Routledge.

Butler, J. (2004), *Precarious Life: The Powers of Mourning and Violence*, London: Verso.

Butler, J. (2009), *Frames of War: When is Life Grievable?*, London: Verso.

Butler, J. (2020), *The Force of Nonviolence*, London: Verso.

Buvinic, M., M. Das Cupta, U. Gasabonne and P. Verwimp (2013), *Violent Conflict and Gender Inequality: An Overview*, Washington: The World Bank.

Carr, R. (2004), 'From Balfour to Suez: Britain's Zionist Misadventure', *History Review* 50: 39–41.

Carrier, D. (2000), *The Aesthetics of Comics*, University Park: Pennsylvania State University Press.

Chakrabarty, D. (2002), *Habitations in Modernity: Essays in the Wake of Subaltern Studies*, Chicago: University of Chicago Press.

Charlesworth, H. (1995), 'Human Rights as Men's Rights', in J. Peters and A. Wolper (eds), *Women's Rights, Human Rights: International Feminist Perspectives*, 103–13, New York: Routledge.

Charsley, K. and H. Wray (2015), 'Introduction: The Invisible (Migrant) Man', *Men and Masculinities* 18(4): 403–23.

Chouliaraki, L. and A. Kissas (2018), 'The Communication of Horrorism: A Typology of ISIS Online Videos', *Critical Studies in Media Communication* 35(1): 24–39.

Chouliaraki, L. and T. Stolic (2017), 'Rethinking Media Responsibility in the "Refugee Crisis": A Visual Typology of European News', *Media, Culture & Society* 39(8): 1162–77.

Christensen, A.-D. and S. Qvotrup Jensen (2014), 'Combining Hegemonic Masculinity and Intersectionality', *NORMA: International Journal for Masculinity Studies* 9(1): 60–75.

Christiansen, P. (2018), 'Vietnameze-American Author Thi Bui Wins High-Profile US Literary Award', *Sigoneer*, 30 August, available online: https://saigoneer.com/vietnam-literature/14235-vietnamese-american-author-thi-bui-wins-high-profile-us-literary-award (accessed 10 March 2021).

Chute, H. (2010), *Graphic Women: Life Narrative in Contemporary Comics*, New York: Columbia University Press.

Chute, H., ed. (2011), *MetaMaus*, London: Viking.

Chute, H. (2016), *Disaster Drawn: Visual Witness, Comics, and Documentary Form*, Cambridge, MA: Harvard University Press.

Ciocchini, P. and J. Greener (2021), 'Mapping the Pains of Neo-Colonialism: A Critical Elaboration of Southern Criminology', *British Journal of Criminology* 61: 1612–29.

Clark, D. L. (2015), 'What Remains to Be Seen: Animal, Atrocity, Witness', *Yale French Studies* 127: 143–71.

Clark, N. (2012), 'The Time of Difference', in *Geopower: A Panel Discussion*, *Environment and Planning D: Society and Space* 30(6): 975–8.

Codde, P. (2007), 'Philomela Revisited: Traumatic Iconicity in Jonathan Safran Foe's *Extremely Loud & Incredibly Close*', *Studies in American Fiction* 35(2): 241–54.

Cohen, J. J. (1996), 'Monster Culture (Seven Theses)', in J. J. Cohen (ed.), *Monster Theory: Reading Culture*, 3–25, Minneapolis: University of Minnesota Press.

Colby, J. (2019), 'Transforming Tonantzin/Guadalupe: Women's Art and Dialogue in Central California', *Femspec* 19(1): 33–52.

Colfer, E., A. Donkin and G. Rigano (2017), *Illegal*, London: Hodder Children's Books.

Collins, J. (2004), *Occupied by Memory: The Intifada Generation and the Palestinian State of Emergency*, New York: New York University Press.

Comaroff, J. and J. L. Comaroff (2012), *Theory from the South, or How Euro-America is Evolving Toward Africa*, London: Paradigm Publishers.

Connell, R. W. (1995), *Masculinities*, Cambridge: Polity.

Cooke, M. (2002), 'Saving Brown Women', *Signs: Journal of Women in Culture and Society* 28(1): 468–70.

Cottee, S. (2019), *ISIS and the Pornography of Violence*, New York: Anthem Press.

Couser, G. T. (2004), *Vulnerable Subjects: Ethics and Life Writing*, Ithaca: Cornell University Press.

Couser, G. T. (2012), *Memoir: An Introduction*, Oxford: Oxford University Press.

Cowdy, C. (2016), 'Everybody Calls Me Rosh: *Harvey, The Hockey Sweater*, and the Invisible Québécois Child', in C. Rifkind and L. Warley (eds), *Canadian Graphic: Picturing Life Narratives*, 267–96. Waterloo: Wilfrid Laurier University Press.

Cox, S. (2018), 'The Slow Journalism of the Moral Draughtsman: Joe Sacco's Coverage of State Sanctioned Sexual Violence', *Journal of Graphic Novels and Comics* 9(3): 195–213.

Craps, S. (2013), *Postcolonial Witnessing: Trauma Out of Bounds*, Basingstoke: Palgrave Macmillan.

Crawley, K. and H. van Rijswijk (2012), 'Justice in the Gutter: Representing Everyday Trauma in the Graphic Novels of Art Spiegelman', *Law Text Culture* 16: 93–118.

Cresswell, T. (2017), 'Elisabeth Bishop in and out of Place: A Topopoetic Approach', in R. T. Tally Jr. (ed.), *The Routledge Handbook of Literature and Space*, 114–24, Abingdon: Routledge.

Crofts, P. and A. Vogl (2019), 'Dehumanized and Demonized Refugees, Zombies and War Z', *Law and Humanities* 13(1): 29–51.

Crook, M., D. Short and N. South (2018), 'Ecocide, Genocide, Capitalism and Colonialism: Consequences for Indigenous People and Glocal Ecosystems Environments', *Theoretical Criminology* 22(3): 298–317.

Culler, J. (1981), *The Pursuit of Signs: Semiotics, Literature, Deconstruction*, London: Routledge and Kegan Paul.

Cusicanqui, S. R. (2012), 'A Reflection on the Practices and Discourses of Decolonisation', *South Atlantic Quarterly* 111(1): 95–109.

Cutter, J. M. (2000), 'Philomela Speaks: Alice Walker's Revisioning of Rape Archetype in *Color Purple*', *MELUS* 25(3/4): 161–80.

Dandurand, Y. and J. Jahn (2021), 'The Erosion of Justice Symbolism', in H. Kury and S. Redo (eds), *Crime Prevention and Justice in 2030: The UN and the Universal Declaration of Human Rights*, 561–74, Cham: Springer.

Danewid, I. (2017), 'White Innocence in the Black Mediterranean: Hospitality and the Erasure of History', *Third World Quarterly* 38(7): 1674–89.

Davies, D. (2019), *Urban Comics: Infrastructure and the Global City in Contemporary Graphic Narratives*, Abingdon: Routledge.

Davies, D. (2020), 'Dreamlands, Borderzones, and Spaces of Exception: Comics and Graphic Narratives of the US-Mexico Border', *a/b: Auto/Biography Studies* 35(2): 383–403.

Dawes, J. (2007), *That the World May Know: Bearing Witness to Atrocity*, Cambridge, MA: Harvard University Press.

Dawes, J. (2013), *Evil Men*, Cambridge, MA: Harvard University Press.

Dawes, J. (2018), *The Novel of Human Rights*, Cambridge, MA: Harvard University Press.

De Genova, P. N. (2002), 'Migrant "Illegality" and Deportability in Everyday Life', *Annual Review of Anthropology* 31(1): 419–47.

De Genova, P. N. (2017), 'Introduction. The Borders of "Europe" and the European Question', in P. N. de Genova (ed.), *The Borders of "Europe": Autonomy of Migration, Tactics of Bordering*, 1–36, Durham, NC: Duke University Press.

De Hart, B. (2009), 'Love Thy Neighbour: Family Reunification and the Rights of Insiders', *European Journal of Migration and Law* 11: 235–52.

Dehm, S. and J. Silverstein (2020), 'Film as Anti-Asylum Technique: International Law, Borders and the Gendering of Refugee Subjectivities', *Griffith Law Review* 29(3): 425–50.

Délano Alonso, A. and B. Nienass (2016), 'Deaths, Visibility, and Responsibility', *Social Research: An International Quarterly* 83(2): 421–51.

De León, J. (2015), *The Land of Open Graves: Living and Dying on the Migrant Trail*, Oakland: University of California Press.

Deleuze, G. and F. Guattari (2016), *Kafka: Toward a Minor Literature*, trans. D. Polan, Minneapolis: University of Minnesota Press.

Denson, S., C. Meyer and D. Stein (2013), 'Introducing Transnational Perspectives on Graphic Narratives: Comics at the Crossroads', in S. Denson, C. Meyer and D. Stein (eds), *Transnational Perspectives on Graphic Narratives: Comics at the Crossroads*, 1–24, London: Bloomsbury Academic.

Department for the Execution of Judgements of the European Court of Human Rights (2021), *Children's Rights: Thematic Factsheet*, February, Brussels: Council of Europe, available online: https://rm.coe.int/thematic-factsheet-children-eng/1680a14a43 (accessed 9 August 2022).

Derrida, J. (2000), *The Instant of My Death/Demeure: Fiction and Testimony*, trans. E. Rottenberg, Stanford: Stanford University Press.

Diamond, A. and L. Poharec (2017), 'Introduction: Freaked and Othered Bodies in Comics', *Journal of Graphic Novels and Comics* 8(5): 402–16.

Dix, B. (2019a), 'Sri-Lanka – A Brief History of Modern Conflict', in B. Dix and L. Pollock, *Vanni: A Family's Struggle through the Sri Lankan Conflict*, 6–7, Oxford: The New Internationalist.

Dix, B. (2019b), 'Afterword', in B. Dix and L. Pollock, *Vanni: A Family's Struggle through the Sri Lankan Conflict*, 160–62, Oxford: The New Internationalist.

Dix, B. and R. Kaur (2019), 'Drawing – Writing Culture: The Truth-Fiction Spectrum of an Ethno-Graphic Novel on the Sri Lankan Civil War and Migration', *Visual Anthropology Review* 35(1): 76–111.

Dix, B. and L. Pollock (2019), *Vanni: A Family's Struggle through the Sri Lankan Conflict*, Oxford: New Internationalist.

Dodds, K. (2007), *Geopolitics: A Very Short Introduction*, Oxford: Oxford University Press.

Donovan, C. and E. Ustundag (2017), 'Graphic Narratives, Trauma, and Social Justice', *Studies in Social Justice* 11(2): 221–37.

Douglas, K. (2010), *Contesting Childhood: Autobiography, Trauma, and Memory*, New Brunswick, NJ: Rutgers University Press.

Douglas, K. (2023), *Children and Biography: Reading and Writing Life Stories*, London: Bloomsbury Academic.

Douzinas, C. (2007), *Human Rights and Empire: The Political Economy of Cosmopolitanism*, London: Routledge.

DuBois, P. (1991), *Torture and Truth*, London: Routledge.

Dukich, M. and T. Shah (2019), 'Progress Report on Enumerating the Deaths in the Sri Lankan Civil War', *Human Rights Data Analysis Group*, 15 May, available online: https://hrdag.org/content/enumerating-deaths-sri-lankan-civil-war.html (accessed 11 May 2021).

Dürr, M. and L. Horneman (2018), *Zenobia*, New York: Seven Stories Press.

Eaten Fish (2016), 'Offshore Center: Kids' Center', *Eaten Fish*, 22 July, available online: https://eatenfish.com/page/2/#jp-carousel-107 (accessed 23 May 2022).

Eaten Fish (2018), 'Manus Island and the Death Angel', *Eaten Fish*, 30 May, available online: https://eatenfish.com/2018/05/30/manus-island-and-the-death-angel/ (accessed 22 July 2022).

Eaten Fish (2019), 'Nazi Concentration Camps Vs Australia's Concentration Refugee Camps: What is the Difference?', *Eaten Fish*, 8 June, available online: https://eatenfish.com/2019/06/08/nazi-concentration-camps-vs-australias-concentration-refugee-camps/ (accessed 23 May 2022).

Edmondson, T. (2010), 'The Jesus Fish Evolution of a Cultural Icon', *Studies in Popular Culture* 32(2): 57–66.

El-Enany, N. and S. Keenan (2019), 'From Pacific to Traffic Islands: Challenging Australia's Colonial Use of the Ocean through Creative Process', *Acta Academica* 51(1): 28–52.

El Guindi, F. (1999), *Veil: Modesty, Privacy, and Resistance*, Oxford: Berg.

El Refaie, E. (2001), 'Metaphors We Discriminate By: Naturalized Themes in Austrian Newspaper Articles about Asylum Seekers', *Journal of Sociolinguistics* 5(3): 352–71.

El Refaie, E. (2003), 'Understanding Visual Metaphor: The Example of Newspaper Cartoons', *Visual Communication* 2(1): 75–95.

El Refaie, E. (2012), *Autobiographical Comics: Life Writing in Pictures*, Jackson: Mississippi University Press.

El Refaie, E. (2014), 'Looking on the Dark and Bright Side: Creative Metaphors of Depression in Two Graphic Memoirs', *a/b: Auto/Biography Studies* 29(1): 149–74.

El Refaie, E. (2022), 'Comics Journalism', in E. La Cour, S. Grennan and R. Spanjers (eds), *Key Terms in Comics Studies*, 65–6, Cham: Palgrave Macmillan.

Fagerlid, C. and M. A. Tisdel (2020), 'Introduction: Literary Anthropology, Migration, and Belonging', in C. Fagerlid and M. A. Tisdel (eds), *A Literary Anthropology of Migration and Belonging: Roots, Routes, and Rhizomes*, 1–18, Cham: Palgrave Macmillan.

Falah, G.-W. (2005), 'The Visual Representation of Muslim/Arab Women in Daily Newspapers in the United States', in G. W. Falah and C. Nagel (eds), *Geographies of Muslim Women: Gender, Religion, and Space*, 300–20, New York: The Guilford Press.

Falola, T. (2009), *Colonialism and Violence in Nigeria*, Bloomington: Indiana University Press.

Fanon, F. (1965), *A Dying Colonialism*, trans. H. Chevalier, New York: Grove Press.

Fanon, F. (2004), *The Wretched of the Earth*, trans. R. Philcox, New York: Grove Press.

Farmer, P. (2003), *Pathologies of Power: Health, Human Rights, and the War on the Poor*, Berkeley: University of California Press.

Fassin, D. (2010), 'Inequality of Lives, Hierarchies of Humanity: Moral Commitments and Ethical Dilemmas of Humanitarianism', in I. Feldman and M. Ticktin (eds), *In the Name of Humanity: The Government of Threat and Care*, 238–55, Durham, NC: Duke University Press.

Fassin, D. (2011), 'Policing Borders, Producing Boundaries. The Governmentality of Immigration in Dark Times', *Annual Review of Anthropology* 40: 213–26.

Fiske, L. (2016), *Human Rights, Refugee Protest, and Immigration Detention*, Cham: Palgrave Macmillan.

Fitzmyer, A. J. (2008), *First Corinthians*, New Haven: Yale University Press.

Foucault, M. (1986), 'Of Other Spaces', *Diacritics* 16(1): 22–7.

Foucault, M. (2003a), *Abnormal: Lectures at the Collège de France 1974–1975*, trans. G. Burchell, London: Verso.

Foucault, M. (2003b), *Society Must Be Defended: Lectures at the Collège de France: 1975–76*, trans. D. Macey, Basingstoke: Palgrave Macmillan.

Foucault, M. (2005), *The Hermeneutics of the Subject: Lectures at the Collège de France: 1981–82*, trans. G. Burchell, Basingstoke: Palgrave Macmillan.

Fox, V. M. (2009), *Proverbs 10–31*, New Haven: Yale University Press.

Freud, S. (1961), *The Future of an Illusion, Civilization and Its Discontents, and Other Works*, vol. 21 of *The Standard Edition of the Complete Psychological Works of Sigmund Freud*, trans. and ed. J. Strachey, London: The Hogarth Press and the Institute of Psychoanalysis.

Freud, S. (2001), *Beyond the Pleasure Principle, Group Psychology and Other Works*, vol. 18 of *The Standard Edition of the Complete Psychological Works of Sigmund Freud*, trans. and ed. J. Strachey and A. Freud, London: Vintage.

Froden, G. (2017), 'An Empty Promise', *PositiveNegatives*, available online: https://positivenegatives.org/story/an-empty-promise/comic/ (accessed 22 July 2022).

Gamlin, J. (2022), 'Coloniality and the Political Economy of Gender: Edgework in Juárez City', *Urban Studies* 59(3): 509–25.

Garber, M. (1997), *Vested Interests: Cross-Dressing and Cultural Anxiety*, New York: Routledge.

Gardner, J. (2006), 'Archives, Collectors, and the New Media Work of Comics', *Modern Fiction Studies* 52(4): 787–806.

Ghanim, G. (2008), 'Thanatopolitics: The Case of Colonial Occupation in Palestine', in R. Lentin (ed.), *Thinking Palestine*, 65–81, London: Zed Books.

Giddens, T. (2012), 'Comics, Law, and Aesthetics: Towards the Use of Graphic Fiction in Legal Studies', *Law and Humanities* 6(1): 85–109.

Giddens, T. (2015a), 'Graphic Justice', in T. Giddens (ed.), *Graphic Justice: Intersections of Comics and Law*, np, London: Routledge.

Giddens, T., ed. (2015b), *Graphic Justice: Intersections of Comics and Law*, London: Routledge.

Gilmore, L. (1994), *Autobiographics: A Feminist Theory of Women's Self-Representation*, Ithaca: Cornell University Press.

Gilmore, L. (2001a), 'Limit-Cases: Trauma, Self-Representation and the Jurisdictions of Identity', *Biography* 24(1): 128–39.

Gilmore, L. (2001b), *The Limits of Autobiography: Trauma and Testimony*, Ithaca: Cornell University Press.

Gilmore, L. (2017), *Tainted Witness: Why We Doubt What Women Say about Their Lives*, New York: Columbia University Press.

Gilmore, L. (2019), 'Frames of Witness: The Kavanaugh Hearings, Survivor Testimony and #MeToo', *Biography: Interdisciplinary Quarterly* 42(3): 610–23.

Gilmore, L. and E. Marshal (2019), *Witnessing Girlhood: Toward an Intersectional Tradition of Life Writing*, New York: Fordham University Press.

Glare, P. G. W., ed. (2012), *The Oxford Latin Dictionary*, Oxford: Oxford University Press.

Gloeckner, P. (2000), *A Child's Life and Other Stories*, Berkeley, CA: Frog Books.

Gloeckner, P. (2002), *The Diary of a Teenage Girl: An Account in Words and Pictures*, Berkeley, CA: Frog Books.

Gloeckner, P. (2008), 'La Tristeza', in M. Kirschner, J. B. MacKinnon, P. Shoebridge and M. Simons (eds), *I Live Here: Juarez* (vol. 3), np, Toronto: Random House.

Gloeckner, P. and J. Flores-Olivier (2011), 'Women, Justice, and Juárez', *Replicante*, 10 April, available online: https://revistareplicante.com/women-justice-and-juarez/ (accessed 10 March 2021).

Gloeckner, P. and W. Joiner (2015), 'The Rumpus Interview with Phoebe Gloeckner', *The Rumpus*, 8 August, available online: https://therumpus.net/2015/08/08/the-saturday-rumpus-interview-phoebe-gloeckner/ (accessed 22 July 2022).

Gokani, R., A. Bogossian and B. Akkeson (2015), 'Occupying Masculinities: Fathering in the Palestinian Territories', *NORMA: International Journal for Masculinity Studies* 10(3/4): 203–18.

Goldberg, S. E. (2007), *Beyond Terror: Gender, Narrative, Human Rights*, New Brunswick, NJ: Rutgers University Press.

Goldberg, S. E. and A. S. Moore (2011), 'Old Questions in New Boxes: Mia Kirshner's I Live Here and the Problematics of Transnational Witnessing', *Humanity: An International Journal of Human Rights, Humanitarianism, and Development* 2(2): 233–53.

González, J. (1995), 'Autotopographies', in G. Brahm Jr. and M. Discoll (eds), *Prosthetic Territories: Politics and Hypertechnologies*, 133–49, Boulder, CO: Westview Press.

González Rodríguez, S. (2012), *The Femicide Machine*, Los Angeles: Semiotext(e).

Gravels, M. (1999), *Nationalism as Political Paranoia in Burma: An Essay on the Historical Practice of Power*, Surrey: Curzon Press.

Gray, R., R. V. Gross, R. J. Goeber and C. Koelb, eds (2005), *A Franz Kafka Encyclopedia*, Connecticut: Greenwood Press.

Grene, D. (2013), 'Introduction to Aeschylus's Prometheus Bound', in D. Grene and R. Lattimore (eds), *Greek Tragedies*, vol. 1, trans. D. Grene, 67–8, Chicago: Chicago University Press.

Griffiths, M. (2015), '"Here Man is Nothing!": Gender and Policy in an Asylum Context', *Men and Masculinities* 18(4): 468–88.

Groensteen, T. (2007), *The System of Comics*, trans. B. Beaty and N. Nguyen, Jackson: Mississippi University Press.

Grosfoguel, R. (2011), 'Decolonizing Post-Colonial Studies and Paradigms of Political Economy: Transmodernity, Decolonial Thinking, and Global Coloniality', *Transmodernity: Journal of Peripheral Cultural Production of the Luso-Hispanic World*, 1(1): np.

Grosz, E. (2012), 'Geopower', in *Geopower: A Panel Discussion, Environment and Planning D: Society and Space* 30(6): 973–5.

Guadagno, L. (2020), *Migrants and the COVID-19 Pandemic: An Initial Analysis*, Geneva: International Organization for Migration, available online: https://publications.iom.int/system/files/pdf/mrs-60.pdf (accessed 24 May 2022).

Guerin, F. and R. Hallas (2007), 'Introduction', in F. Guerin and R. Hallas (eds), *Image and the Witness: Trauma, Memory and Visual Culture*, 1–22, London: Wallflower Press.

Gusain, A. and S. Jha (2020), 'Trauma, Memory, History and its Counter Narration in Thi Bui's Graphic Memoir *The Best We Could Do*', *Journal of Graphic Novels and Comics* 12(5): 1–13.

Haase, D. (2000), 'Children, War, and the Imaginative Space of Fairy Tales', *The Lion and the Unicorn* 24(3): 360–77.

Hammami, R. (1990), 'Women, the Hijab, and the Intifada', *Middle East Report* 164/165: 24–8.

Harper, A. B. (2011), 'Connections: Speciesism, Racism, and Whiteness as the Norm', in L. Kemmerer (ed.), *Sister Species: Women, Animals and Social Justice*, 72–8, Urbana: University of Illinois Press.

Hatfield, C. (2005), *Alternative Comics: An Emerging Literature*, Jackson: Mississippi University Press.

Hauskeller, M. (2016), *Mythologies of Transhumanism*, Cham: Palgrave Macmillan.

Hayter, T. (2000), *Open Borders: The Case against Immigration Controls*, London: Pluto Press.

Heddon, D. (2002), 'Autotopography: Graffiti, Landscapes and Selves', *Reconstruction: Studies in Contemporary Culture* 2(3): np.

Heddon, D. (2007), 'One Square Foot: Thousands of Routes', *PAJ: A Journal of Performance Art* 29(2): 40–50.

Herzog, B. (2020), *Invisibilization of Suffering: The Moral Grammar of Disrespect*, Cham: Palgrave Macmillan.

Hirsch, M. (2004), 'Editor's Column: Collateral Damage', *PMLA* 119(5): 1209–15.

Hong, C. (2016), 'The World Form of Human Rights Comics', in S. A. McClennen and A. S. Moore (eds), *The Routledge Companion to Human Rights and Literature*, 193–205, London: Routledge.

Hornblower, S. and A. Spawforth (1999), *The Oxford Classical Dictionary*, Oxford: Oxford University Press.

Horstkotte, S. and N. Pedri (2012), 'Focalization in Graphic Narrative', *Narrative* 19(3): 330–57.

Huggan, G. (2008), *Interdisciplinary Measures: Literature and the Future of Postcolonial Studies*, Liverpool: Liverpool University Press.

Human Rights Watch (2002), *'My Gun Was as Tall as Me': Child Soldiers in Burma*, *Human Rights Watch*, 16 October, available online: https://www.hrw.org/reports/2002/burma/Burma0902.pdf (accessed 11 May 2021).

Human Rights Watch (2004), *Living in Fear: Child Soldiers and the Tamil Tigers in Sri Lanka*, *Human Rights Watch*, 11 November, available online: https://www.hrw.org/report/2004/11/10/living-fear/child-soldiers-and-tamil-tigers-sri-lanka (accessed 11 May 2021).

Human Rights Watch (2021), *A Threshold Crossed: Israeli Authority and the Crimes of Apartheid and Persecution*, 27 April, available at: https://www.hrw.org/report/2021/04/27/threshold-crossed/israeli-authorities-and-crimes-apartheid-and-persecution (accessed 11 May 2021).

Humphrey, A. (2017), 'Emotion and Secrecy in Australian Asylum-Seeking Comics: The Politics of Visual Style', *International Journal of Cultural Studies* 21(5): 457–85.

Humphrey, A. S. (2020), 'Drawing out of Detention: The Transnational Drawing Practices of Eaten Fish, Refugee Cartoonist', *a/b: Auto/Biography Studies* 35(2): 435–58.

Hutcheon, L. (1996), 'Flexing Femininity: Female Body-Builders Refiguring the Body', *Gender, Place and Culture – Journal of Feminist Geography* 3(3): 327–40.

IOM: International Organization for Migration (2022a), *World Migration Report 2022*, Geneva: International Organization for Migration, available online: https://publications.iom.int/books/world-migration-report-2022 (accessed 5 May 2022).

IOM: International Organization for Migration (2022b), *Ukraine Internal Displacement Report: General Population Survey (Round 3)*, DTM: Understanding Displacement, available online: https://displacement.iom.int/sites/default/files/public/reports/IOM_Ukraine%20Displacement%20Report_R3_ENG1_compressed.pdf (accessed 24 May 2022).

In 't Veld, L. (2019), *The Representation of Genocide in Graphic Novels: Considering the Role of Kitsch*, Cham: Palgrave Macmillan.

Jacobsen, M. C. and M. A. Karlsen (2021), 'Introduction: Unpacking the Temporalities of Irregular Migration', in M. C. Jacobsen, M. A. Karlsen and C. Khosravi (eds), *Waiting and the Temporalities of Irregular Migration*, 1–20, London: Routledge.

Jeffrey, J. (2018), 'Eddie Adams' Iconic Vietnam War Photo: What Happened Next', BBC News 29 January, available online: https://www.bbc.com/news/world-us-canada-42864421 (accessed 10 March 2021).

Jensen, M. (2014), 'The Fictional Is Political: Forms of Appeal in Autobiographical Fiction and Literature', in M. Jensen and M. Jolly (eds), *We Shall Bear Witness: Life Narratives and Human Rights*, 141–57, Madison: Wisconsin University Press.

Johansen, A. G. (2021), 'What is a Firewall? Firewalls Explained and Why You Need One', *NortonLifeLock*, 17 June, available online: https://us.norton.com/internetsecurity-emerging-threats-what-is-firewall.html (accessed 22 July 2022).

Jolly, M. (2014), 'Introduction: Life/Rights Narrative in Action', in M. Jensen and M. Jolly (eds), *We Shall Bear Witness: Life Narratives and Human Rights*, 3–24, Madison: Wisconsin University Press.

Jones, S. (2019), 'Testimony through Culture: Towards a Theoretical Framework', *Rethinking History: The Journal of Theory and Practice* 23(3): 257–78.

Kafka, F. (1983), 'Prometheus', in N. N. Glatzer (ed.), *The Complete Stories by Franz Kafka*, trans. W. Muir and E. Muir, 475–6, New York: Schocken Books.

Kappeler, S. (1995), 'Specicism, Racism, Nationalism . . . or the Power of Scientific Subjectivity', in C. J. Adams and J. Donovan (eds), *Animals and Women: Feminist Theoretical Explorations*, 320–352, Durham: Duke University Press.

Karjalainen, P. T. (2015), 'On Topobiography; Or, How to Write One's Place', *Nordia Geographical Publications* 44(4): 101–7.

Karpinski, C. E. (2016), 'Life in Boxes: History, Pedagogy, and Nation-Building in Canadian Biographics for Young Adults', in C. Rifkind and L. Warley (eds), *Canadian Graphic: Picturing Life Narratives*, 235–66, Waterloo: Wilfrid Laurier University Press.

Katsulis, Y., V. Lopez, A. Durfee and A. Robillard (2010), 'Female Sex Workers and the Social Context of Workplace Violence in Tijuana Mexico', *Medical Anthropology Quarterly* 24(1): 344–62.

Keeble, R. and S. Wheeler (2007), *The Journalistic Imagination: Literary Journalists from Defoe to Capote and Carter*, London: Routledge.

Kemal, B. (2020), *Writing Cyprus: Postcolonial and Partitioned Literatures of Place and Space*, London: Routledge.

Khélif, K. (2008), 'The Story of Mi-Su', in M. Kirschner, J. B. MacKinnon, P. Shoebridge and M. Simons (eds), *I Live Here: Burma*, vol. 2, np, New York: Pantheon Books.

Khorana, S. (2015), 'The Problem with Empathy', *Overland*, 1 October, available online: https://overland.org.au/2015/10/the-problem-with-empathy/ (accessed 28 August 2022).

Kirschner, M. (2008a), 'Journals', in M. Kirschner, J. B. MacKinnon, P. Shoebridge and M. Simons (eds), *I Live Here: Burma*, vol. 2, np, New York: Pantheon Books.

Kirschner, M. (2008b), 'Journals', in M. Kirschner, J. B. MacKinnon, P. Shoebridge and M. Simons (eds), *I Live Here: Juarez*, vol. 3, np, New York: Pantheon Books.

Kirschner, M., J. B. MacKinnon, P. Shoebridge and M. Simons, eds. (2008), *I Live Here: Burma*, vol. 2–3, New York: Pantheon Books.

Kleefeld, S. (2020), *Webcomics*, London: Bloomsbury.

Konstantinou, Y. (2022), 'Not in My Name', *Πενάκια Εναντίον Γκλομπ// Pens Vs Batons*, 18 August, available online: https://www.facebook.com/photo?fbid=10226124141426693&set=a.10201051125376962 (accessed 24 August 2022).

Kooistra, J. L. (1995), *The Artist as Critic: Bitextuality in Fin-de-Siècle Illustrated Books*, Aldershot: Scolar Press.

Kozol, W. (2008), 'Visual Witnessing and Women's Human Rights', *Peace Review*, 20(1): 67–75.

Kozol, W. (2011), 'Complicities of Witnessing in Joe Sacco's Palestine', in E. Swanson Goldberg and A. S. Moore (eds), *Theoretical Perspectives on Human Rights and Literature*, 165–79, London: Routledge.

Kozol, W. (2014), *Distant Wars Visible. The Ambivalence of Witnessing*, Minneapolis: The University of Minnesota Press.

Kremnitzer, M. (1989), 'The Landau Commission Report – Was the Security Service Subordinated to the Law, or the Law to the "Needs" of the Security Service?', *Israel Law Review* 23(2–3): 216–79.

Krimmer, E. (2015), 'Philomela's Legacy: Rape, the Second World War, and the Ethics of Reading', *German Quarterly* 88(1): 82–103.

Krivade, A. (2022), 'MEPs Withhold Discharge of EU Border Control Agency Frontex' Accounts', *European Parliament: News*, 31 March, available online: https//www.europarl.europa.eu/news/en/press-room/20220328IPR26301/meps-withhold-discharge-of-eu-border-control-agency-frontex-accounts (accessed 5 April 2022).

Krug, G. E., L. L. Dahlberg, J. A. Mercy, A. B. Zwi and R. Lozano, eds (2002), *World Report on Violence and Health*, Geneva: World Health Organization, available online:

https://apps.who.int/iris/bitstream/handle/10665/42495/9241545615_eng.pdf (accessed 9 August 2022).

Kukkonen, K. (2014), 'Web Comics', in M. L. Ryan, L. Emerson and B. J. Robertson (eds), *The Johns Hopkins Guide to Digital Media*, 521–4, Baltimore: Johns Hopkins University Press.

Lacan, J. (2001), *Écrits: A Selection*, trans. A. Sheridan, London: Routledge.

LaCapra, D. (1998), *History and Memory After Auschwitz*, New York: Cornell University Press.

Lara, I. (2008), 'Goddess of the Américas in the Decolonial Imaginary: Beyond the Virtuous Virgen/Pagan Puta Dichotomy', *Feminist Studies* 34(1/2): 99–127.

Laub, D. (1992), 'Bearing Witness, or the Vicissitudes of Listening', in S. Felman and D. Laub (eds), *Testimony: Crises of Witnessing in Literature, Psychoanalysis and History*, 57–74, London: Routledge.

Lebech, M. (2004), 'What is Human Dignity', *Maynooth Philosophical Papers* 2: 59–69.

Lefebvre, H. (1991), *The Production of Space*, trans. D. Nicholson-Smith, Oxford: Blackwell.

Le Guin, U. (1988), *Buffalo Gals and Other Animal Presences*, New York: New American Library.

Lentin, R. (2008), 'Introduction: Thinking Palestine', in R. Lentin (ed.), *Thinking Palestine*, 1–22, London: Zed Books.

Limb, M. (2022), 'UK-Rwanda Plan Fails to Safeguard Refugees' Medical Care, Say Campaigners', *British Medical Journal* 337: np.

Litvak, M. (1998), 'The Islamization of the Palestinian-Israeli Conflict: The Case of Hamas', *Middle Eastern Studies* 34(1): 148–63.

Lubeigt, G. (2007), 'Industrial Zones in Burma and Burmese Labour in Thailand', in M. Skidmore and T. Wilson (eds), *Myanmar: The State, Community and the Environment*, 159–88, Canberra: Australian National University Press.

Lugones, M. (2007), 'Heterosexualism and the Colonial/ Modern Gender System', *Hypatia* 22(1): 186–209.

Lugones, M. (2010), 'The Coloniality of Gender', in W. H. Mignolo and A. Escobar (eds), *Globalization and the Decolonial Option*, 369–90, New York: Routledge.

Luria, S. (2017), 'Literature and Land Surveying', in R. T. Tally Jr. (ed.), *The Routledge Handbook of Literature and Space*, 148–56, Abingdon: Routledge.

Luscombe, B. (2007), 'Pop Culture Finds Lost Boys', *Time*, 2 February, available online: http://content.time.com/time/subscriber/article/0,33009,1584807,00.html (accessed 11 May 2021).

Maantay, J. (2002), 'Mapping Environmental Injustices: Pitfalls and Potential of Geographic Information Systems in Assessing Environmental Health and Equity', *Environmental Health Perspectives* 110(2): 161–71.

MacFarlane, E. (2014), 'The Medium and the Message: Comics about Asylum Seekers', *The Conversation*, 14 February, available online: https://theconversation.com/

the-medium-and-the-message-comics-about-asylum-seekers-23168 (accessed 23 May 2022).

Madanipour, A., M. Shucksmith and E. Brooks (2022), 'The Concept of Spatial Justice and the European Union's Territorial Cohesion', *European Planning Studies* 30(5): 807–24.

Maldonado-Torres, N. (2010), 'On the Coloniality of Being: Contributions to the Development of a Concept', in W. H. Mignolo and A. Escobar (eds), *Globalization and the Decolonial Option*, 94–124, New York: Routledge.

Malkki, L. (2010), 'Children, Humanity, and the Infantilization of Peace', in I. Feldman and M. Ticktin (eds), *In the Name of Humanity: The Government of Threat and Care*, 58–85, Durham, NC: Duke University Press.

Manea, D. and M. Precup (2020), 'Infantilizing the Refugee: On the Mobilization of Empathy in Kate Evans' *Threads from the Refugee Crisis*', *a/b: Auto/biography Studies* 35(2): 481–7.

March, J. (2000), 'Vases and Tragic Drama: Euripides' *Medea* and Sophocles' Lost *Tereus*', in N. K. Rutter and B. A. Sparkes (eds), *Word and Image in Ancient Greece*, 119–39, Edinburgh: Edinburgh University Press.

Margolis, H. (2021), 'European Court OKs Bans on Religious Dress at Work', *Human Rights Watch*, 19 July, available online: https://www.hrw.org/news/2021/07/19/european-union-court-oks-bans-religious-dress-work (accessed 24 July 2021).

Mbembe, A. (2006), 'On Politics as a Form of Expenditure', in J. Comaroff and J. L. Comaroff (eds), *Law and Disorder in the Postcolony*, 299–336, Chicago: University of Chicago Press.

Mbembe, A. (2018), 'Deglobalization', *Esprit* 12: 86–94.

Mbembe, A. (2019a), 'Bodies as Borders', *From the European South* 4: 5–18.

Mbembe, A. (2019b), *Necropolitics*, trans. S. Corcoran, Durham, NC: Duke University Press.

Mbembe, A. (2021), *Out of the Dark Night: Essays on Decolonization*, New York: Columbia University Press.

Mbembe, A. and S. Nuttall (2008), 'Introduction: Afropolis', in A. Mbembe, S. Nuttall and C. A. Breckenridge (eds), *Johannesburg: The Elusive Metropolis*, 1–26, Durham, NC: Duke University Press.

McCloud, S. (1994), *Understanding Comics*, New York: HarperCollins.

McLaren, A. M. (2017a), 'Introduction: Decolonizing Feminism' in A. M. McLaren (ed.), *Decolonizing Feminism: Transnational Feminism and Globalization*, 15–36, London: Rowman & Littlefield.

McLaren, A. M. (2017b), 'Decolonizing Rights: Transnational Feminism and "Women's Rights as Human Rights"', in M. A. McLaren (ed.), *Decolonizing Feminism: Transnational Feminism and Globalization*, 108–47, London: Rowman & Littlefield.

Mehta, B. and P. Mukherji (2015), 'Introduction', in B. Mehta and P. Mukherji (eds), *Postcolonial Comics: Texts, Events, Identities*, 1–26, London: Routledge.

Menicucci, G. (2005), 'Sexual Torture, Rendering, Practices', *ISIM Review* 16: 18–19.

Mernissi, F. (1991), *The Veil and the Male Elite: A Feminist Interpretation of Women's Rights in Islam*, Abingdon: Perseus Books Publishing.

Messerschmidt, J. W. (2010), *Hegemonic Masculinities and Camouflaged Politics*, Boulder, CO: Paradigm.

Michael, O. (2014), 'Lolita is Set Free: Questioning and Re-inventing Constructions of Adolescent and Pre-adolescent Female Beauty in Phoebe Gloeckner's Graphic Memoirs', in M. Ioannou and M. Kyriakidou (eds), *Female Beauty in Art: History, Feminism, Women Artists*, 38–66, Newcastle Upon Tyne: Cambridge Scholars.

Michael, O. (2018), 'Graphic Autofiction and the Visualisation of Trauma in Lynda Barry and Phoebe Gloeckner's Graphic Memoirs', in H. Dix (ed.), *Autofiction in English*, 105–24, Basingstoke: Palgrave Macmillan.

Michael, O. (2019), 'Reading Phoebe Gloeckner's *A Child's Life and Other Stories* at the Time of #MeToo', *Life Writing* 16(3): 345–67.

Michael, O. (2020a), 'Crossing, Conflict and Diaspora in Cyprus and beyond in Miranda Hoplaros and Lara Alphas' *The Sign-Maker*', *a/b: Auto/Biography Studies* 35(2): 405–34.

Michael, O. (2020b), 'Queer Trauma, Paternal Loss and Graphic Healing in Alison Bechdel's *Fun Home: A Family Tragicomic*', in A. Ionescu and M. Margaroni (eds), *Arts of Healing: Cultural Narratives of Trauma*, 187–210, London: Rowman & Littlefield.

Michael, O. (2022a), 'Looking at the Perpetrator in Nina Bunjevac's *Fatherland*', *Journal of Perpetrator Research* 5(2): np.

Michael, O. (2022b), 'The (In)Visibility of Border Violence', *A Women's Thing*, 25 May, available online: https://awomensthing.org/blog/border-violence/ (accessed 24 August 2022).

Michael, O. (2023), 'Gendered Testimonies at the Dawn of the Twenty-First Century', in S. Jones and R. Woods (eds), *The Palgrave Handbook of Testimony and Culture*, np, Cham: Palgrave Macmillan.

Michael, O. (2024), 'Spatiotemporal Palimpsests, Remembered Times, and Hybrid Temporalities in Narrative Fiction on Europe's "Refugee Crisis"', in J. Schimanski, J. Nyman and C. Zamorano Llena (eds), *Temporalities and Subjectivities in Migration Literature in Europe*, np, London: Lexington.

Michael, O. and J. Mastilovic (2022), 'Injurious Metaphors and (Non-)Art as Activist Counter-Discourse to Greece's "Refugee Crisis"', in N. González Ortega and A. Belén Martínez García (eds), *Representing 21st-Century Migration in Europe: Performing Migrants' Identities, Bodies and Texts*, 187–207, Oxford: Berghahn.

Mickwitz, N. (2016), *Documentary Comics: Graphic Truth-Telling in a Skeptical Age*, Cham: Palgrave Macmillan.

Mickwitz, N. (2020a), 'Introduction: Discursive Context, "Voice," and Empathy in Graphic Life Narratives of Migration and Exile', *a/b: Auto/Biography Studies* 35(2): 459–65.

Mickwitz, N. (2020b), 'Comics Telling Refugee Stories', in D. Davies and C. Rifkind (eds), *Documenting Trauma in Comics. Traumatic Pasts, Embodied Histories, and Graphic Reportage*, 277–96, Cham: Palgrave Macmillan.

Mickwitz, N. (2022), 'Witness', in E. La Cour, S. Grennan and R. Spanjers (eds), *Key Terms in Comics Studies*, 352, Cham: Palgrave Macmillan.

Miéville, C. (2005), *Between Equal Rights: A Marxist Theory of International Law*, Leiden: Brill.

Mignolo, W. D. (2002), 'The Geopolitics of Knowledge and the Colonial Difference', *South Atlantic Quarterly*, 101(1): 57–96.

Mignolo, W. D. (2011), *The Darker Side of Western Modernity: Global Futures, Decolonial Options*, New York: Duke University Press.

Mignolo, W. D. (2013), 'Who Speaks for the "Human" in Human Rights?', in J. M. Barreto (ed.), *Human Rights from a Third World Perspective: Critique, History, and International Law*, 44–64, Newcastle Upon Tyne: Cambridge Scholars.

Mignolo, W. D. and R. Gaztambide-Fernández (2014), 'Decolonial Options and Artistic/ AestheSic Entanglements: An Interview with Walter Mignolo', *Decolonization: Indigeneity, Education & Society* 3(1): 196–212.

Mignolo, W. D. and R. Vazquez (2013), 'Decolonial AestheSis: Colonial Wounds/ Decolonial Healings', *Social Text Online*, np.

Miller, A. (2007), *Reading Bande Dessinée: Critical Approaches to French-language Comic Strips*, Bristol: Intellect.

Mitchell, W. J. T. (1994), *Picture Theory: Essays on Verbal and Visual Representation*, Chicago: Chicago University Press.

Mohanty, T. C. (1988), 'Under Western Eyes: Feminist Scholarship and Colonial Discourses', *Feminist Review* 30(1): 61–88.

Mohanty, T. C. (2003), '"Under Western Eyes" Revisited: Feminist Solidarity through Anticapitalist Struggles', *Signs: Journal of Women in Culture and Society* 28(2): 499–535.

Montanari, F. (2016), *The Brill Dictionary of Ancient Greek*, Leiden: Brill.

Mrad, Abu, N. (2016), 'The Greek Refugees Who Fled to the Middle East in WWII', BBC News, 20 June, available online: https://www.bbc.com/news/world-europe-36499727 (accessed 10 August 2021).

Mukherjee, N. (2011), '"A Desideratum More Sublime": Imperialism's Expansive Vision and Lambton's Trigonometrical Survey of India', *Postcolonial Studies* 14(4): 429–47.

Mulvey, L. (1989), *Visual and Other Pleasures*, Basingstoke: Macmillan.

Mulvey, L. (2006), *Death 24x a Second: Stillness and the Moving Image*, London: Reaktion Books.

Munro, P. (2012), 'Harbouring the Illicit: Borderlands and Human Trafficking in South East Asia', *Crime, Law, and Social Change* 58: 159–77.

Murrey, S. J. (2006), 'Thanatopolitics: On the Use of Death for Mobilizing Political Life', *Polygraph: An International Journal of Politics and Culture* 18: 191–215.

Murrey, S. J. (2018), 'Thanatopolitics', in J. R. Di Leo (ed.), *Bloomsbury Handbook to Literary and Cultural Theory*, 718–19, London: Bloomsbury.

Musleh-Motut, N. (2019), 'Comics Images and the Art of Witnessing: A Visual Analysis of Joe Sacco's *Footnotes in Gaza*', *Arab Studies* 27(1): 62–89.

Nabizadeh, G. (2019), *Representation and Memory in Graphic Novels*, London: Routledge.

Nathan, D. (1999), 'Work, Sex, and Danger in Ciudad *Juárez*', *NACLA Report on the Americas* 33(3): 24–30.

Nayar, P. (2016), *Human Rights and Literature: Writing Rights*, London: Routledge.

Nayar, P. (2021), *The Human Rights Graphic Novel: Drawing It Just Right*, Abingdon: Routledge.

Naylor, L., M. Daigle, S. Zaragocin, M. M. Ramírez and M. Gilmartin (2018), 'Interventions: Bringing the Decolonial to Political Geography', *Political Geography* 66: 199–209.

Nethery, A. and Silverman S., eds (2015), *Immigration Detention: The Migration of a Policy and its Human Impact*, London: Routledge.

Nicholson, S. (2014), 'Europe's Rights Court Upholds Burka Bans', *Deutsche Welle*, 1 July, available online: https://www.dw.com/en/europes-rights-court-upholds-french-burqa-ban/a-17749889 (accessed 24 July 2021).

Nicolaïdis, K. (2015), 'Southern Barbarians? A Post-Colonial Critique of EUniversalism', in K. Nicolaïdis, B. Sèbe and G. Maas (eds), *Echoes of Empire: Memory, Identity and the Legacy of Imperialism*, 283–304, London: I. B. Tauris.

Núñez-Mchiri, G. G. (2012), 'Housing, *Colonias*, and Social Justice in the U.S.-Mexico Border Region', in M. Lusk, K. Staudt and E. Moya (eds), *Social Justice in the U.S.-Mexico Border Region*, 109–26, New York: Springer.

Oliver, K. (2001), *Witnessing: Beyond Recognition*, Minneapolis: Minnesota University Press.

Op de Beeck, N. (2012), 'On Comics-Style Picture Books and Picture-Bookish Comics', *Children's Literature Association Quarterly* 37(4): 468–76.

Orozco, E. F. (2019), 'Mapping the Trail of Violence: The Memorialization of Public Space as a Counter-Geography of Violence in *Ciudad* Juárez', *Journal of Latin American Geography* 18(3): 132–57.

Page, R. (2014), 'Blogs', in M. L. Ryan, L. Emerson and B. J. Robertson (eds), *The Johns Hopkins Guide to Digital Media*, 42–5, Baltimore: Johns Hopkins University Press.

Parikh, K. (2017), *Writing Human Rights: The Political Imaginaries of Writers of Color*, Minneapolis: University of Minnesota Press.

Parker, J. E. K. (2018), 'Gavel', in J. Hohmann and D. Joyce (eds), *International Law's Objects*, 214–24, Oxford: Oxford University Press.

Pascoal, R. (2020), *Motherhood in the Context of Human Trafficking and Sexual Exploitation: Studies on Nigerian and Romanian Women*, Cham: Springer.

Pearson, E. A. (2001), 'Revealing and Concealing: The Persistence of Vaginal Iconography in Medieval Imagery: The Mandorla, the Vesica Piscis, The Rose,

Sheela-Na-Gis and the Double-Tailed Mermaid', PhD Diss., University of Ottawa, Ottawa.

Pécoud, A. (2020), 'Death at the Border: Revisiting the Debate in Light of the Euro-Mediterranean Migration Crisis', *American Behavioural Scientist* 64(4): 379–88.

Pécoud, A. and P. de Guchteneire (2006), 'International Migration, Border Controls and Human Rights: Assessing the Relevance of a Right to Mobility', *Journal of Borderlands Studies* 21(1): 69–86.

Pedri, N. (2015a), 'Thinking about Photography in Comics', *Image [&] Narrative* 16(2): 1–13.

Pedri, N. (2015b), 'What's the Matter of Seeing in Graphic Memoir?', *South Central Review* 32(3): 8–29.

Pedri, N. and H. Staveley (2018), 'Not Playing Around: Games in Graphic Illness Narratives', *Literature and Medicine* 36(1): 230–56.

Perera, S. and J. Pugliese (2016), 'The Tragedy of Eaten Fish, the Award-Winning Cartoonist on Manus Island', *The Conversation*, 9 September, available online: https://theconversation.com/the-tragedy-of-eaten-fish-the-award-winning-cartoonist-on-manus-island-65150 (accessed 25 May 2022).

Peters, J. and A. Wolper (1995), 'Introduction', in J. Peters and A. Wolper (eds), *Women's Rights, Human Rights: International Feminist Perspectives*, 1–10, New York: Routledge.

Phelps, J. (2017), 'Why Is So Much Art about the "Refugee Crisis" So Bad?', *Open Democracy*, 11 May, available online: https://www.opendemocracy.net/5050/jerome-phelps/refugee-crisis-art-weiwei (accessed 23 August 2022).

Pitcher, L. (1998), '"The Divine Impatience": Ritual, Narrative, and Symbolization in the Practice of Martyrdom in Palestine', *Medical Anthropology Quarterly* 12(1): 8–30.

Polak, K. (2017), *Ethics in the Gutter: Empathy and Historical Fiction in Comics*, Columbus: Ohio State University Press.

Popescu, A. (2012), 'I Don't Live Here – But I Will Tell the Story: A Cultural Poetic Approach to *I Live Here* by Mia Kirschner', *Multilingual Discourses* 1(1): 55–80.

Precup, M. (2020), *The Graphic Lives of Fathers: Memory, Representation, and Fatherhood in North American Autobiographical Comics*, Cham: Palgrave Macmillan.

Pugliese, J. (2009), 'Crisis Heterotopias and Border Zones of the Dead', *Continuum: Journal of Media & Cultural Studies* 23(5): 663–79.

Quijano, A. (2007), 'Coloniality and Modernity/Rationality', *Cultural Studies* 21(2–3): 168–78.

Radcliffe, S. and I. Radhuber (2020), 'The Political Geographies of D/decolonization: Variegation and Decolonial Challenges of/in Geography', *Political Geography* 70: 1–12.

Rankin, J. (2022), 'Head of EU Border Agency Frontex Resigns Amid Criticisms', *The Guardian*, 29 April, available online: https://www.theguardian.com/world/2022/apr/29/head-of-eu-border-agency-frontex-resigns-amid-criticisms-fabrice-leggeri (accessed 24 August 2022).

Rauhut, D. (2018), 'A Rawls-Sen Approach to Spatial Injustice', *Social Science Spectrum* 4(3): 109–22.

Restrepo, E. and A. Rojas (2010), *Inflexión Decolonial: Fuentes, Conceptos y Cuestionamientos*, Popayán: Universidad del Cauca.

Rifkind, C. (2020), 'Migrant Detention Comics and the Aesthetic Technologies of Compassion', in D. Davies and C. Rifkind (eds), *Documenting Trauma in Comics: Traumatic Pasts, Embodied Histories, and Graphic Reportage*, 297–316, Cham: Palgrave Macmillan.

Rifkind, C. and L. Warley (2016), 'Editors' Introduction', in C. Rifkind and L. Warley (eds), *Canadian Graphic: Picturing Life Narratives*, 1–22, Waterloo: Wilfrid Laurier University Press.

Risley, A. (2010), 'Sex Trafficking: The "Other" Crisis in Mexico?', *The Latin Americanist* 54(1): 99–117.

Robben, C. G. M. A. (2004a), 'Death and Anthropology: An Introduction', in C. G. M. A. Robben (ed.), *Death, Mourning and Burial: A Cross-Cultural Reader*, 1–16, Malden, MA: Blackwell Publishing.

Robben, C. G. M. A. (2004b), 'State Terror in the Netherworld: Disappearance and Reburial in Argentina', in C. G. M. A. Robben (ed.), *Death, Mourning and Burial: A Cross-Cultural Reader*, 134–48, Malden, MA: Blackwell Publishing.

Romero, G. L. and I. Dahlman (2012), 'Introduction – Justice Framed: Law in Comics and Graphic Novels', *Law Text Culture* 16: 3–32.

Rosenblatt, A. (2015), *Digging for the Disappeared: Forensic Science After Atrocity*, Stanford: Stanford University Press.

Ruffell, I. A., ed. (2012), *Aeschylus: Prometheus Bound*, London: Bloomsbury.

Sacco, J. (2001), *Palestine*, Seattle: Fantagraphics.

Sacco, J. ed. (2009a), *A Child in Palestine: The Cartoons of Naji al-Ali*, London: Verso.

Sacco, J. (2009b), 'Foreword', in J. Sacco, *Footnotes in Gaza*, xi–xiii, London: Jonathan Cape.

Sacco, J. (2009c), *Footnotes in Gaza*, London: Jonathan Cape.

Sacco, J. (2012a), 'A Manifesto Anyone?', in J. Sacco, *Journalism*, ix–xii, London: Jonathan Cape.

Sacco, J. (2012b), *Journalism*, London: Jonathan Cape.

Sack, J. (2015), *La Lucha: The Story of Lucha Castro and Human Rights in Mexico*, London: Verso.

Sack, R. D. (1997), *Homo Geographicus*, Baltimore: Johns Hopkins University Press.

Sadan, M. (2013), 'Ethnic Armies and Ethnic Conflict in Burma: Reconsidering the History of Colonial Militarization in the Kashin Region of Burma during the Second World War', *South East Asia Research* 21(4): 601–2.

Said, E. (1979), *Orientalism*, New York: Vintage Books.

Said, E. (1993), *Culture and Imperialism*, New York: Vintage Books.

Said, E. (2001), 'Homage to Sacco', in J. Sacco, *Palestine*, i–v, New York: Fantagraphics.

Saltzman, L. (2006), *Making Memory Matter: Strategies of Remembrance in Contemporary Art*, Chicago: University of Chicago Press.

Sandford, S. (2022), 'Drawing Digital: Exploring the Subjects and Spaces of Autobiographical Webcomics', PhD Diss., Adelaide: College of Humanities, Arts and Social Sciences, Flinders University.

San Martín Bacaicoa, J. and M. Perea Horno (2003), 'The Olympus and the Sea', 1–16, *World Congress of Thalassotherapy*, 24–26 January, Morocco.

Sanna, F. (2016), *The Journey*, London: Flying Eye Books.

Schaffer, K. and S. Smith (2004), *Human Rights and Narrated Lives: The Ethics of Recognition*, New York: Palgrave Macmillan.

Scherr, R. (2013), 'Shaking Hands with Other People's Pain: Joe Sacco's "Palestine"', *Mosaic: An Interdisciplinary Critical Journal* 46(1): 19–36.

Scherr, R. (2015), 'Framing Human Rights: Comics Form and the Politics of Recognition in Joe Sacco's Footnotes in Gaza', *Textual Practice* 29(1): 111–31.

Scherr, R. (2020), 'Drawing Ground in the Graphic Novel', *a/b: Auto/Biography Studies* 35(2): 475–9.

Scherr, R. (2021), 'Representing the Extreme Point of Sexual Violence: Ethical Strategies in Phoebe Gloeckner's "La Tristeza"', in F. L. Aldama (ed.), *The Routledge Companion to Gender and Sexuality in Comic Book Studies*, 459–68, Abingdon: Routledge.

Schimanski, J. (2006), 'Crossing and Reading: Notes towards a Theory and Method', *Nordlit*, 19: 41–63.

Schimanski, J. and S. F. Wolfe (2017), 'Intersections: A Conclusion in the Form of a Glossary', in J. Schimanski and S. F. Wolfe (eds), *Border Aesthetics: Concepts and Intersections*, 147–70, New York: Berghahn.

Schiwy, F. (2010), 'Decolonization and the Question of Subjectivity: Gender, Race, and Binary Thinking', in W. H. Mignolo and A. Escobar (eds), *Globalization and the Decolonial Option*, 125–48, New York: Routledge.

Schmid, J. (2019), 'Documentary Webcomics: Mediality and Contexts', in J. S. J. Kirchoff and M. P. Cook (eds), *Perspectives on Digital Comics: Theoretical, Critical and Pedagogical Essays*, 63–87, Jefferson: McFarland.

Scholtmeijer, M. (1995), 'The Power of Otherness: Animals in Women's Fiction', in C. J. Adams and J. Donovan (eds), *Animals and Women: Feminist Theoretical Explorations*, 231–62, Durham, NC: Duke University Press.

Schulz, A. K. (2017), 'Decolonizing the Anthropocene: The Mytho-Politics of Human Mastery', *E-International Relations*, 1 July, available online: https://www.e-ir. info/2017/07/01/decolonising-the-anthropocene-the-mytho-politics-of-human-mastery/ (accessed 22 July 2022).

Schwartz-Marin, A. and A. Cruz-Santiago (2016), 'Pure Corpses, Dangerous Citizens: Transgressing the Boundaries between Experts and Mourners in the Search for the Disappeared in Mexico', *Social Research: An International Quarterly* 83(2): 483–510.

Shaiken, H. (2019), 'The "Giant Sucking Sound" of NAFTA: Ross Perot Was Ridiculed as Alarmist in 1992 but His Warning Turned Out to Be Prescient', *The Conversation*,

12 July, np, available online: https://theconversation.com/the-giant-sucking-sound-of-nafta-ross-perot-was-ridiculed-as-alarmist-in-1992-but-his-warning-turned-out-to-be-prescient-120258 (accessed 7 March 2022).

Shattleworth, S. (2010), *The Mind of the Child: Child Development, Science, and Medicine, 1840 – 1900*, Oxford: Oxford University Press.

Sidaway, D. J. (2019), 'Decolonizing Border Studies?', *Geopolitics* 24(1): 270–5.

Sifaki, E. (2019), 'Erotimata gia tin Pediki Prosfigiki Logotexnia', *Keimena: Electroniko Periodiko Paidikis Logotexnias* ['Questions on Children's Literature', *Texts: Electronic Journal of Children's Literature*] 30: 1–10. Original in Greek, my translation.

Silove, D., A. F. Sinnerbrink, V. Manicavasagar and Z. Steel (1997), 'Anxiety, Depression and PTSD in Asylum-Seekers: Associations with Pre-Migration Trauma and Post-Migration Stressors', *British Journal of Psychiatry* 170: 351–7.

Simpson, J. and E. Weiner (eds) (1989), *Oxford English Dictionary*, Oxford: Clarendon Press.

Slabodsky, S. (2014), *Decolonial Judaism: Triumphal Failures of Barbaric Thinking*, Basingstoke: Palgrave Macmillan.

Slaughter, R. J. (2007), *Human Rights, Inc.: The World Novel, Narrative Form and International Law*, New York: Fordham University Press.

Smith, S. (2011), 'Human Rights and Comics: Autobiographical Avatars, Crisis Witnessing, and Transnational Rescue Networks', in M. Chaney (ed.), *Graphic Subjects: Critical Essays on Autobiography and Graphic Novels*, 61–72, Madison: University of Wisconsin Press.

Smith, S. and J. Watson (2010), *Reading Autobiography: A Guide for Interpreting Life Narratives*, Minneapolis: Minnesota University Press.

Soja, W. E. (2009), 'The City and Spatial Justice', *Spatial Justice* 1: 1–5.

Somasundaram, D. (2002), 'Child Soldiers: Understanding the Context', *British Medical Journal* 324(7348): 1268–71.

Sowder, M. (2005), *Whitman's Ecstatic Union: Conversation and Ideology in Leaves of Grass*, London: Routledge.

Spivak, Gayatri C. (1988), 'Can the Subaltern Speak?', in C. Nelson and L. Grossberg (eds), *Marxism and the Interpretation of Culture*, 271–313, Urbana: University of Illinois Press.

Srivastava, N. (2018), *Italian Colonialisms and Resistances to Empire, 1930–1970*, Cham: Palgrave Macmillan.

Stemple, L. (2008), 'Male Rape and Human Rights', *Hastings Law Journal* 60(3): 605–46.

St. Fleur, L. S. (2020), 'Landscape and Lore: River Acheron and the Oracle of the Dead', MA Diss., New York: Graduate Faculty in Liberal Studies, The City University of New York.

Strathdee, A. S., R. Lozada, S. J. Semple, R. Orozovich, M. Pu, H. Staines-Orozco, M. Fraga-Vallejo, H. Amaro, A. Delatorre, C. Magis-Rodríguez and T. L. Patterson (2008), 'Characteristics of Female Sex Workers with US Clients in Two Mexico-US Border Cities', *Sexually Transmitted Diseases: The Journal of the American Sexually Transmitted Diseases Association* 35(3): 263–8.

Sultan, A. and K. O'Sullivan (2001). 'Psychological Disturbances in Asylum Seekers Held in Long-Term Detention: A Participant-Observer Account', *Medical Journal of Australia* 175: 593–6.

Sutherland, J. M. (2003), 'Refiguring Death: The Poetics of Transience in the Work of Rainer Maria Rilke,' PhD Diss., London: University College London.

Taha, H. (2018), 'Ethnography of Death in Palestine', *Journal of Historical Archaeology & Anthropological Sciences* 3(1): 143–8.

Tally, T. R. Jr. (2017), 'Introduction: The Reassertion of Space in Literary Studies', in T. R. Tally Jr. (ed.), *The Routledge Handbook of Literature and Space*, 1–7, Abingdon: Routledge.

Taxidou, O. (2004), *Tragedy, Modernity and Mourning*, Edinburgh: Edinburgh University Press.

Taylor, H. R. (2006), 'Colonial Forces in British Burma: A National Army Postponed', in K. Hack and T. Rettig (eds), *Colonial Armies in Southeast Asia*, 185–200, London: Routledge.

Tazzioli, M. (2016), 'Border Displacements. Challenging the Politics of Rescue between Mare Nostrum and Triton', *Migration Studies* 4(1): 1–19.

Ticktin, M. (2017), 'A World Without Innocence', *American Ethnologist: Journal of the American Ethnological Society* 44(4): 577–90.

Topak, Ö. E. (2014), 'The Biopolitical Border in Practice: Surveillance and Death at the Greece–Turkey Borderzones', *Environment and Planning D: Society and Space* 32(5): 815–33.

Traunmüller, R., S. Kijewski and M. Freitag (2019), 'The Silent Victims of Sexual Violence during War: Evidence from a List Experiment in Sri Lanka', *Journal of Conflict Resolution* 63(9): 2015–42.

Tuan, Y.-F. (1977), *Space and Place: The Perspectives of Experience*, Minneapolis: University of Minnesota Press.

United Nations General Assembly (1989), *Convention on the Rights of the Child*, 12 December, available online: http //wunrn.org/reference/pdf/Convention_Rights_ Child.PDF (accessed 11 May 2021).

United Nations Office for Humanitarian Affairs (2007), 'Israeli–Palestinian Fatalities Since 2000 – Key Trends', *United Nations: The Question of Palestine*, available online: https://www.un.org/unispal/document/auto-insert-208380/ (accessed 11 May 2021).

Valencia, S. (2014), 'NAFTA: Capitalismo Gore and the Femicide Machine', *Scapegoat* 6: 131–6.

Van Dijk, A. T. (1991), *Racism and the Press*, London: Routledge.

Van Tuyl, J. (2015), 'Dolls in Holocaust Children's Literature: From Identification to Manipulation', *Children's Literature Association Quarterly* 40(1): 24–38.

Vassiloudi, V. (2019), 'International and Local Relief Organizations and the Promotion of Children's and Young Adult Refugee Narratives', *Bookbird: A Journal of International Children's Literature* 57(2): 35–49.

Veit, M. and F. Strass (2021), 'At the European Union-Turkey Border, Human Rights Violations are no Longer Clandestine Operations', in J. L. Diab (ed.), *Dignity in Movement: Borders, Bodies and Rights*, 316–38, Bristol: E-International Relations.

Verdery, K. (2004), 'Dead Bodies Animate the Study of Politics', in C. G. M. A. Robben (ed.), *Death, Mourning and Burial: A Cross-Cultural Reader*, 303–10, Malden, MA: Blackwell Publishing.

Vernant, J. P. (2006), *Myth and Thought Among the Greeks*, New York: Zone Books.

Vila, P. (2000), *Crossing Borders, Reinforcing Borders: Social Categories, Metaphors and Narrative Identities on the U.S.-Mexico Frontier*, Austin: University of Texas Press.

Vila, P. (2005), *Border Identifications: Narratives of Religion, Gender, and Class on the U.S.-Mexico Border*, Austin: University of Texas Press.

Wahab, S. (2005), 'Violence within the Sex Industry: Guest Editor's Introduction', *Journal of Inter-Personal Violence* 20(3): 263–9.

Wahbe, R. M. (2020), 'The Politics of *Karameh*: Palestinian Burial Sites under the Gun', *Critique of Anthropology* 40(3): 323–40.

Waldner, L. K. and B. A. Dobratz (2013), 'Graffiti as a Form of Contentious Political Participation', *Sociology Compass* 7(5): 377–89.

Weishut, D. J. N. (2015), 'Sexual Torture of Palestinian Men by Israeli Authorities', *Reproductive Health Matters* 23(46): 71–84.

Whitlock, G. (2001), 'In the Second Person: Narrative Transactions in Stolen Generations Memories', *Biography: Interdisciplinary Quarterly* 24(1): 197–214.

Whitlock, G. (2008), 'Autographics: The Seeing "I" of Comics', *Modern Fiction Studies* 52(4): 965–79.

Whitlock, G. (2011), 'Embridry', *Profession* 13: 85–97

Whitlock, G. (2015a), *Postcolonial Life Narratives: Testimonial Transactions*, Oxford: Oxford University Press.

Whitlock, G. (2015b), 'The Hospitality of Cyberspace: Mobilizing Asylum Seeker Testimony Online', *Biography* 38(2): 245–66.

Whitlock, G. (2017), 'Joe Sacco's Australian Story', *Life Writing* 14(3): 283–95.

Whitlock, G. and A. Poletti (2008), 'Self-Regarding Art', *Biography: Interdisciplinary Quarterly* 31(1): v–xxiii.

Wilcox, B. L. (2015), *Bodies of Violence: Theorizing Embodied Subjects in International Relations*, New York: Oxford University Press.

Williams, I. (2015), 'Comics and the Iconography of Illness', in M. Czerweic (ed.), *Graphic Medicine Manifesto*, 115–42, Philadelphia: Penn State University Press.

Williams, R. (2010), *The Divided World: Human Rights and Its Violence*, Minneapolis: Minnesota University Press.

Wing, A. K. (1997), 'Critical Race Feminism and International Human Rights', *University of Miami Inter-American Law Review* 28(2): 337–60.

Woessner, M. (2013), 'Provincializing Human Rights? The Heideggerian Legacy from Charles Malik to Dipesh Chakrabarty', in J. M. Barreto (ed.), *Human Rights from a*

Third World Perspective: Critique, History, and International Law, 65–101, Newcastle Upon Tyne: Cambridge Scholars.

Wolf, R. E. (1958), 'The Virgin of Guadalupe: A Mexican National Symbol', *Journal of American Folklore* 71(279): 34–35.

Womack, S. (2006), 'Ethnicity and Martial Races: the Garde Indigène of Cambodia in the 1880s and 1890s', in K. Hack and T. Rettig (eds), *Colonial Armies in Southeast Asia*, 100–18, London: Routledge.

Wong, S., R. Shapcott and E. Parker (2020), 'Graphic Lives, Visual Stories: Reflections on Practice, Participation, and the Potentials of Creative Engagement', *a/b: Auto/Biography Studies* 35(2): 311–29.

Woodard, D. R. (2007), 'Hesiod and Greek Myth', in R. D. Woodard (ed.), *The Cambridge Companion to Greek Mythology*, 83–165, Cambridge: Cambridge University Press.

Woods, J. E. (2011), *Deuteronomy: An Introduction and Commentary*, Dowers Grove, IL: Inter-Varsity Press.

World Bank (2011), *World Development Report 2011: Conflict, Security and Development*, Washington: The World Bank.

Woudstra, H. M. (1981), *The Book of Joshua*, Grand Rapids, MI: William B. Eerdmans Publishing Co.

Wray, H. (2009), 'Moulding the Migrant Family', *Legal Studies* 29: 592–618.

Yalouri, E. (2019), '"Difficult" Representations. Visual Art Engaging with the Refugee Crisis', *Visual Studies* 34(3): 223–38.

Yusoff, K. (2012), 'Introduction', in *Geopower: A Panel Discussion, Environment and Planning D: Society and Space* 30(6): 971–3.

Zarecki, J. P. (2007), 'Pandora and the Good Eris in Hesiod', *Greek, Roman, and Byzantine Studies* 47: 5–29.

Zebedúa-Yañez, V. (2005), 'Killing as Performance: Violence and the Shaping of Community', *E-Misférica* 2(2): np.

Zervou, A. (2020), 'Existorontas tin Prosfigia kai tin Anagkastiki Metanastefsi sta Paidika Vivlia – Ypervenontas tin Paidagogiki Logokrisia', ['Telling the Story of Refugeeness and Forced Migration in Children's Books – Overcoming Educational Censorship'], *Texts: Electronic Journal of Children's Literature* 31: 1–24. Original in Greek, my translation.

Zocchi, B. (2021), 'On the Margins of EU-Rope: Colonial Violence at the Bosnian-Croatian Frontier', in J. L. Diab (ed.), *Dignity in Movement: Borders, Bodies and Rights*, 27–40, Bristol: E-International Relations.

Index

www.ingramcontent.com/pod-product-compliance
Lightning Source LLC
Chambersburg PA
CBHW071849270326
41929CB00013B/2163